Deepak Chopra's Buddha

A Story of Enlightenment

Written By
DEEPAK CHOPRA

Adapted By
JOSHUA DYSART

Art By
HARSHVARDHAN KADAM
DEAN HYRAPIET

Colors By
S.M. BHASKAR
VENKAT VASA
DEAN HYRAPIET

Letters By
NILESH S. MAHADIK
NILESH P. KUDALE

Project Managers
S. P. KARTHIKEYAN
SUNISH KUMAR P.

Assistant Editor
CHARLIE BECKERMAN

Editors
GOTHAM CHOPRA
MARIAH HUEHNER

LIQUID COMICS

Co-Founder & Partner
GOTHAM CHOPRA

Co-Founder & CEO
SHARAD DEVARAJAN

Co-Founder & President
SURESH SEETHARAMAN

DYNAMITE ENTERTAINMENT

President
NICK BARRUCCI

Chief Operating Officer
JUAN COLLADO

Editor
JOSEPH RYBANDT

Creative Director
JOSH JOHNSON

Director Business Development
RICH YOUNG

Graphic Designer
JASON ULLMEYER

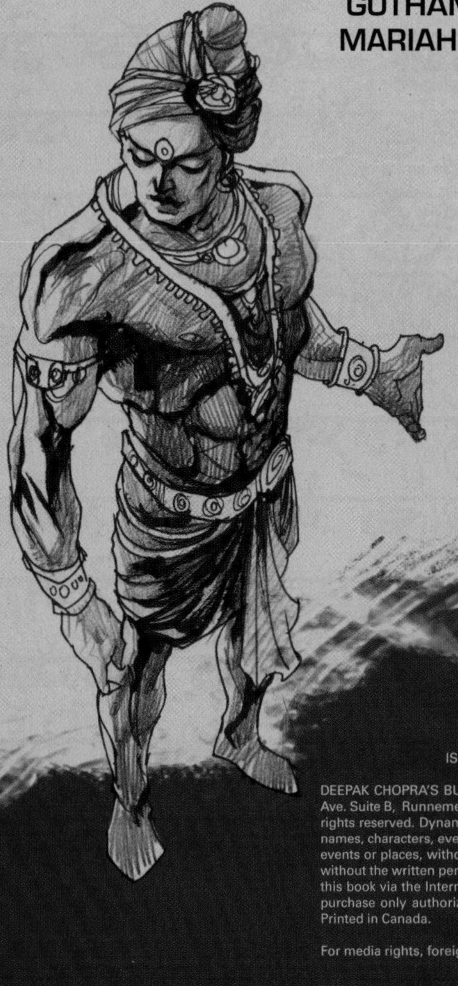

ISBN10: 1-60690-185-0 ISBN13: 978-1-60690-185-4 First Printing 10 9 8 7 6 5 4 3 2 1

DEEPAK CHOPRA'S BUDDHA – A STORY OF ENLIGHTENMENT. First printing. Published by Dynamite Entertainment. 155 Ninth Ave. Suite B, Runnemede, NJ 08078. Printed in Canada.

For media rights, foreign rights, promotions, licensing, and advertising: marketing@dynamiteentertainment.com.

Buddha: A Story of Enlightenment

There are few stories that can be described as epic, mythic, simple, and spiritual all at the same time. Buddha's is one of them.

It's the story of a man who had it all, gave it all up, and then *really* gained it all. It's the story of a man who would be king, who became something far more powerful. It is a story full of tragedy and triumph, rich and poor, sacred and profane, divine and diabolical, but ultimately about one simple thing: the quest for enlightenment.

In the west, enlightenment is a tricky word. It's taken on a New Age connotation, filled with all sorts of false meaning and promise. But etymologically it means to be brought "into the light" which is Buddha's journey. He showed us how being in the light, living with simplicity, grace, compassion, focus, and humanity gives us the experience of our true identity. Buddha did this with a purity that was not dressed up in ritual or bureaucracy, big institutions nor layered tomes deconstructing the divine. In fact, he did not look to outside authority for it at all, nor did he mention God. His transformation was experiential, and his story was totally unique, full of suspense, drama, and intrigue.

My favorite part of Buddha's story comes at the end. On his last breaths when Buddha was surrounded by his followers, one of them asked him how he was feeling. Buddha responded without hesitation and with one simple word: "awake."

If we are to solve our existential crises and all of their consequences, including war and terrorism, extreme poverty, social injustice, ecological devastation and more, then our collective civilization must "wake up" as well. Fortunately Buddha's story has shown us the way.

Deepak Chopra
September 2010

From the darkness...

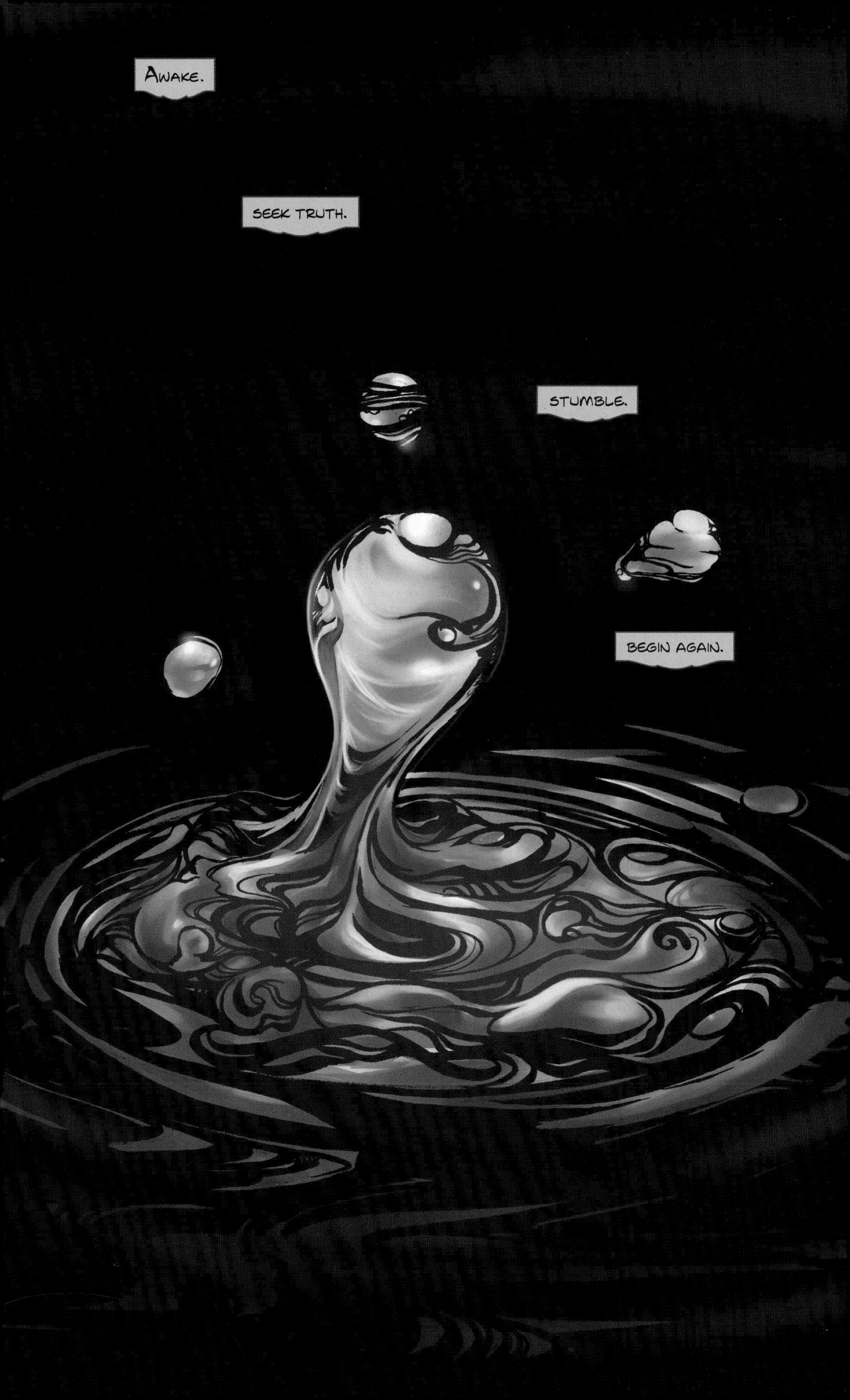
Awake.
Seek truth.
Stumble.
Begin again.

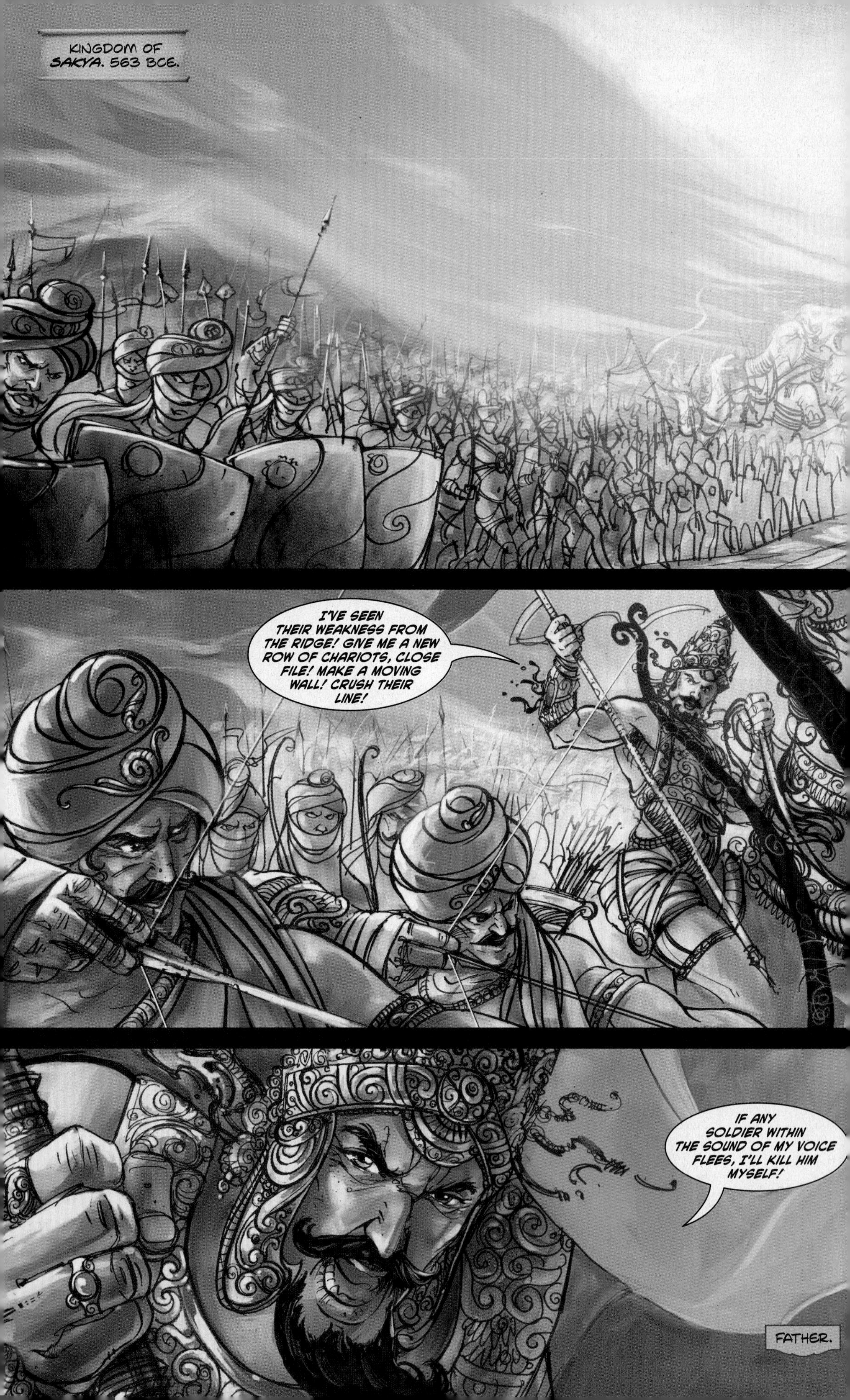
KINGDOM OF SAKYA. 563 BCE.
I'VE SEEN THEIR WEAKNESS FROM THE RIDGE! GIVE ME A NEW ROW OF CHARIOTS, CLOSE FILE! MAKE A MOVING WALL! CRUSH THEIR LINE!
IF ANY SOLDIER WITHIN THE SOUND OF MY VOICE FLEES, I'LL KILL HIM MYSELF!
FATHER.

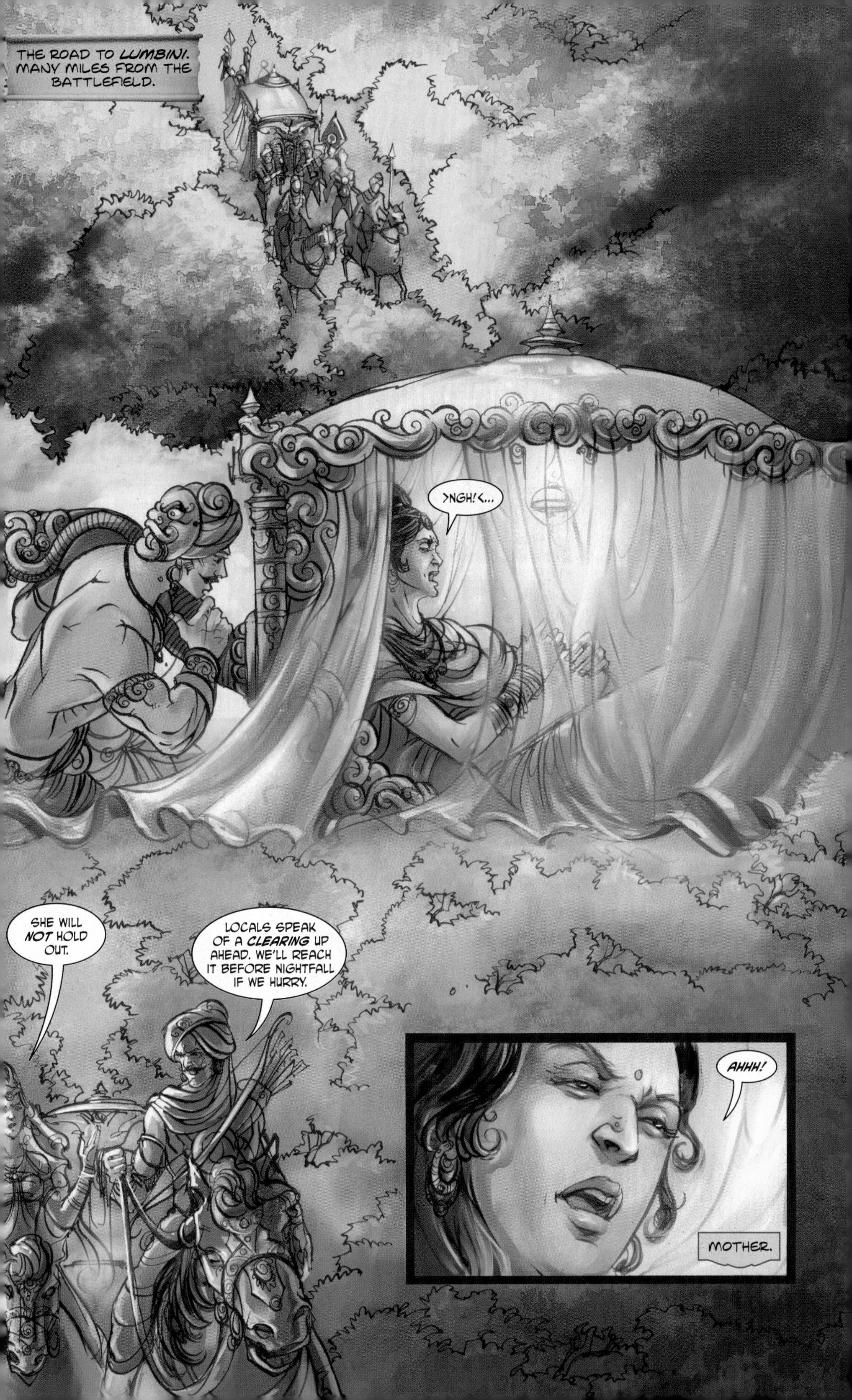
THE ROAD TO LUMBINI. MANY MILES FROM THE BATTLEFIELD.
>NGH!<...
SHE WILL NOT HOLD OUT.
LOCALS SPEAK OF A CLEARING UP AHEAD. WE'LL REACH IT BEFORE NIGHTFALL IF WE HURRY.
AHHH!
MOTHER.

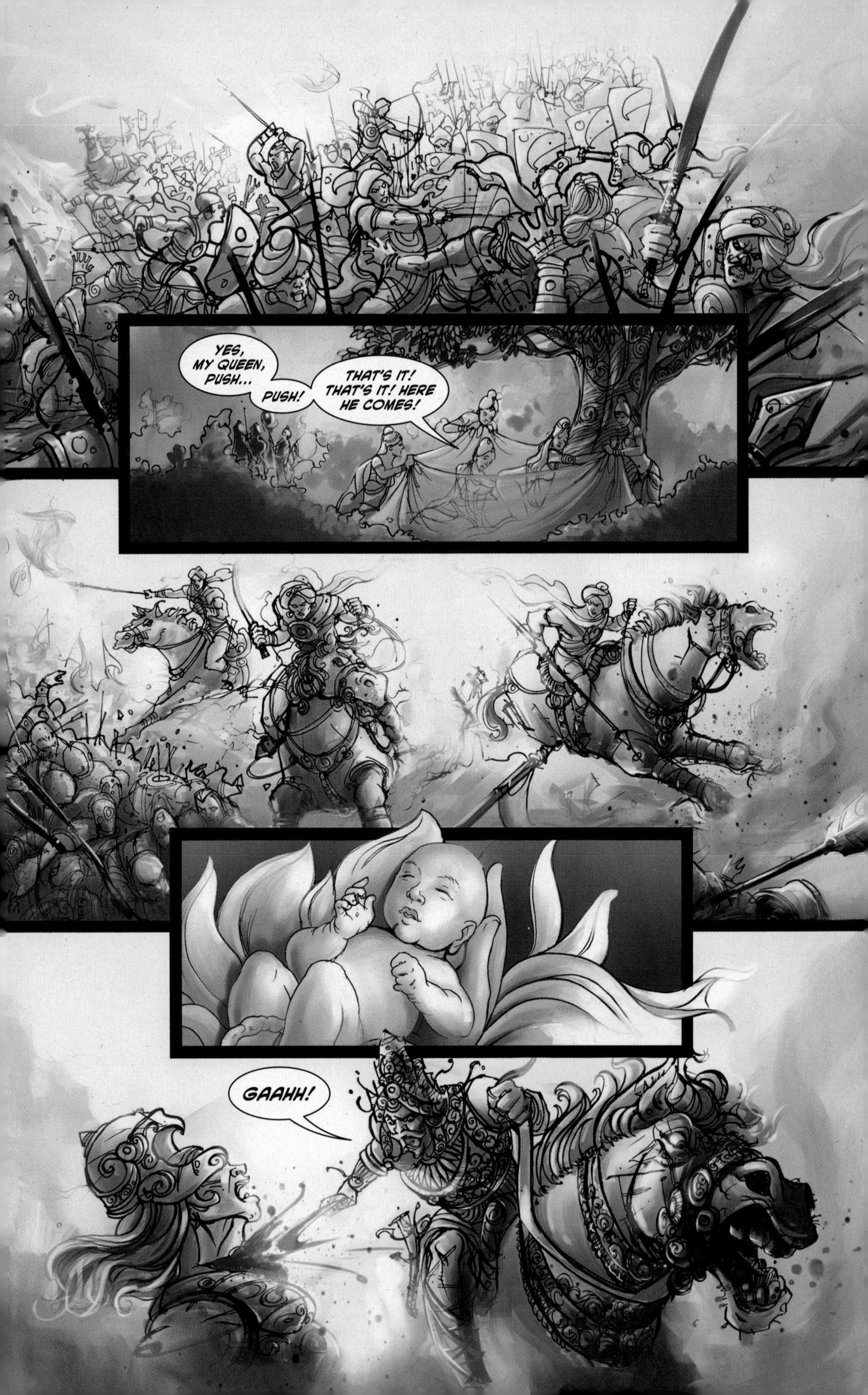
YES, MY QUEEN, PUSH...
PUSH!
THAT'S IT! THAT'S IT! HERE HE COMES!
GAAHH!

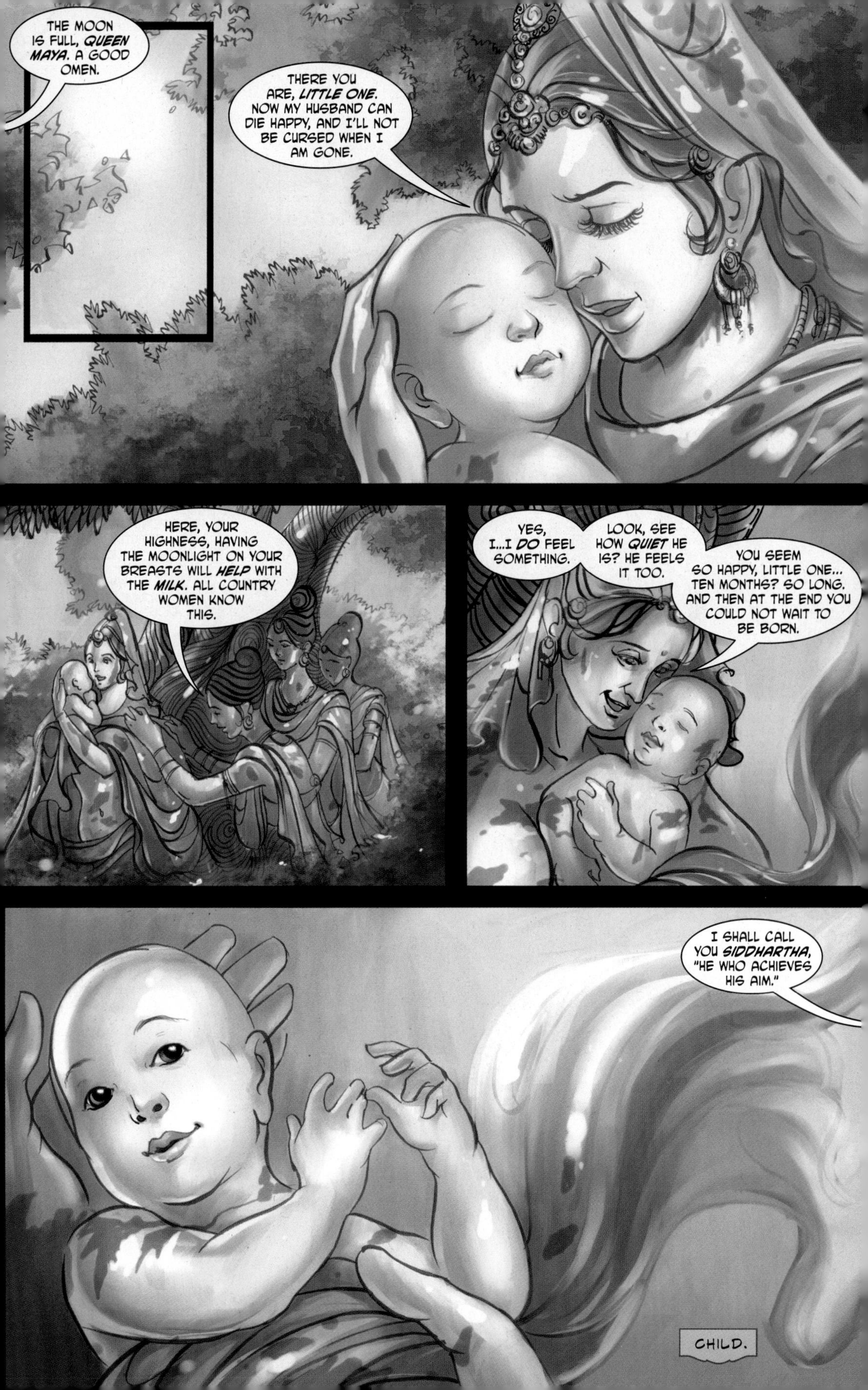
THE MOON IS FULL, QUEEN MAYA. A GOOD OMEN.
THERE YOU ARE, LITTLE ONE. NOW MY HUSBAND CAN DIE HAPPY, AND I'LL NOT BE CURSED WHEN I AM GONE.
HERE, YOUR HIGHNESS, HAVING THE MOONLIGHT ON YOUR BREASTS WILL HELP WITH THE MILK. ALL COUNTRY WOMEN KNOW THIS.
YES, I...I DO FEEL SOMETHING.
LOOK, SEE HOW QUIET HE IS? HE FEELS IT TOO.
YOU SEEM SO HAPPY, LITTLE ONE... TEN MONTHS? SO LONG. AND THEN AT THE END YOU COULD NOT WAIT TO BE BORN.
I SHALL CALL YOU SIDDHARTHA, "HE WHO ACHIEVES HIS AIM."
CHILD.

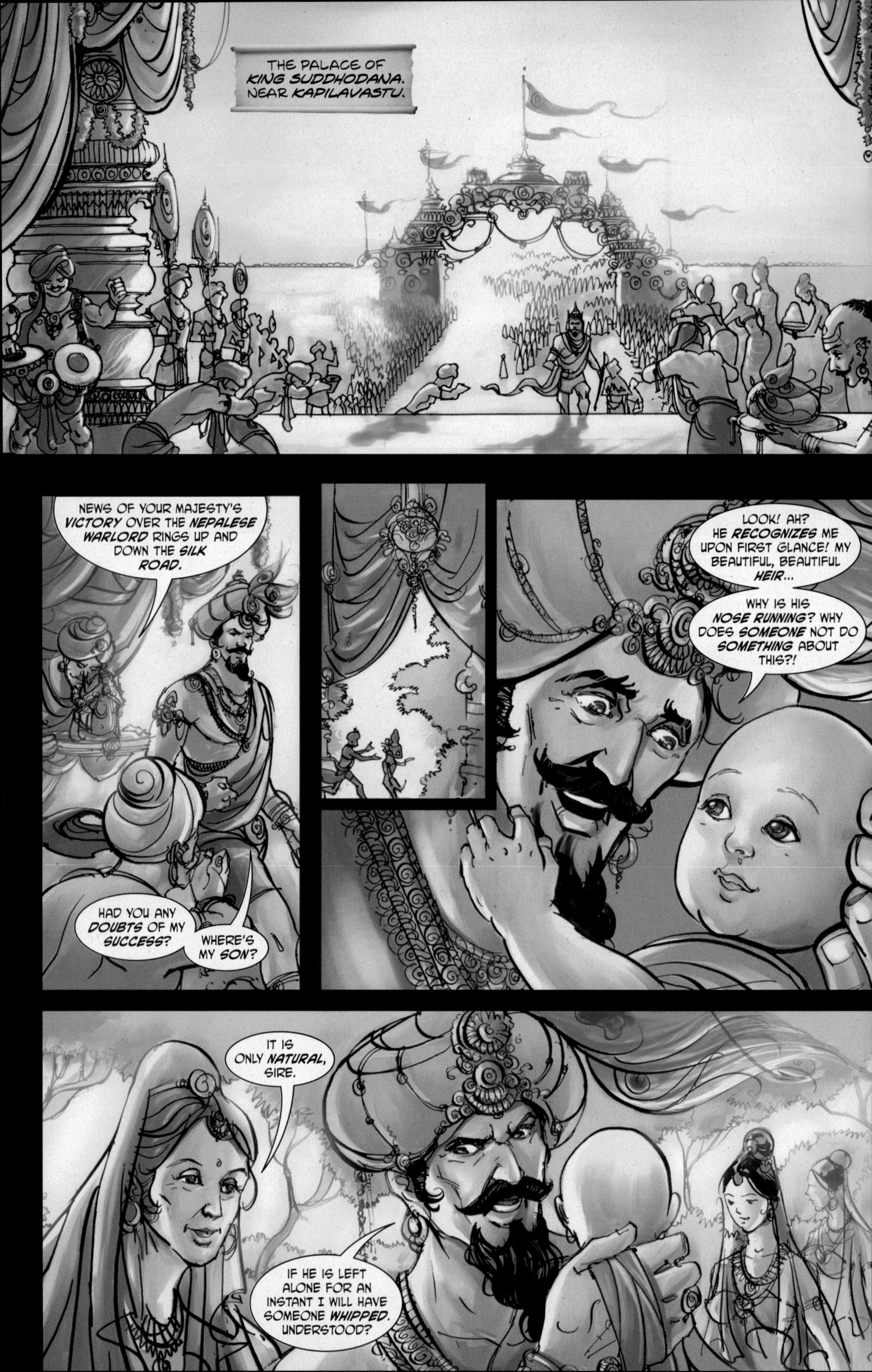
THE PALACE OF KING SUDDHODANA. NEAR KAPILAVASTU.
NEWS OF YOUR MAJESTY'S VICTORY OVER THE NEPALESE WARLORD RINGS UP AND DOWN THE SILK ROAD.
HAD YOU ANY DOUBTS OF MY SUCCESS?
WHERE'S MY SON?
LOOK! AH? HE RECOGNIZES ME UPON FIRST GLANCE! MY BEAUTIFUL, BEAUTIFUL HEIR...
WHY IS HIS NOSE RUNNING? WHY DOES SOMEONE NOT DO SOMETHING ABOUT THIS?!
IT IS ONLY NATURAL, SIRE.
IF HE IS LEFT ALONE FOR AN INSTANT I WILL HAVE SOMEONE WHIPPED. UNDERSTOOD?

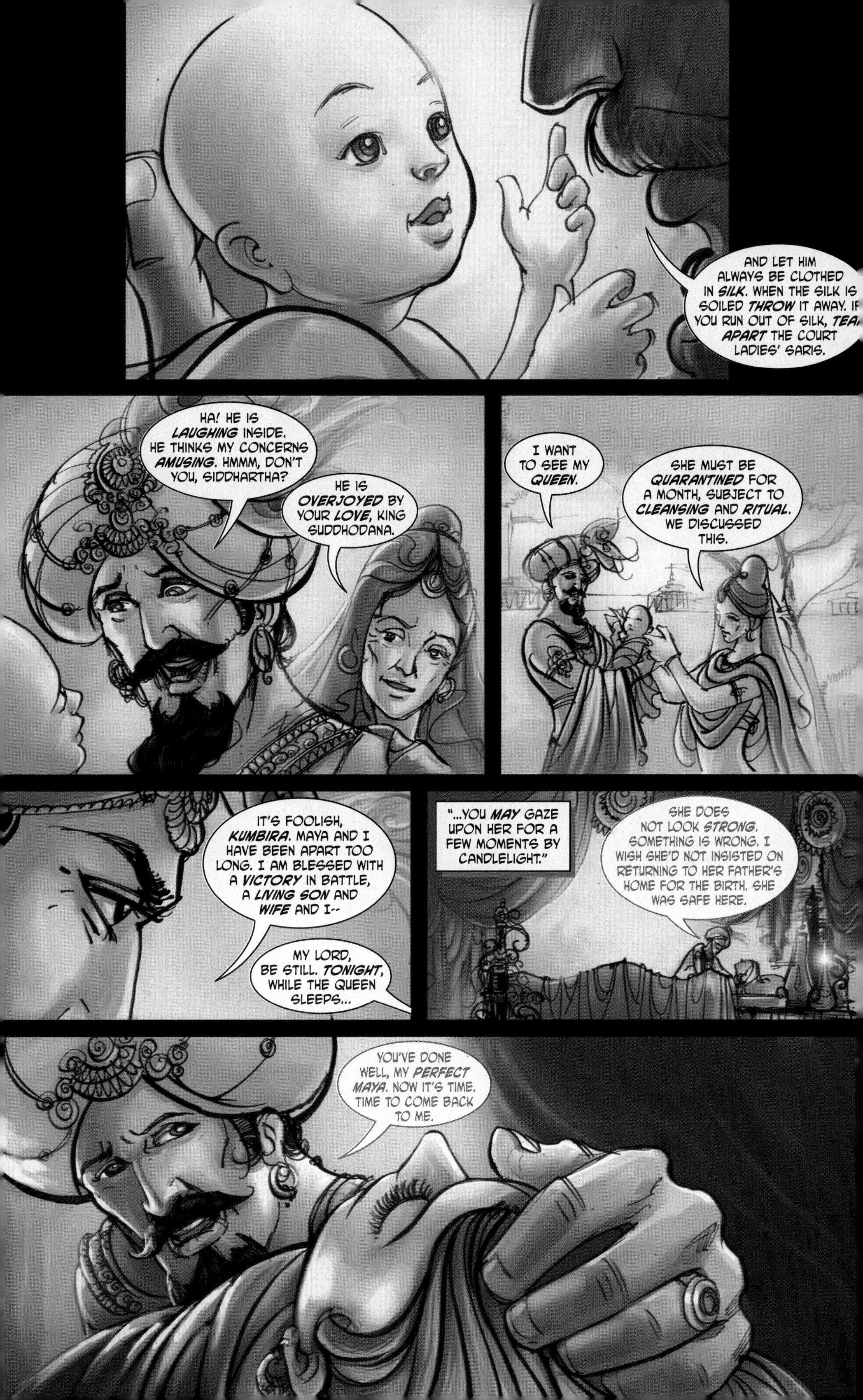
AND LET HIM ALWAYS BE CLOTHED IN SILK. WHEN THE SILK IS SOILED THROW IT AWAY. IF YOU RUN OUT OF SILK, TEAR APART THE COURT LADIES' SARIS.
HA! HE IS LAUGHING INSIDE. HE THINKS MY CONCERNS AMUSING. HMMM, DON'T YOU, SIDDHARTHA?
HE IS OVERJOYED BY YOUR LOVE, KING SUDDHODANA.
I WANT TO SEE MY QUEEN.
SHE MUST BE QUARANTINED FOR A MONTH, SUBJECT TO CLEANSING AND RITUAL. WE DISCUSSED THIS.
IT'S FOOLISH, KUMBIRA. MAYA AND I HAVE BEEN APART TOO LONG. I AM BLESSED WITH A VICTORY IN BATTLE, A LIVING SON AND WIFE AND I--
MY LORD, BE STILL. TONIGHT, WHILE THE QUEEN SLEEPS...
"...YOU MAY GAZE UPON HER FOR A FEW MOMENTS BY CANDLELIGHT."
SHE DOES NOT LOOK STRONG. SOMETHING IS WRONG. I WISH SHE'D NOT INSISTED ON RETURNING TO HER FATHER'S HOME FOR THE BIRTH. SHE WAS SAFE HERE.
YOU'VE DONE WELL, MY PERFECT MAYA. NOW IT'S TIME. TIME TO COME BACK TO ME.

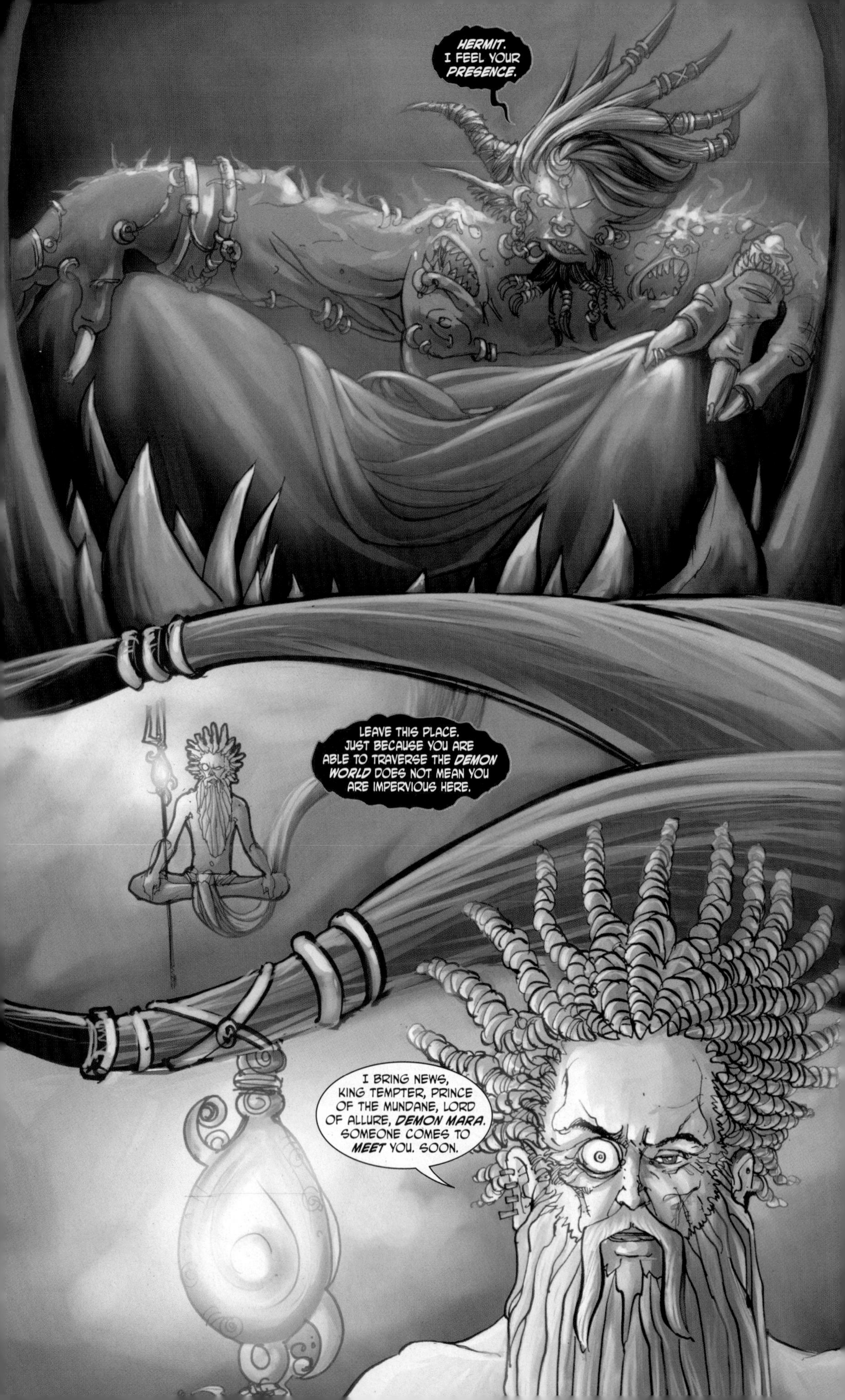
HERMIT. I FEEL YOUR PRESENCE.
LEAVE THIS PLACE. JUST BECAUSE YOU ARE ABLE TO TRAVERSE THE DEMON WORLD DOES NOT MEAN YOU ARE IMPERVIOUS HERE.
I BRING NEWS, KING TEMPTER, PRINCE OF THE MUNDANE, LORD OF ALLURE, DEMON MARA. SOMEONE COMES TO MEET YOU. SOON.

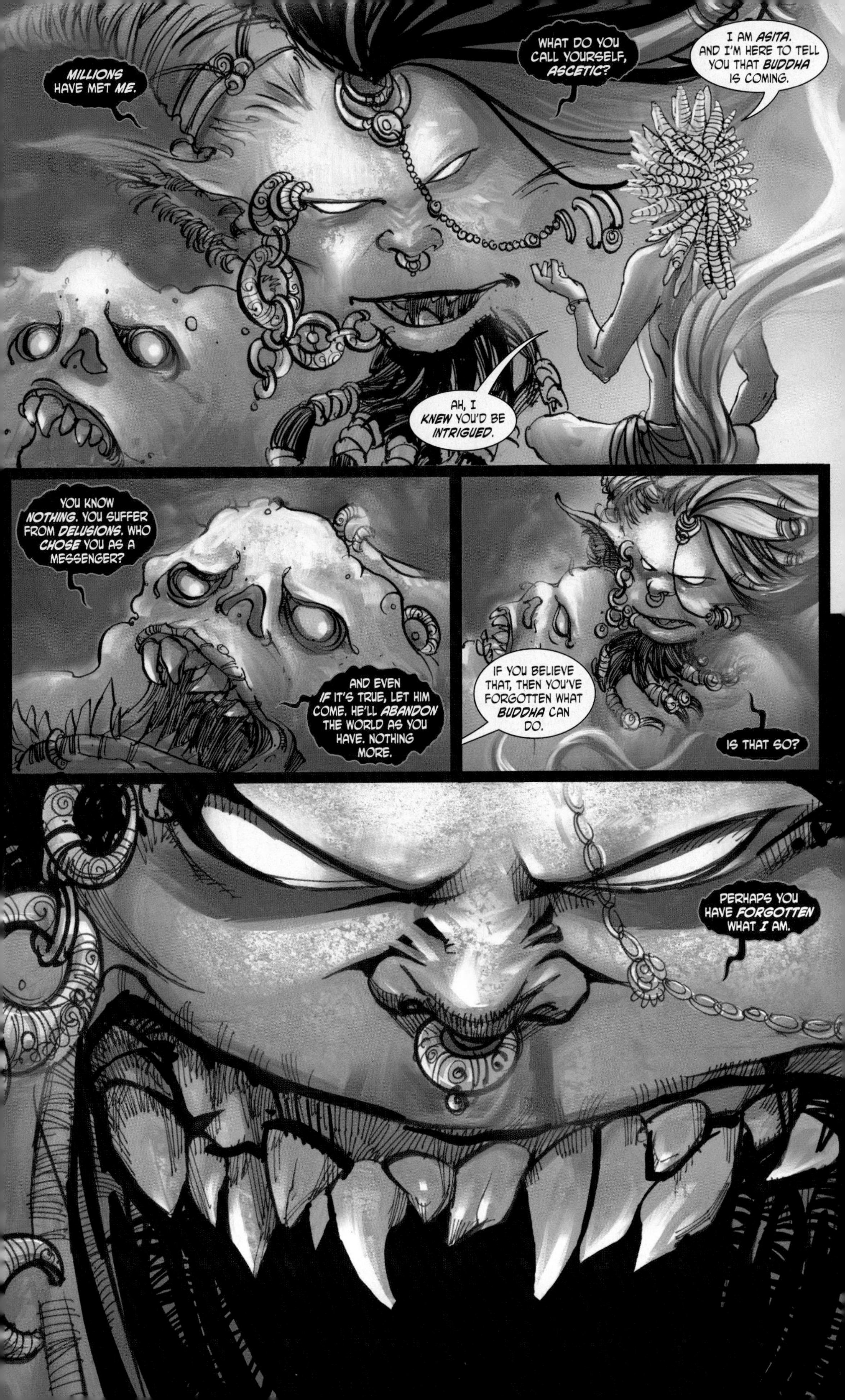
MILLIONS HAVE MET ME.
WHAT DO YOU CALL YOURSELF, ASCETIC?
I AM ASITA. AND I'M HERE TO TELL YOU THAT BUDDHA IS COMING.
AH, I KNEW YOU'D BE INTRIGUED.
YOU KNOW NOTHING. YOU SUFFER FROM DELUSIONS. WHO CHOSE YOU AS A MESSENGER?
AND EVEN IF IT'S TRUE, LET HIM COME. HE'LL ABANDON THE WORLD AS YOU HAVE. NOTHING MORE.
IF YOU BELIEVE THAT, THEN YOU'VE FORGOTTEN WHAT BUDDHA CAN DO.
IS THAT SO?
PERHAPS YOU HAVE FORGOTTEN WHAT I AM.

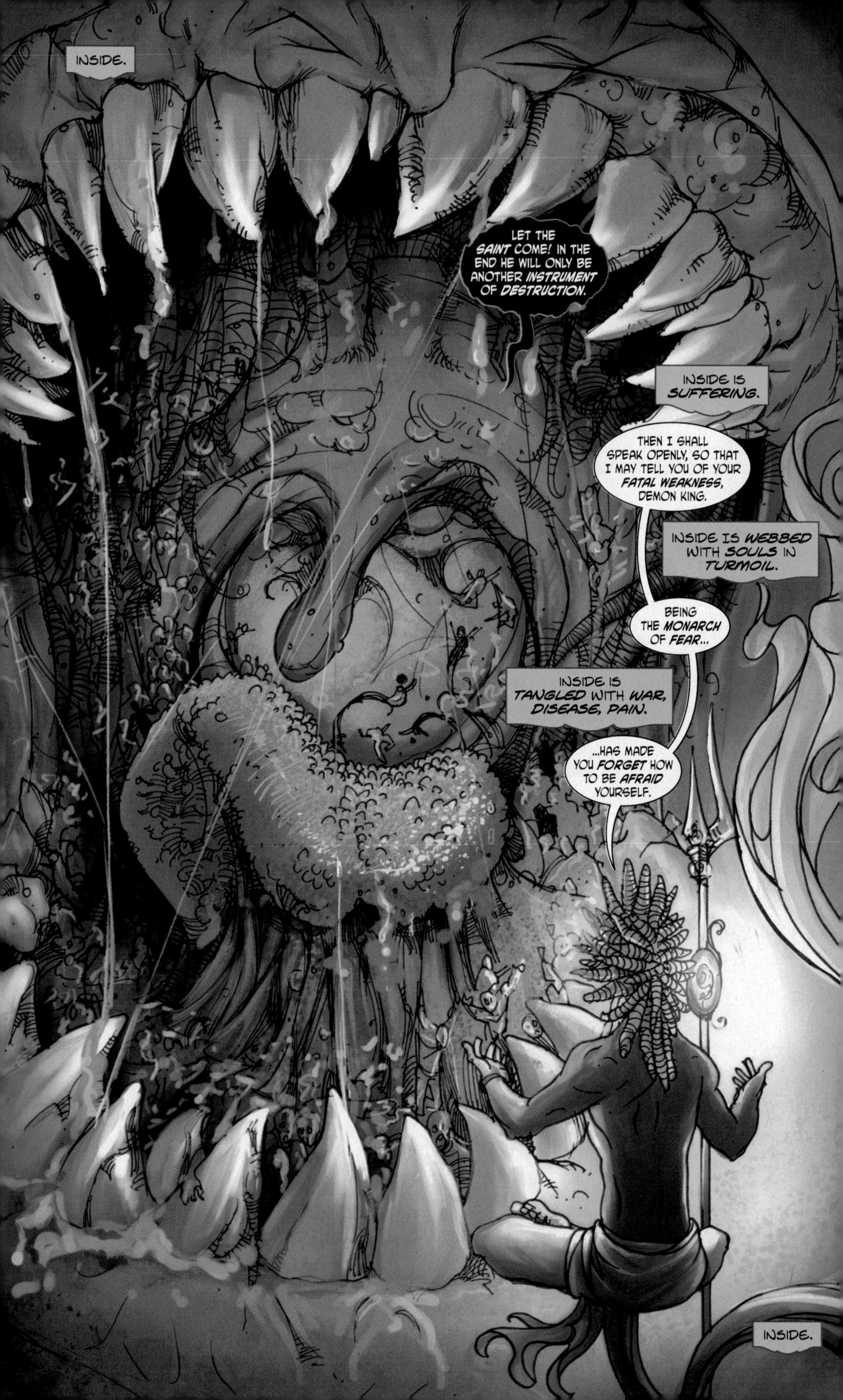
INSIDE.
LET THE SAINT COME! IN THE END HE WILL ONLY BE ANOTHER INSTRUMENT OF DESTRUCTION.
INSIDE IS SUFFERING.
THEN I SHALL SPEAK OPENLY, SO THAT I MAY TELL YOU OF YOUR FATAL WEAKNESS, DEMON KING.
INSIDE IS WEBBED WITH SOULS IN TURMOIL.
BEING THE MONARCH OF FEAR...
INSIDE IS TANGLED WITH WAR, DISEASE, PAIN.
...HAS MADE YOU FORGET HOW TO BE AFRAID YOURSELF.
INSIDE.

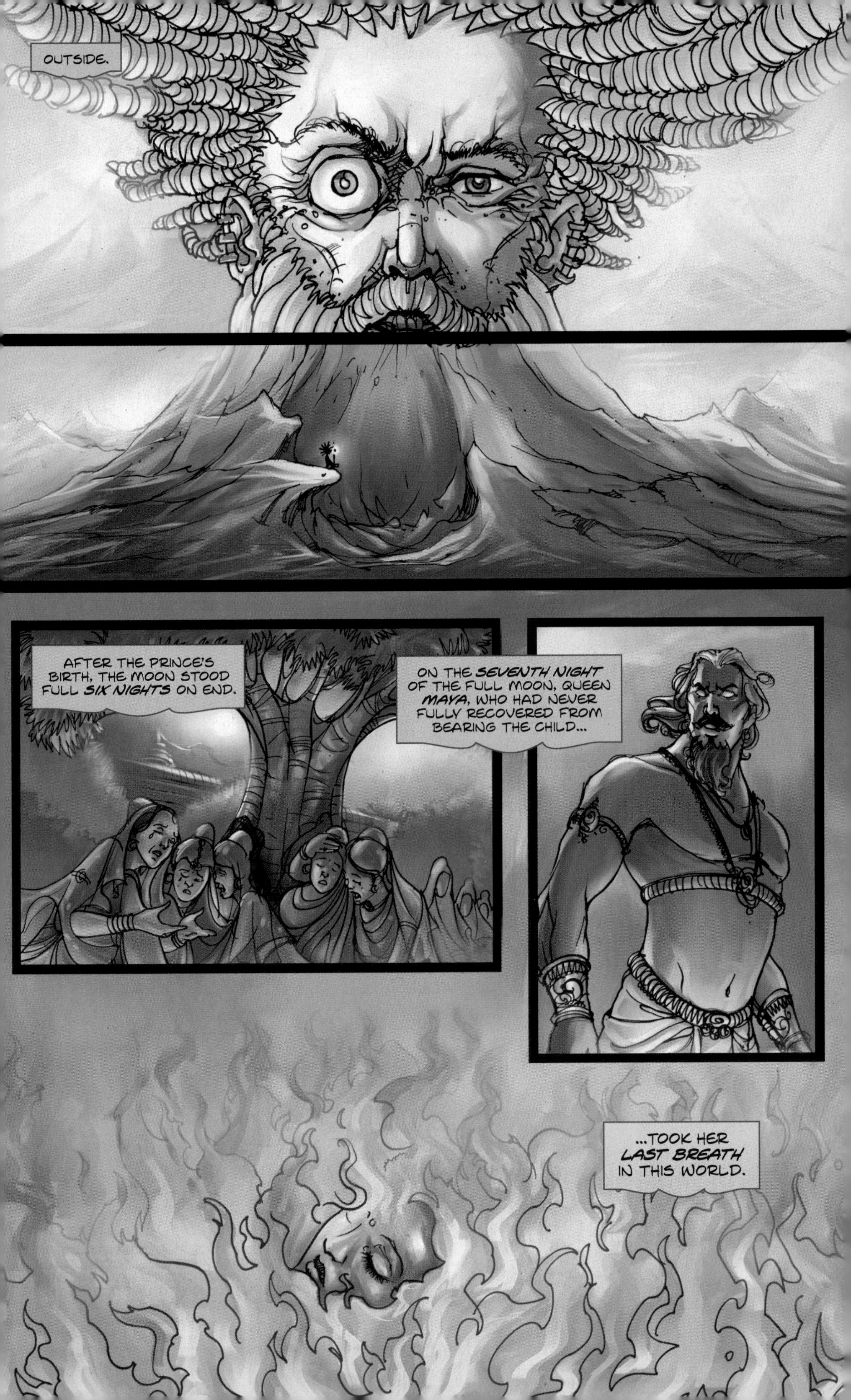
OUTSIDE.
AFTER THE PRINCE'S BIRTH, THE MOON STOOD FULL SIX NIGHTS ON END.
ON THE SEVENTH NIGHT OF THE FULL MOON, QUEEN MAYA, WHO HAD NEVER FULLY RECOVERED FROM BEARING THE CHILD...
...TOOK HER LAST BREATH IN THIS WORLD.

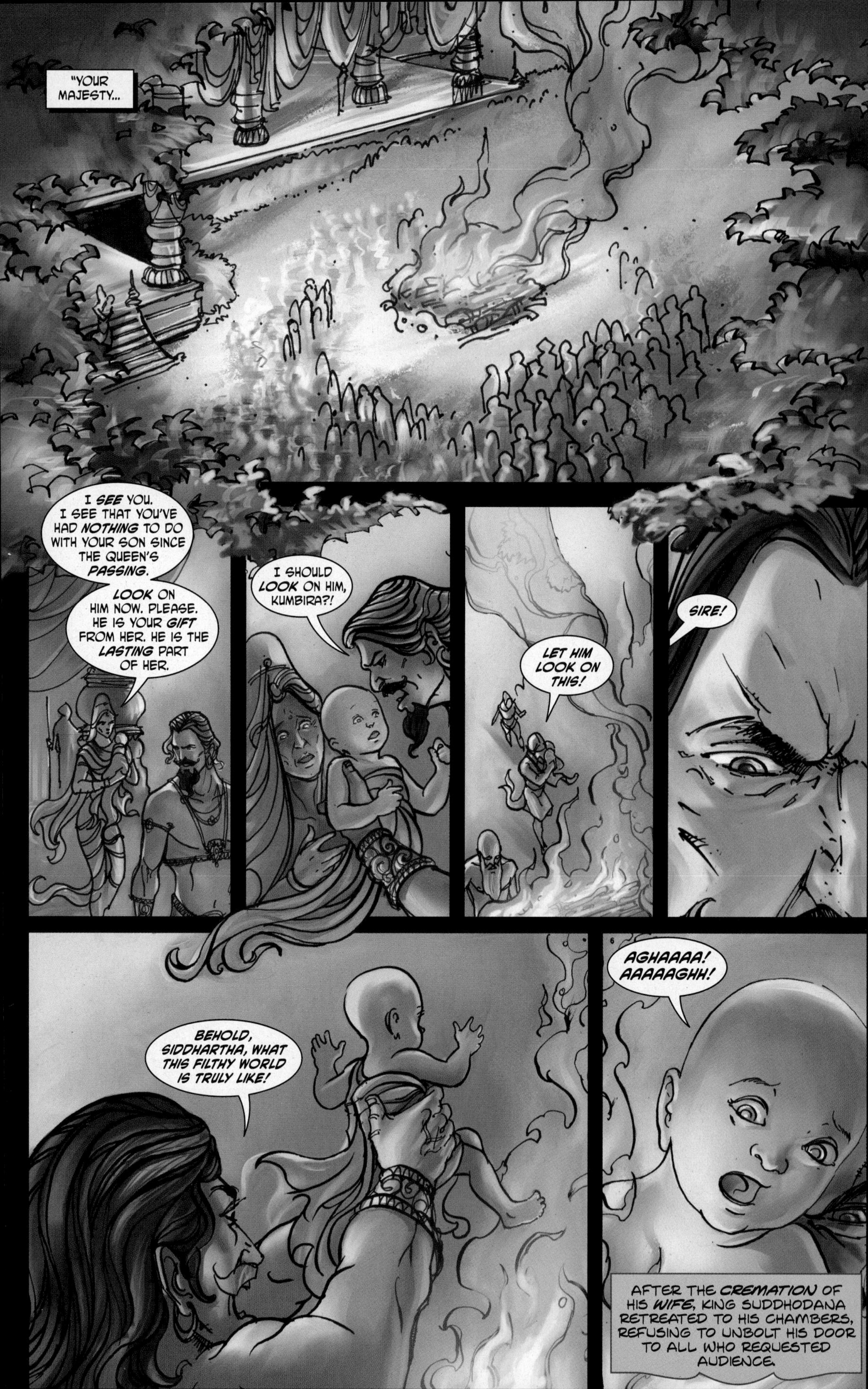
"YOUR MAJESTY...
I SEE YOU. I SEE THAT YOU'VE HAD NOTHING TO DO WITH YOUR SON SINCE THE QUEEN'S PASSING.
LOOK ON HIM NOW. PLEASE. HE IS YOUR GIFT FROM HER. HE IS THE LASTING PART OF HER.
I SHOULD LOOK ON HIM, KUMBIRA?!
LET HIM LOOK ON THIS!
SIRE!
BEHOLD, SIDDHARTHA, WHAT THIS FILTHY WORLD IS TRULY LIKE!
AGHAAAA! AAAAAGHH!
AFTER THE CREMATION OF HIS WIFE, KING SUDDHODANA RETREATED TO HIS CHAMBERS, REFUSING TO UNBOLT HIS DOOR TO ALL WHO REQUESTED AUDIENCE.

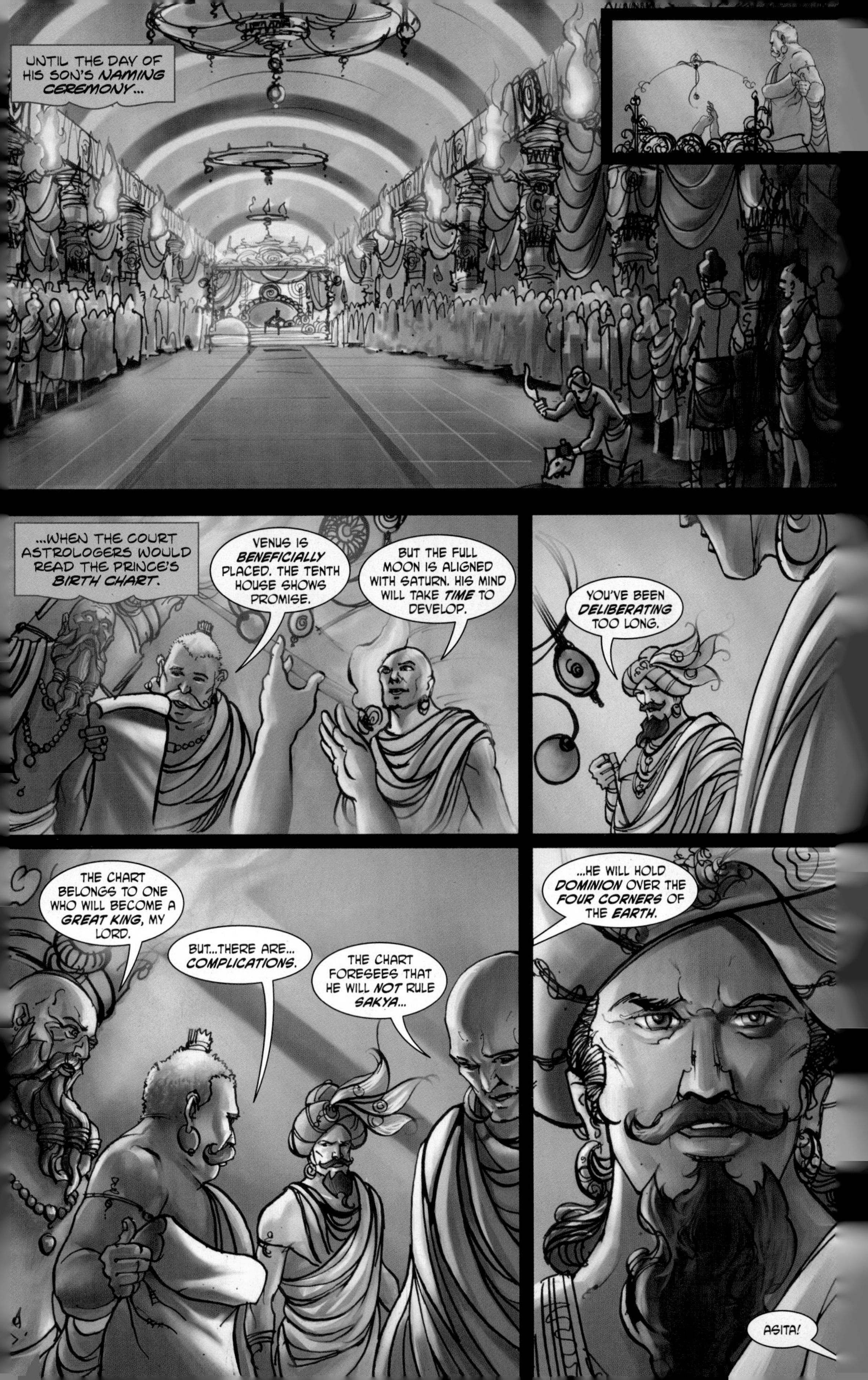
UNTIL THE DAY OF HIS SON'S NAMING CEREMONY...
...WHEN THE COURT ASTROLOGERS WOULD READ THE PRINCE'S BIRTH CHART.
VENUS IS BENEFICIALLY PLACED. THE TENTH HOUSE SHOWS PROMISE.
BUT THE FULL MOON IS ALIGNED WITH SATURN. HIS MIND WILL TAKE TIME TO DEVELOP.
YOU'VE BEEN DELIBERATING TOO LONG.
THE CHART BELONGS TO ONE WHO WILL BECOME A GREAT KING, MY LORD.
BUT...THERE ARE... COMPLICATIONS.
THE CHART FORESEES THAT HE WILL NOT RULE SAKYA...
...HE WILL HOLD DOMINION OVER THE FOUR CORNERS OF THE EARTH.
ASITA!

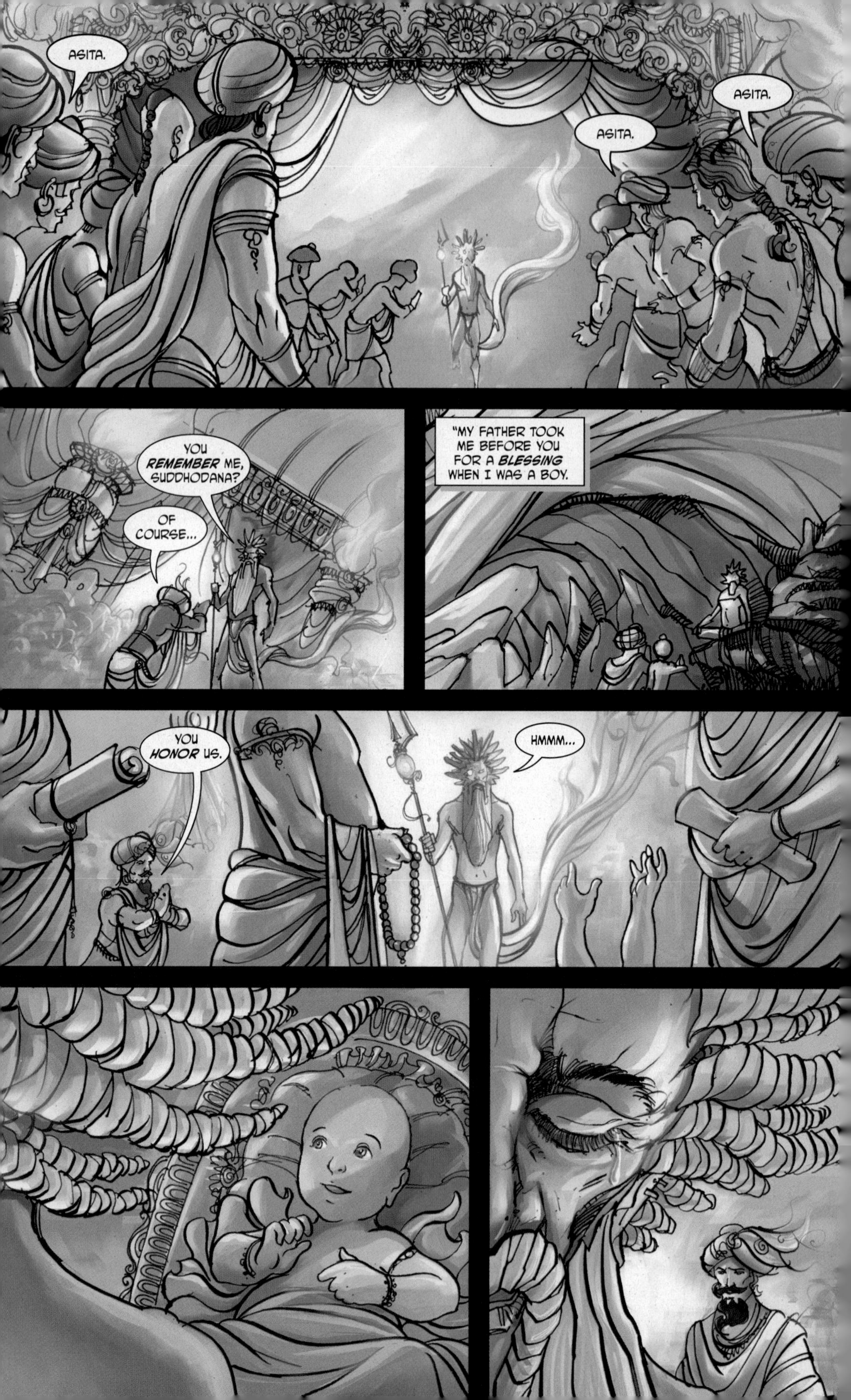
ASITA.
ASITA.
ASITA.
YOU REMEMBER ME, SUDDHODANA?
OF COURSE...
"MY FATHER TOOK ME BEFORE YOU FOR A BLESSING WHEN I WAS A BOY.
YOU HONOR US.
HMMM...

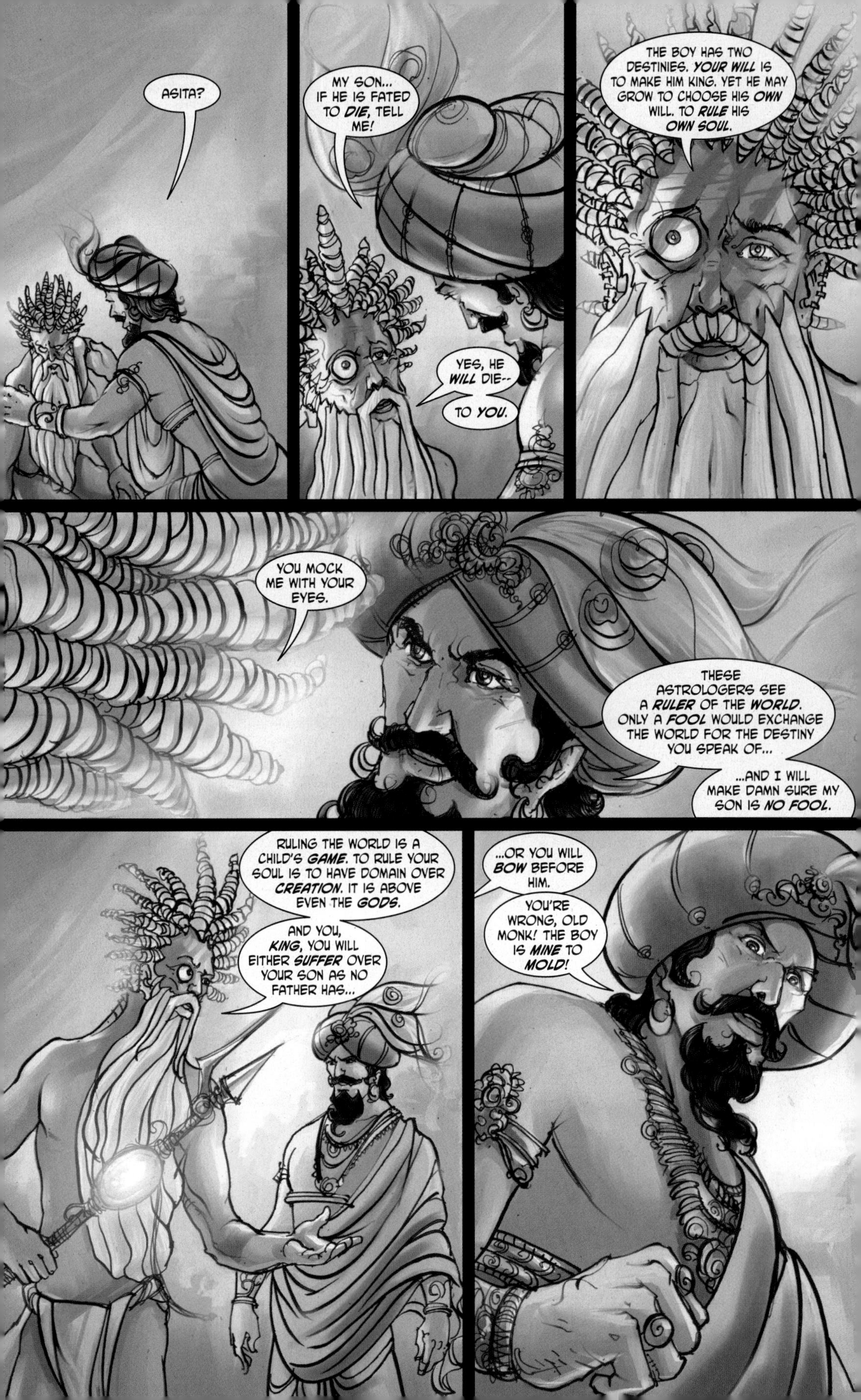
ASITA?
MY SON... IF HE IS FATED TO *DIE*, TELL ME!
YES, HE *WILL* DIE--
TO *YOU*.
THE BOY HAS TWO DESTINIES. *YOUR WILL* IS TO MAKE HIM KING. YET HE MAY GROW TO CHOOSE HIS *OWN* WILL. TO *RULE* HIS *OWN SOUL*.
YOU MOCK ME WITH YOUR EYES.
THESE ASTROLOGERS SEE A *RULER* OF THE *WORLD*. ONLY A *FOOL* WOULD EXCHANGE THE WORLD FOR THE DESTINY YOU SPEAK OF...
...AND I WILL MAKE DAMN SURE MY SON IS *NO FOOL*.
RULING THE WORLD IS A CHILD'S *GAME*. TO RULE YOUR SOUL IS TO HAVE DOMAIN OVER *CREATION*. IT IS ABOVE EVEN THE *GODS*.
AND YOU, *KING*, YOU WILL EITHER *SUFFER* OVER YOUR SON AS NO FATHER HAS...
...OR YOU WILL *BOW* BEFORE HIM.
YOU'RE WRONG, OLD MONK! THE BOY IS *MINE* TO *MOLD*!

SO YOU SAY...I WILL LEAVE YOU TO *YOUR* UNDERSTANDING THEN--

WAIT! WHY DO YOU *WEEP* UPON SEEING MY CHILD?

I WEEP BECAUSE I SHALL NOT LIVE LONG ENOUGH TO HEAR THE *IMMORTAL TRUTH* THE BUDDHA WILL SPEAK.

TEMPLE OF *SHIVA.* BUILT WITHIN THE PALACE WALLS BY KING *SINAHANA,* SUDDHODANA'S FATHER.

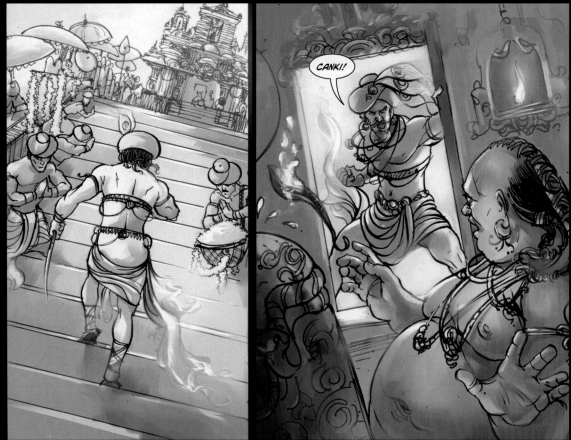

CANKI!

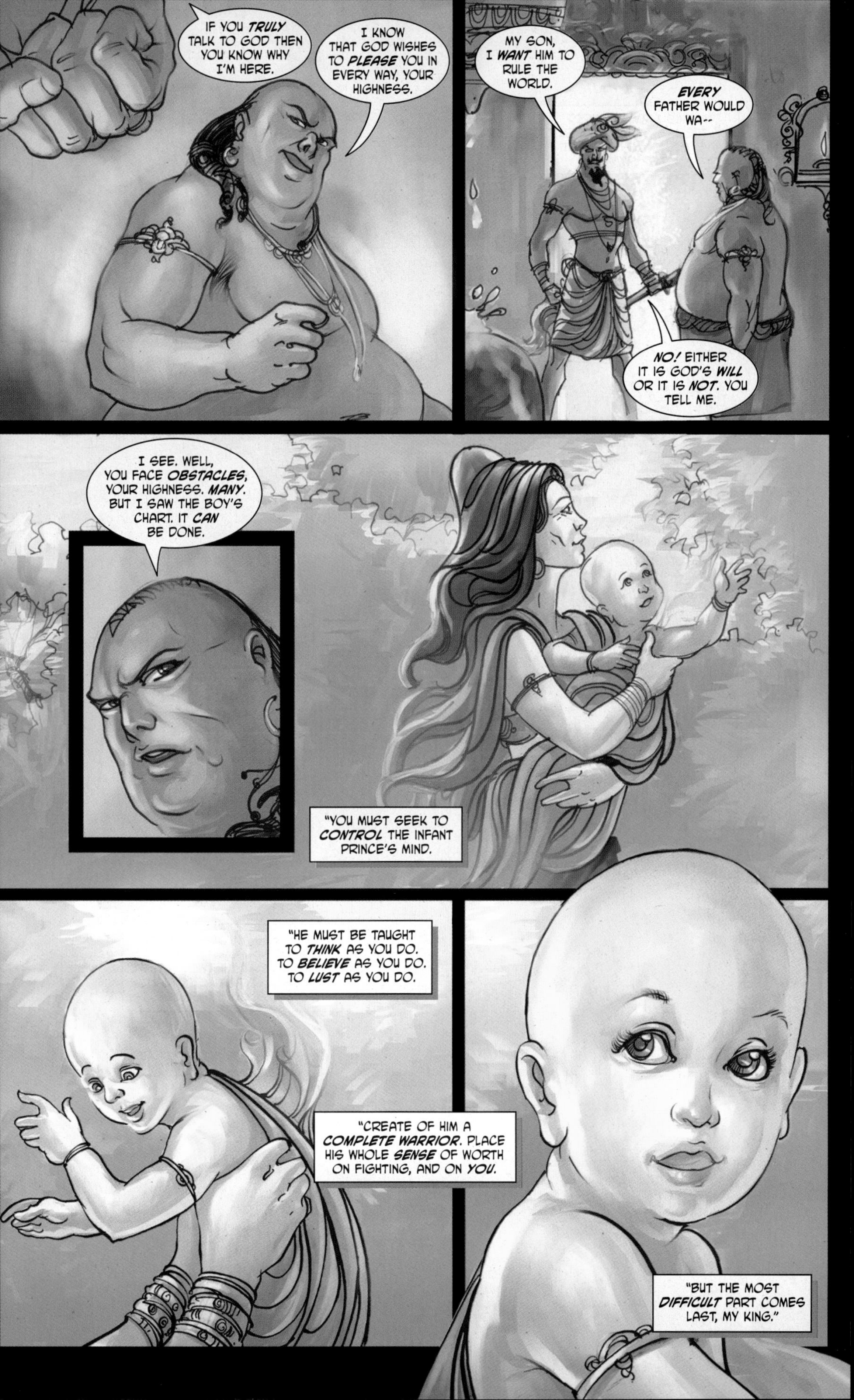
IF YOU TRULY TALK TO GOD THEN YOU KNOW WHY I'M HERE.
I KNOW THAT GOD WISHES TO PLEASE YOU IN EVERY WAY, YOUR HIGHNESS.
MY SON, I WANT HIM TO RULE THE WORLD.
EVERY FATHER WOULD WA--
NO! EITHER IT IS GOD'S WILL OR IT IS NOT. YOU TELL ME.
I SEE. WELL, YOU FACE OBSTACLES, YOUR HIGHNESS. MANY. BUT I SAW THE BOY'S CHART. IT CAN BE DONE.
"YOU MUST SEEK TO CONTROL THE INFANT PRINCE'S MIND.
"HE MUST BE TAUGHT TO THINK AS YOU DO. TO BELIEVE AS YOU DO. TO LUST AS YOU DO.
"CREATE OF HIM A COMPLETE WARRIOR. PLACE HIS WHOLE SENSE OF WORTH ON FIGHTING, AND ON YOU.
"BUT THE MOST DIFFICULT PART COMES LAST, MY KING."

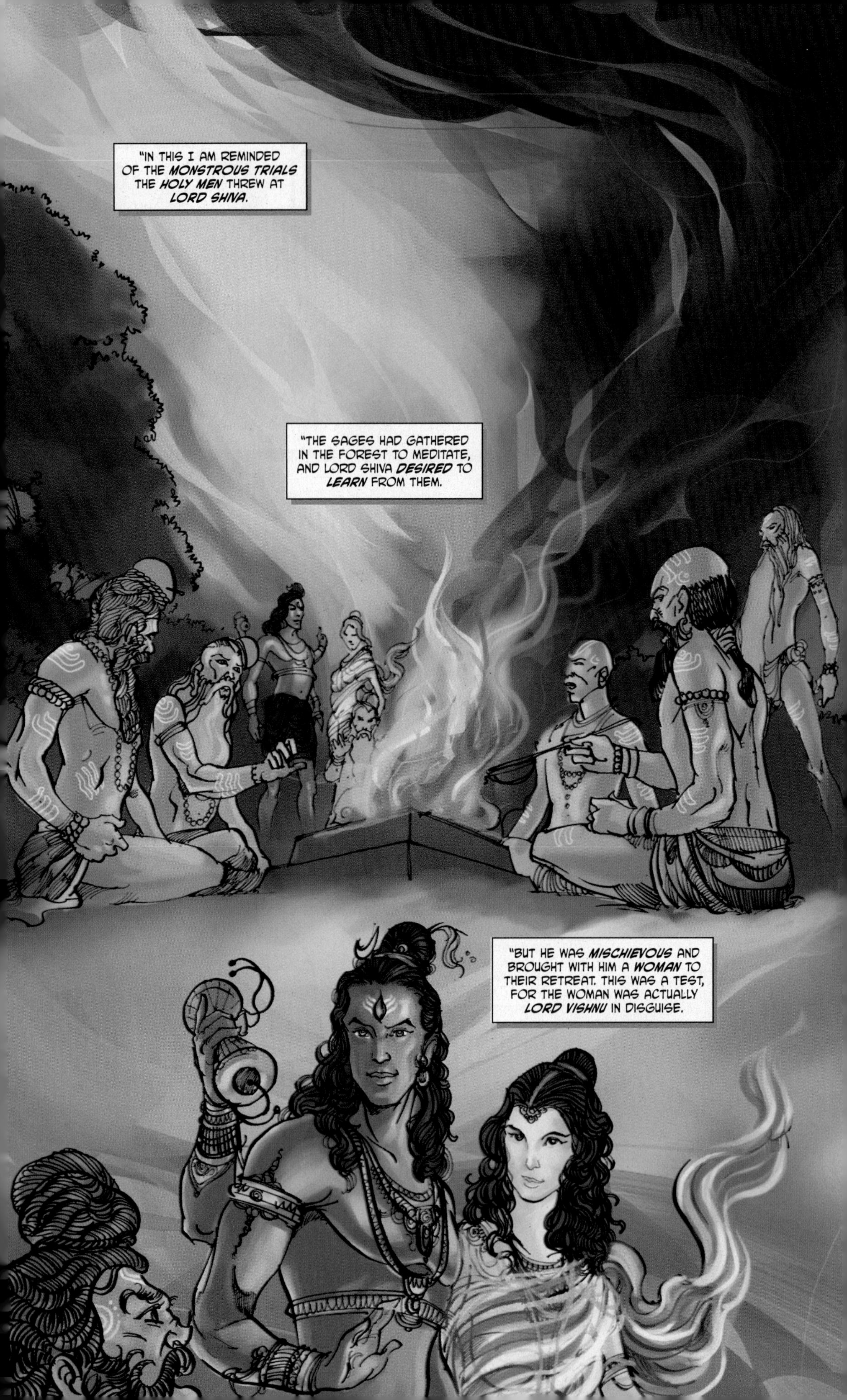
"IN THIS I AM REMINDED OF THE MONSTROUS TRIALS THE HOLY MEN THREW AT LORD SHIVA.
"THE SAGES HAD GATHERED IN THE FOREST TO MEDITATE, AND LORD SHIVA DESIRED TO LEARN FROM THEM.
"BUT HE WAS MISCHIEVOUS AND BROUGHT WITH HIM A WOMAN TO THEIR RETREAT. THIS WAS A TEST, FOR THE WOMAN WAS ACTUALLY LORD VISHNU IN DISGUISE.

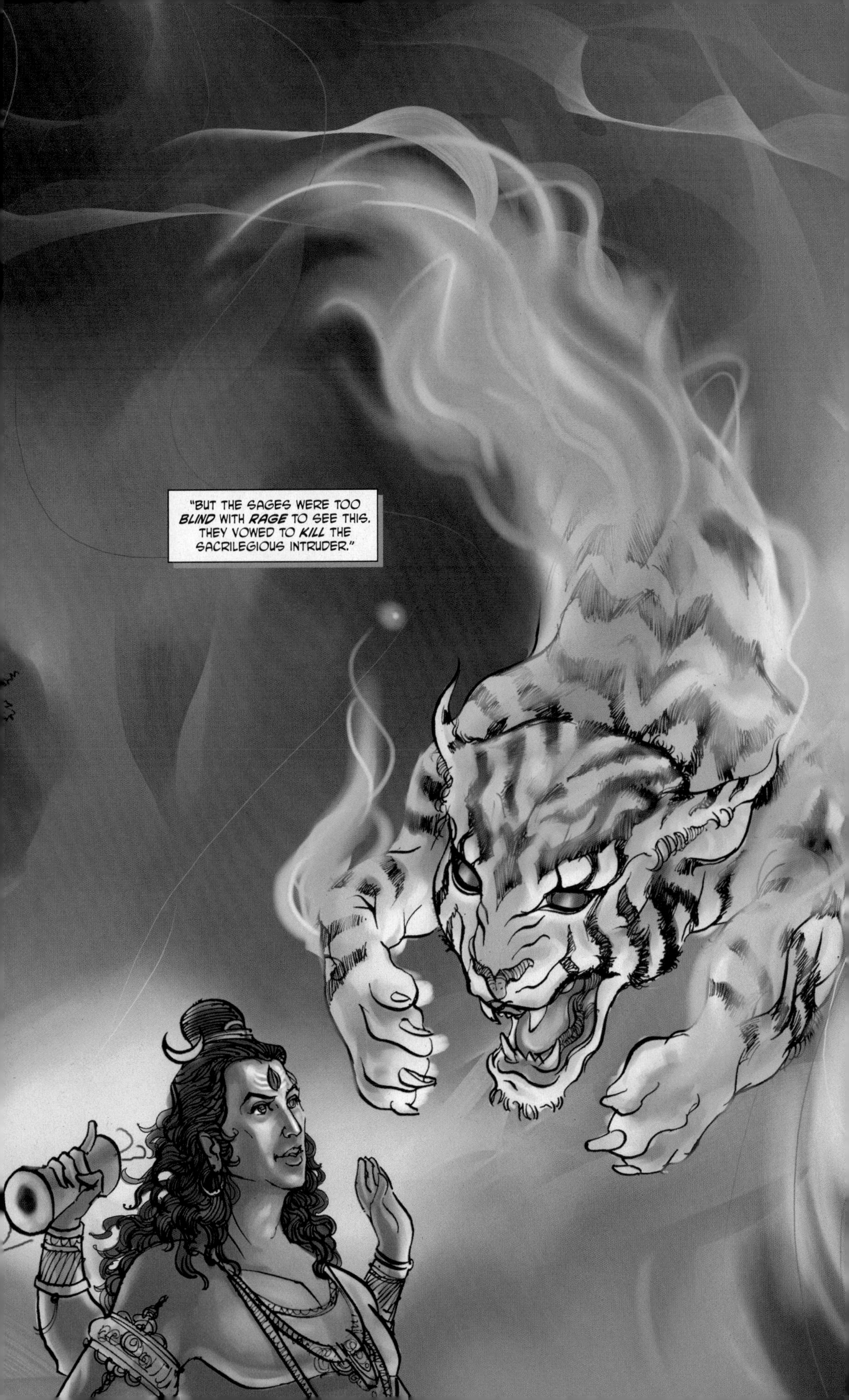
"BUT THE SAGES WERE TOO BLIND WITH RAGE TO SEE THIS. THEY VOWED TO KILL THE SACRILEGIOUS INTRUDER."

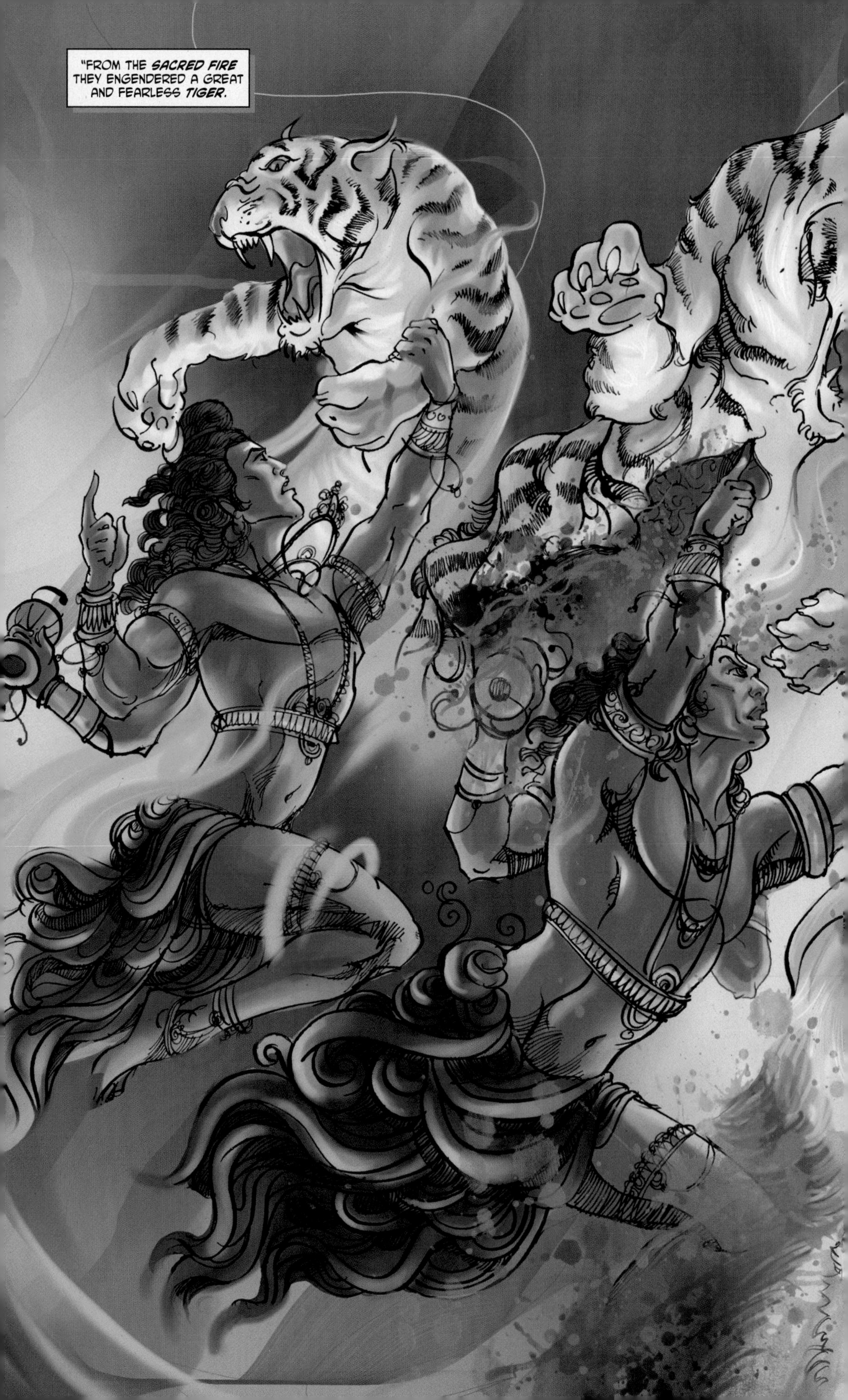
"FROM THE SACRED FIRE THEY ENGENDERED A GREAT AND FEARLESS TIGER.

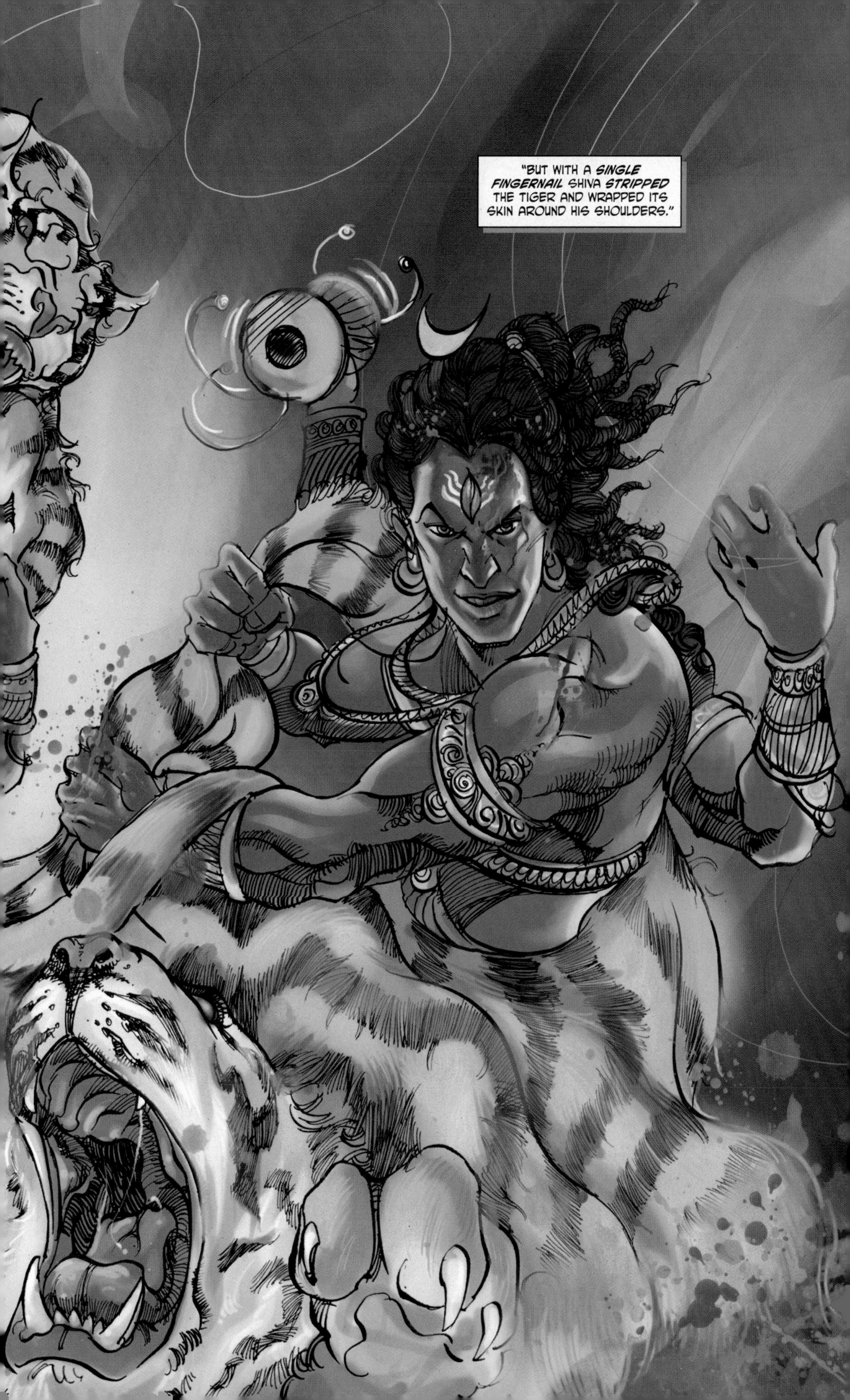
"BUT WITH A SINGLE FINGERNAIL SHIVA STRIPPED THE TIGER AND WRAPPED ITS SKIN AROUND HIS SHOULDERS."

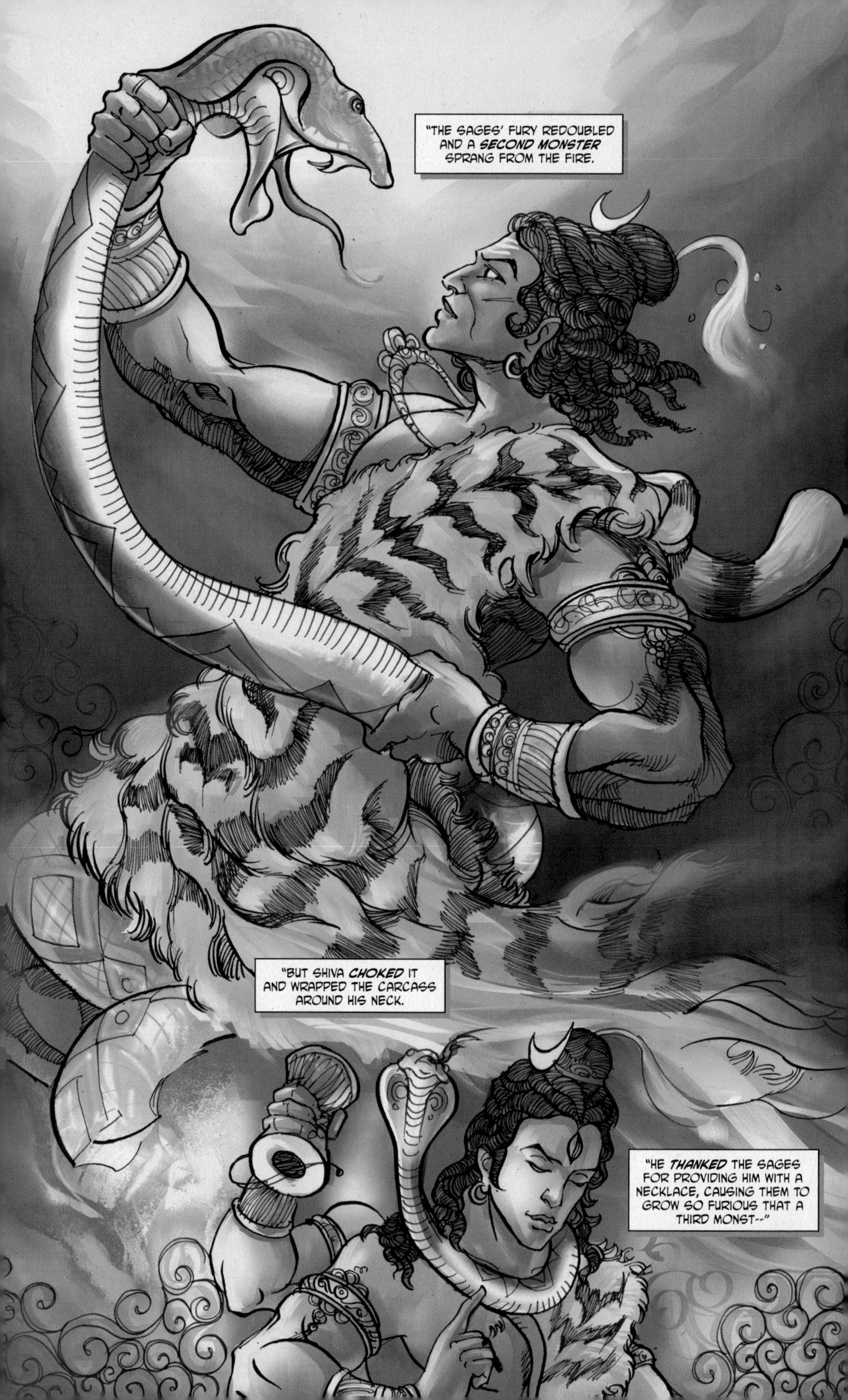
"THE SAGES' FURY REDOUBLED AND A SECOND MONSTER SPRANG FROM THE FIRE.
"BUT SHIVA CHOKED IT AND WRAPPED THE CARCASS AROUND HIS NECK.
"HE THANKED THE SAGES FOR PROVIDING HIM WITH A NECKLACE, CAUSING THEM TO GROW SO FURIOUS THAT A THIRD MONST--"

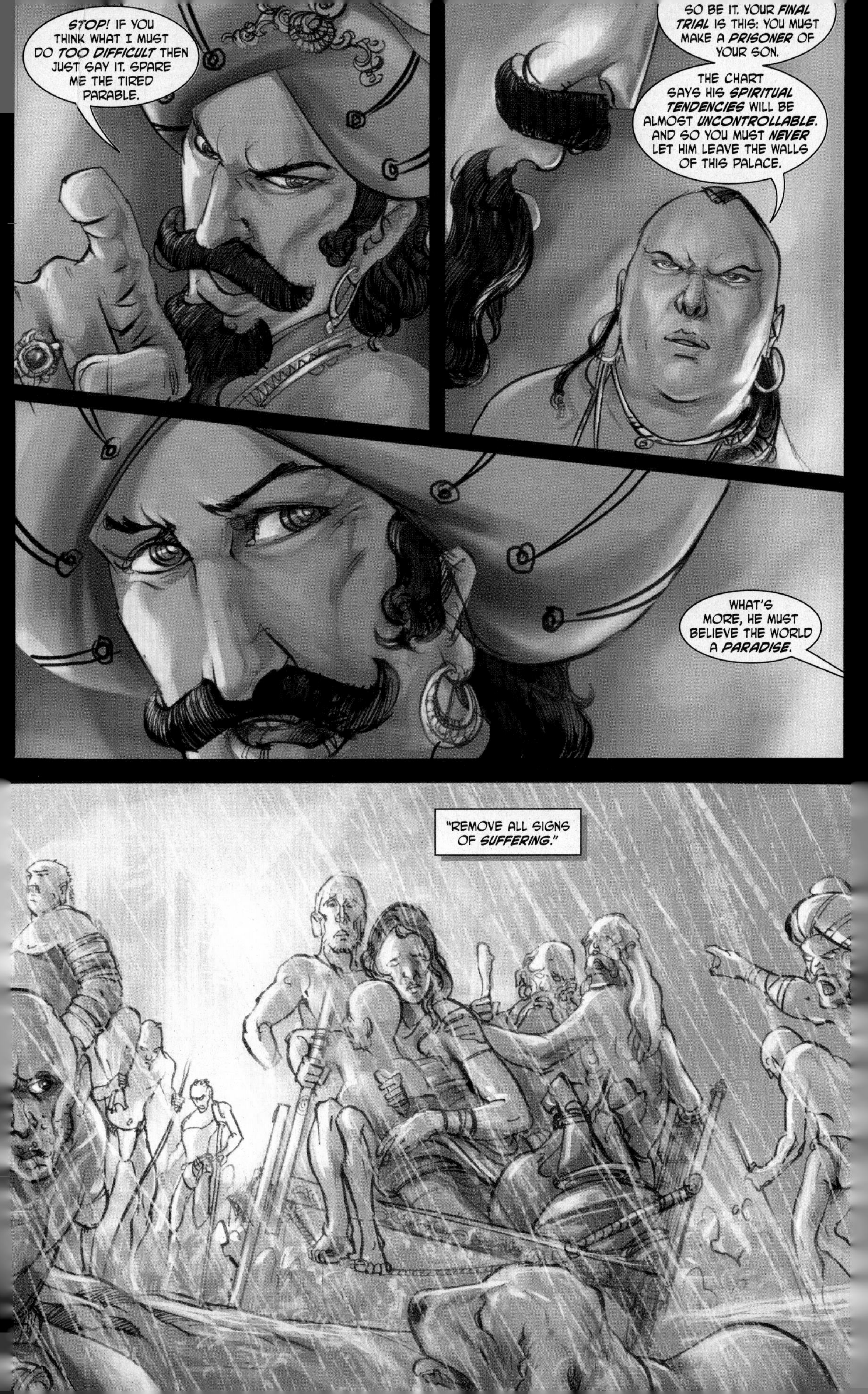
STOP! IF YOU THINK WHAT I MUST DO TOO DIFFICULT THEN JUST SAY IT. SPARE ME THE TIRED PARABLE.
SO BE IT. YOUR FINAL TRIAL IS THIS: YOU MUST MAKE A PRISONER OF YOUR SON.
THE CHART SAYS HIS SPIRITUAL TENDENCIES WILL BE ALMOST UNCONTROLLABLE. AND SO YOU MUST NEVER LET HIM LEAVE THE WALLS OF THIS PALACE.
WHAT'S MORE, HE MUST BELIEVE THE WORLD A PARADISE.
"REMOVE ALL SIGNS OF SUFFERING."

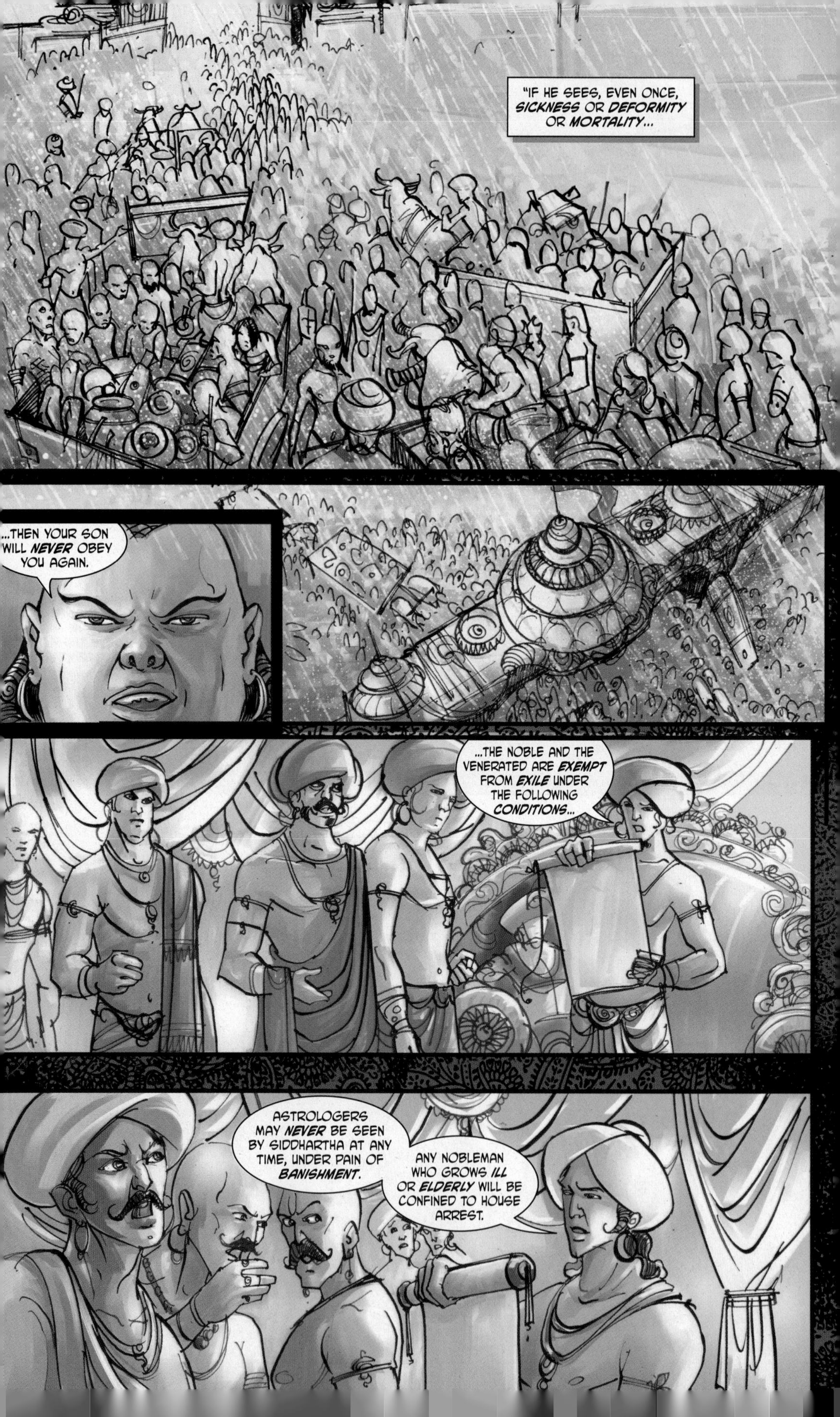
"IF HE SEES, EVEN ONCE, SICKNESS OR DEFORMITY OR MORTALITY...
...THEN YOUR SON WILL NEVER OBEY YOU AGAIN.
...THE NOBLE AND THE VENERATED ARE EXEMPT FROM EXILE UNDER THE FOLLOWING CONDITIONS...
ASTROLOGERS MAY NEVER BE SEEN BY SIDDHARTHA AT ANY TIME, UNDER PAIN OF BANISHMENT.
ANY NOBLEMAN WHO GROWS ILL OR ELDERLY WILL BE CONFINED TO HOUSE ARREST.

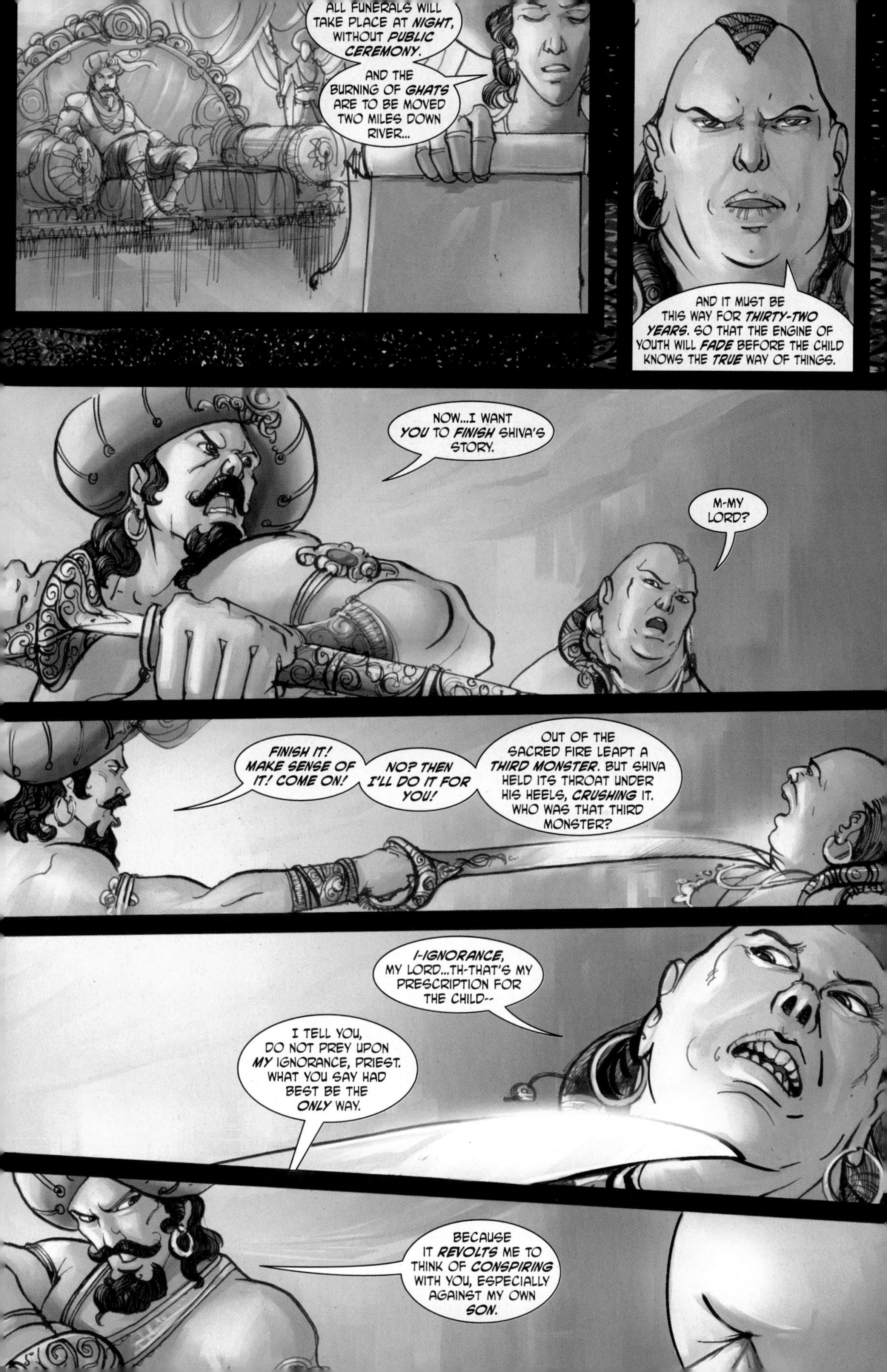
ALL FUNERALS WILL TAKE PLACE AT NIGHT, WITHOUT PUBLIC CEREMONY.
AND THE BURNING OF GHATS ARE TO BE MOVED TWO MILES DOWN RIVER...
AND IT MUST BE THIS WAY FOR THIRTY-TWO YEARS. SO THAT THE ENGINE OF YOUTH WILL FADE BEFORE THE CHILD KNOWS THE TRUE WAY OF THINGS.
NOW...I WANT YOU TO FINISH SHIVA'S STORY.
M-MY LORD?
FINISH IT! MAKE SENSE OF IT! COME ON!
NO? THEN I'LL DO IT FOR YOU!
OUT OF THE SACRED FIRE LEAPT A THIRD MONSTER. BUT SHIVA HELD ITS THROAT UNDER HIS HEELS, CRUSHING IT. WHO WAS THAT THIRD MONSTER?
I-IGNORANCE, MY LORD...TH-THAT'S MY PRESCRIPTION FOR THE CHILD--
I TELL YOU, DO NOT PREY UPON MY IGNORANCE, PRIEST. WHAT YOU SAY HAD BEST BE THE ONLY WAY.
BECAUSE IT REVOLTS ME TO THINK OF CONSPIRING WITH YOU, ESPECIALLY AGAINST MY OWN SON.

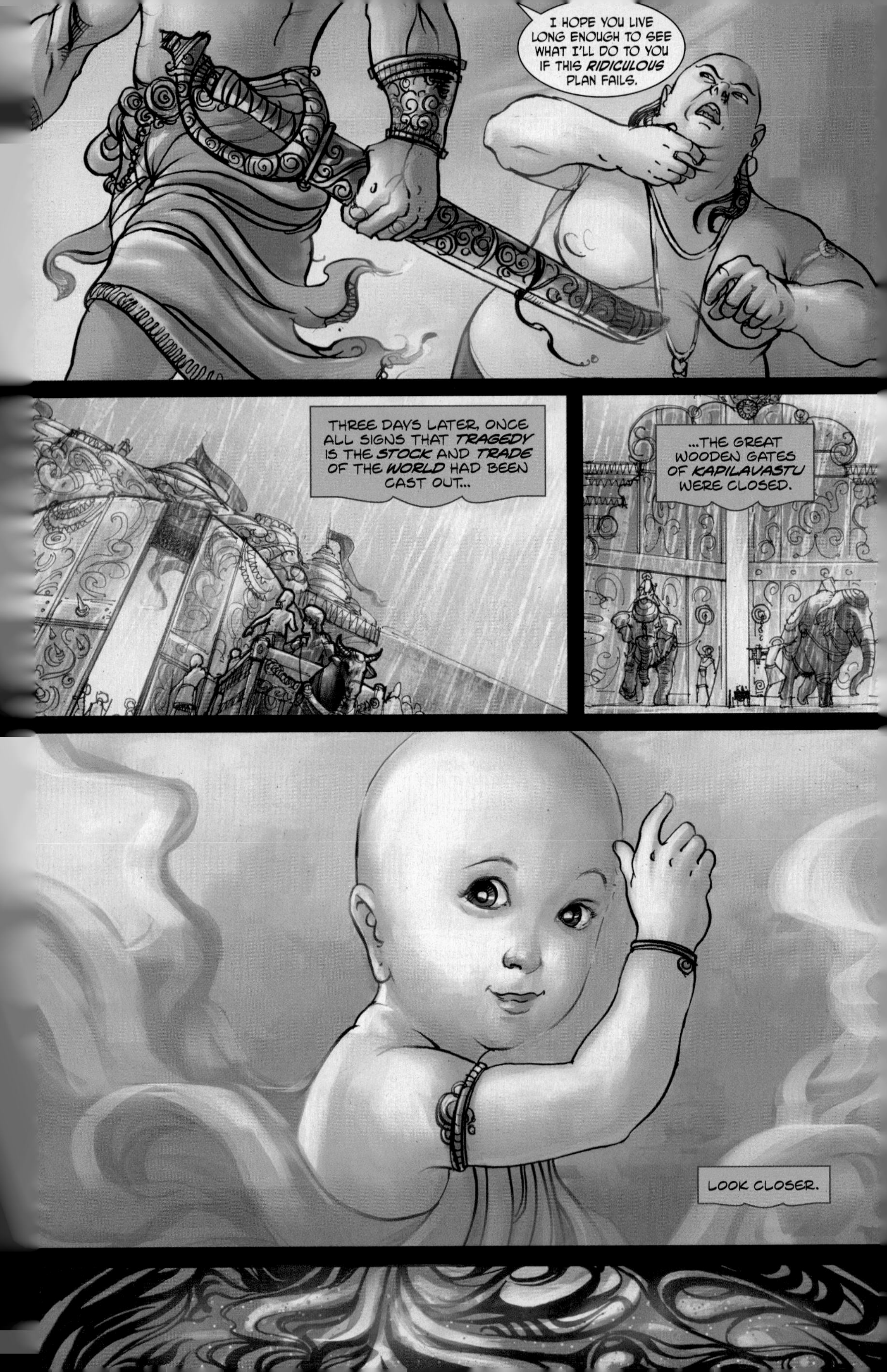
I HOPE YOU LIVE LONG ENOUGH TO SEE WHAT I'LL DO TO YOU IF THIS RIDICULOUS PLAN FAILS.
THREE DAYS LATER, ONCE ALL SIGNS THAT TRAGEDY IS THE STOCK AND TRADE OF THE WORLD HAD BEEN CAST OUT...
...THE GREAT WOODEN GATES OF KAPILAVASTU WERE CLOSED.
LOOK CLOSER.

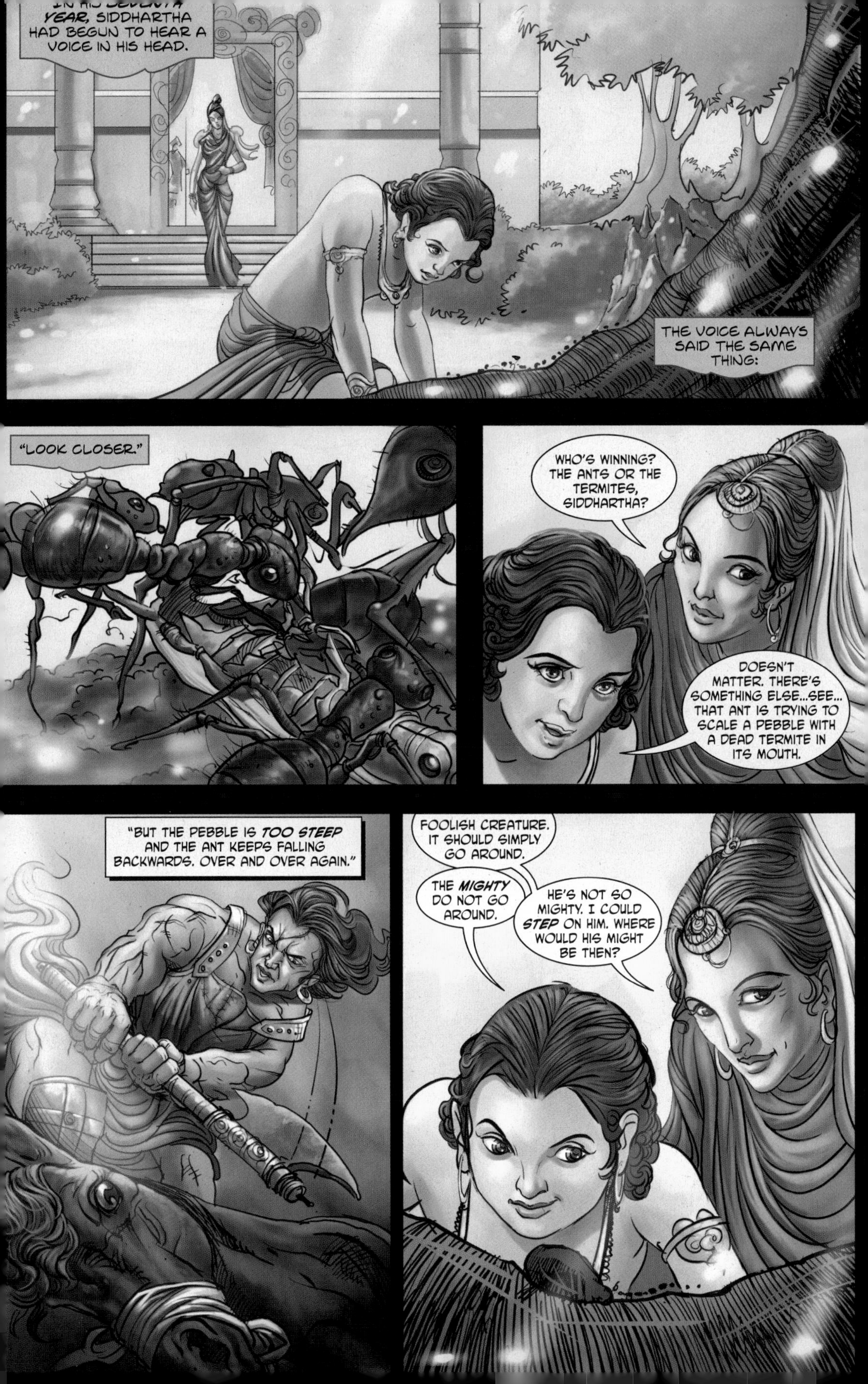

YEAR, SIDDHARTHA HAD BEGUN TO HEAR A VOICE IN HIS HEAD.
THE VOICE ALWAYS SAID THE SAME THING:
"LOOK CLOSER."
WHO'S WINNING? THE ANTS OR THE TERMITES, SIDDHARTHA?
DOESN'T MATTER. THERE'S SOMETHING ELSE...SEE... THAT ANT IS TRYING TO SCALE A PEBBLE WITH A DEAD TERMITE IN ITS MOUTH.
"BUT THE PEBBLE IS *TOO STEEP* AND THE ANT KEEPS FALLING BACKWARDS. OVER AND OVER AGAIN."
FOOLISH CREATURE. IT SHOULD SIMPLY GO AROUND.
THE *MIGHTY* DO NOT GO AROUND.
HE'S NOT SO MIGHTY. I COULD *STEP* ON HIM. WHERE WOULD HIS MIGHT BE THEN?

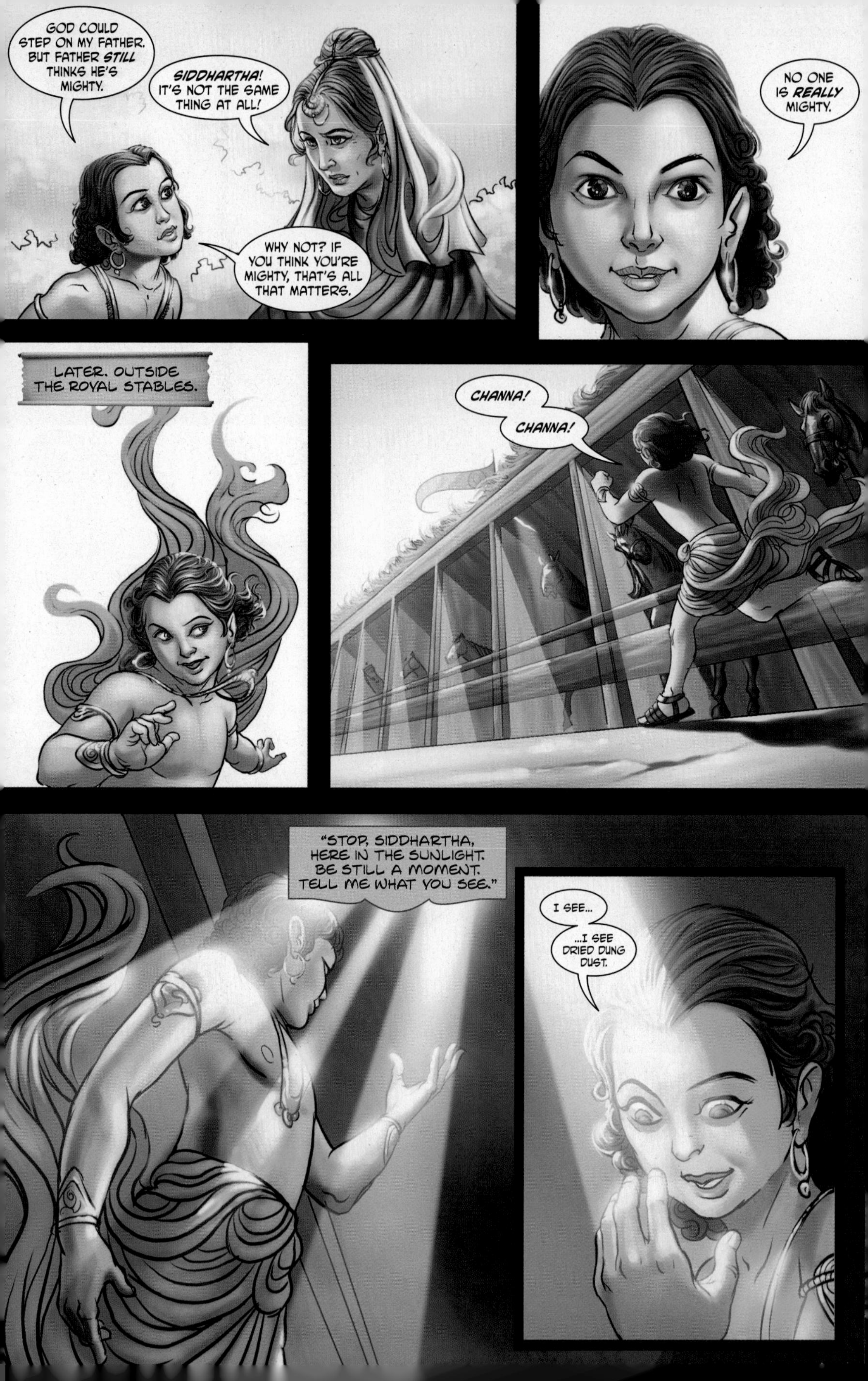
GOD COULD STEP ON MY FATHER. BUT FATHER STILL THINKS HE'S MIGHTY.
SIDDHARTHA! IT'S NOT THE SAME THING AT ALL!
WHY NOT? IF YOU THINK YOU'RE MIGHTY, THAT'S ALL THAT MATTERS.
NO ONE IS REALLY MIGHTY.
LATER. OUTSIDE THE ROYAL STABLES.
CHANNA!
CHANNA!
"STOP, SIDDHARTHA, HERE IN THE SUNLIGHT. BE STILL A MOMENT. TELL ME WHAT YOU SEE."
I SEE...
...I SEE DRIED DUNG DUST.

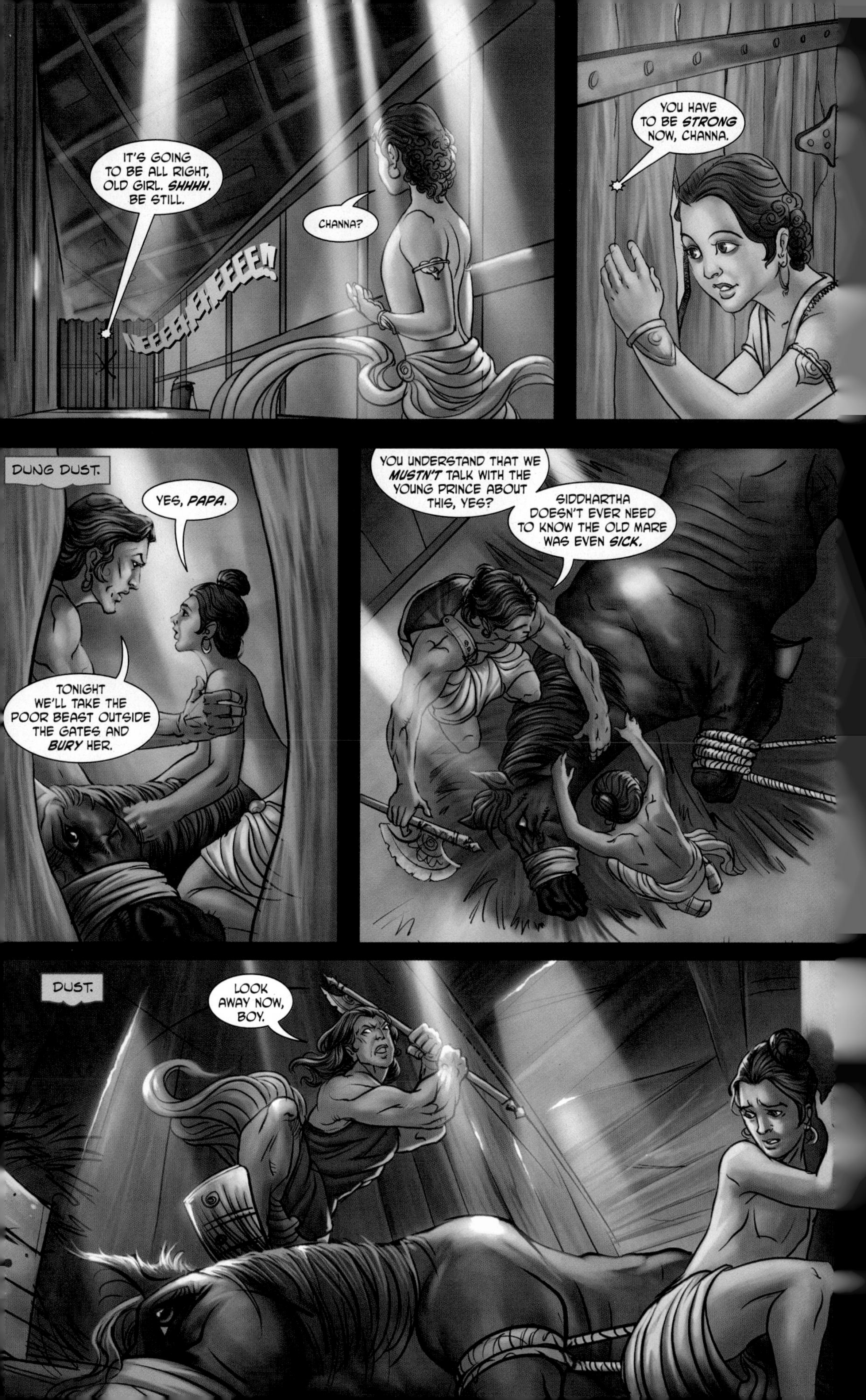
IT'S GOING TO BE ALL RIGHT, OLD GIRL. SHHHH. BE STILL.
NEEEEHEHEEEEE!!
CHANNA?
YOU HAVE TO BE STRONG NOW, CHANNA.
DUNG DUST.
YES, PAPA.
TONIGHT WE'LL TAKE THE POOR BEAST OUTSIDE THE GATES AND BURY HER.
YOU UNDERSTAND THAT WE MUSTN'T TALK WITH THE YOUNG PRINCE ABOUT THIS, YES?
SIDDHARTHA DOESN'T EVER NEED TO KNOW THE OLD MARE WAS EVEN SICK.
DUST.
LOOK AWAY NOW, BOY.

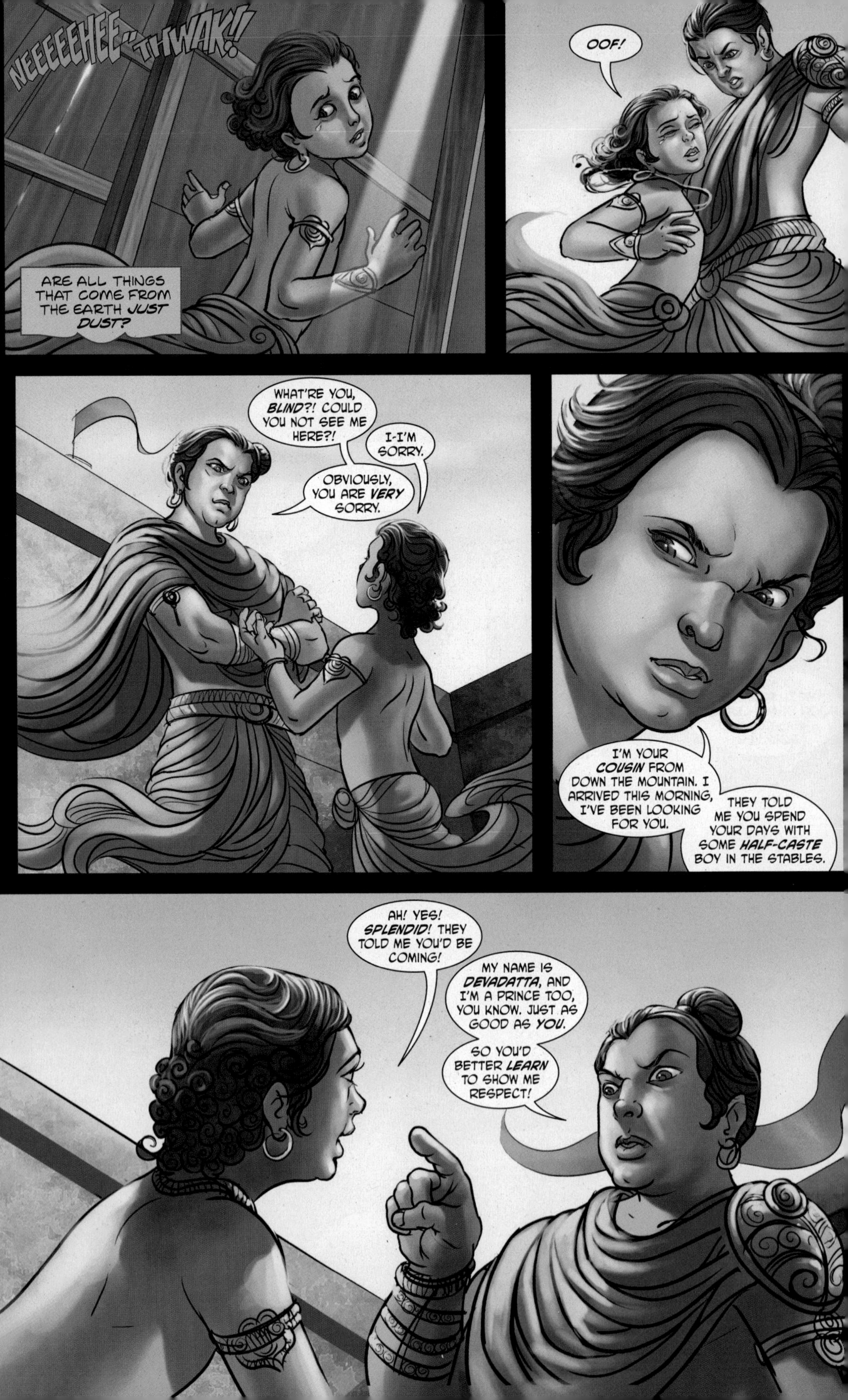

NEEEEEHEE-THWAK!!
ARE ALL THINGS THAT COME FROM THE EARTH JUST DUST?
OOF!
WHAT'RE YOU, BLIND?! COULD YOU NOT SEE ME HERE?!
I-I'M SORRY.
OBVIOUSLY, YOU ARE VERY SORRY.
I'M YOUR COUSIN FROM DOWN THE MOUNTAIN. I ARRIVED THIS MORNING, I'VE BEEN LOOKING FOR YOU.
THEY TOLD ME YOU SPEND YOUR DAYS WITH SOME HALF-CASTE BOY IN THE STABLES.
AH! YES! SPLENDID! THEY TOLD ME YOU'D BE COMING!
MY NAME IS DEVADATTA, AND I'M A PRINCE TOO, YOU KNOW. JUST AS GOOD AS YOU.
SO YOU'D BETTER LEARN TO SHOW ME RESPECT!

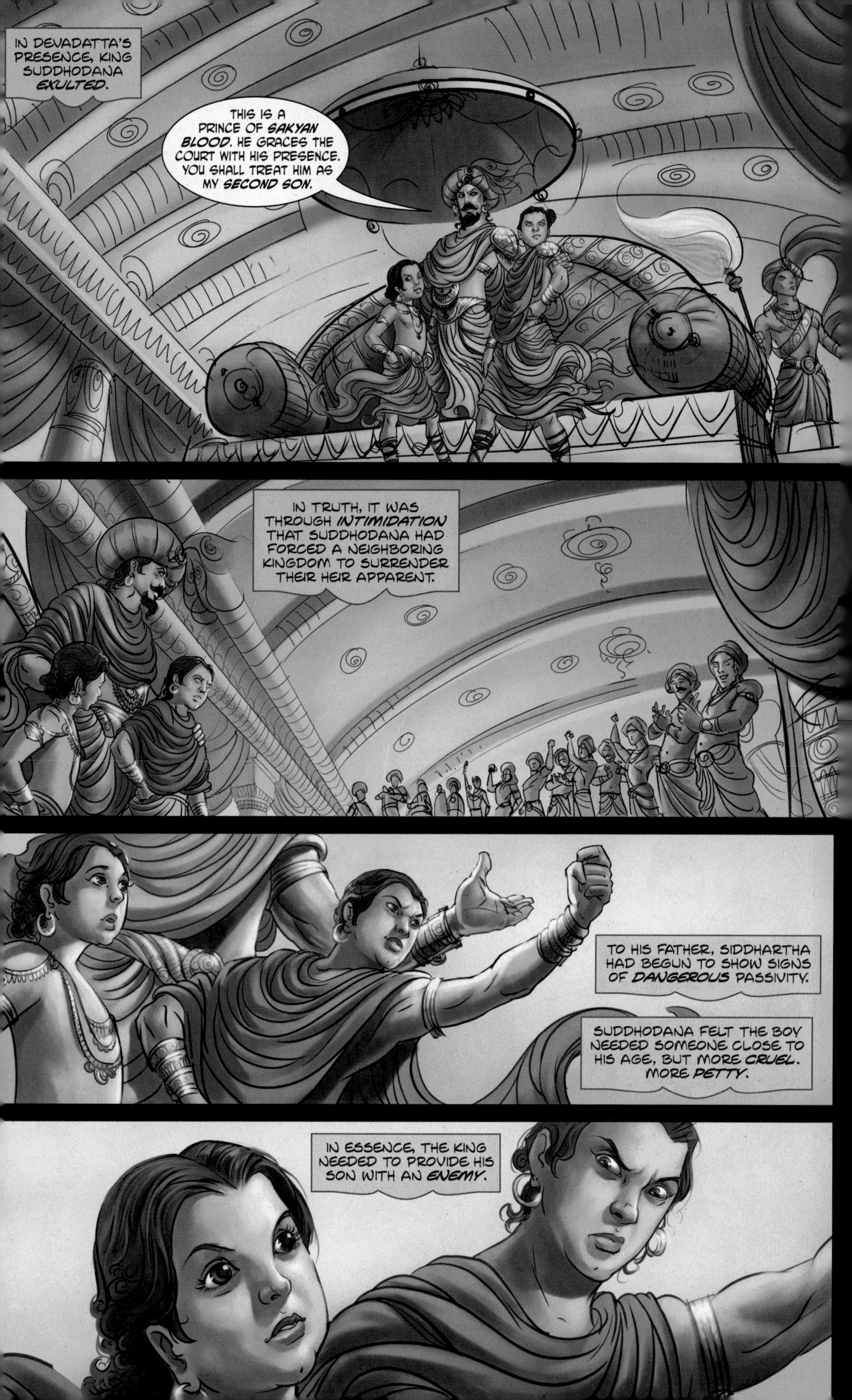
IN DEVADATTA'S PRESENCE, KING SUDDHODANA EXULTED.
THIS IS A PRINCE OF SAKYAN BLOOD. HE GRACES THE COURT WITH HIS PRESENCE. YOU SHALL TREAT HIM AS MY SECOND SON.
IN TRUTH, IT WAS THROUGH INTIMIDATION THAT SUDDHODANA HAD FORCED A NEIGHBORING KINGDOM TO SURRENDER THEIR HEIR APPARENT.
TO HIS FATHER, SIDDHARTHA HAD BEGUN TO SHOW SIGNS OF DANGEROUS PASSIVITY.
SUDDHODANA FELT THE BOY NEEDED SOMEONE CLOSE TO HIS AGE, BUT MORE CRUEL. MORE PETTY.
IN ESSENCE, THE KING NEEDED TO PROVIDE HIS SON WITH AN ENEMY.

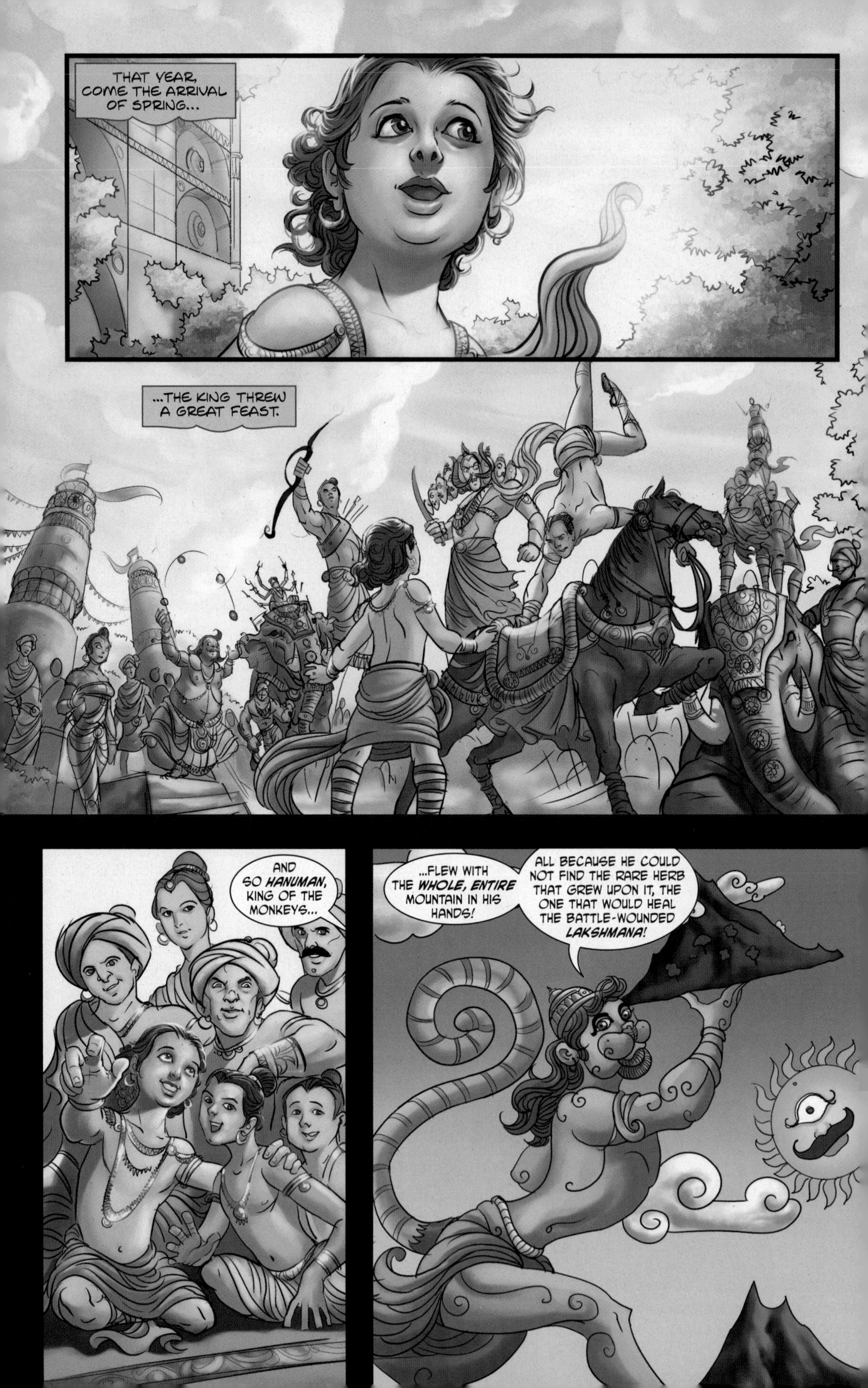
THAT YEAR, COME THE ARRIVAL OF SPRING...
...THE KING THREW A GREAT FEAST.
AND SO HANUMAN, KING OF THE MONKEYS...
...FLEW WITH THE WHOLE, ENTIRE MOUNTAIN IN HIS HANDS!
ALL BECAUSE HE COULD NOT FIND THE RARE HERB THAT GREW UPON IT, THE ONE THAT WOULD HEAL THE BATTLE-WOUNDED LAKSHMANA!

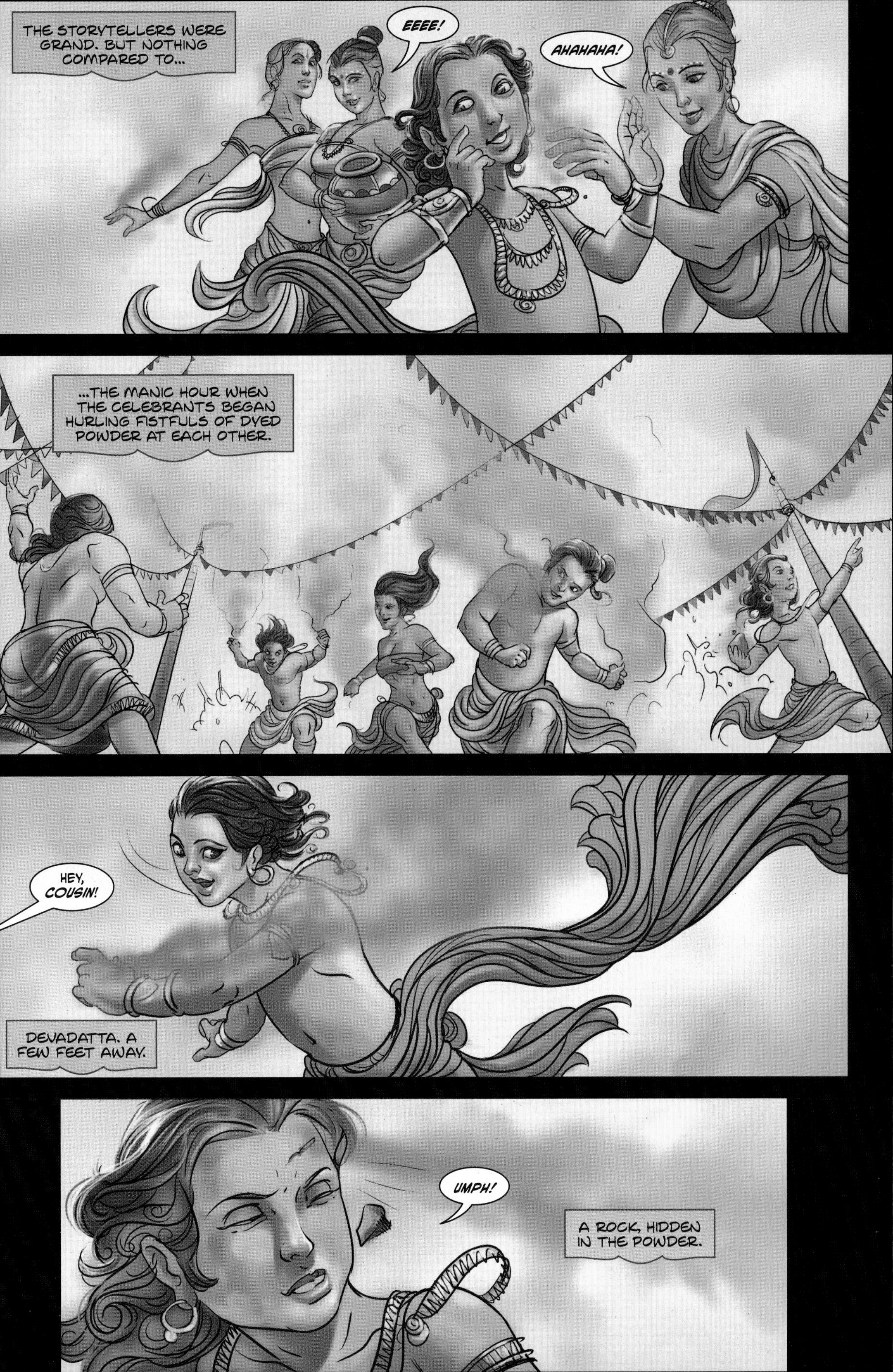
THE STORYTELLERS WERE GRAND. BUT NOTHING COMPARED TO...
EEEE!
AHAHAHA!
...THE MANIC HOUR WHEN THE CELEBRANTS BEGAN HURLING FISTFULS OF DYED POWDER AT EACH OTHER.
HEY, COUSIN!
DEVADATTA. A FEW FEET AWAY.
UMPH!
A ROCK, HIDDEN IN THE POWDER.

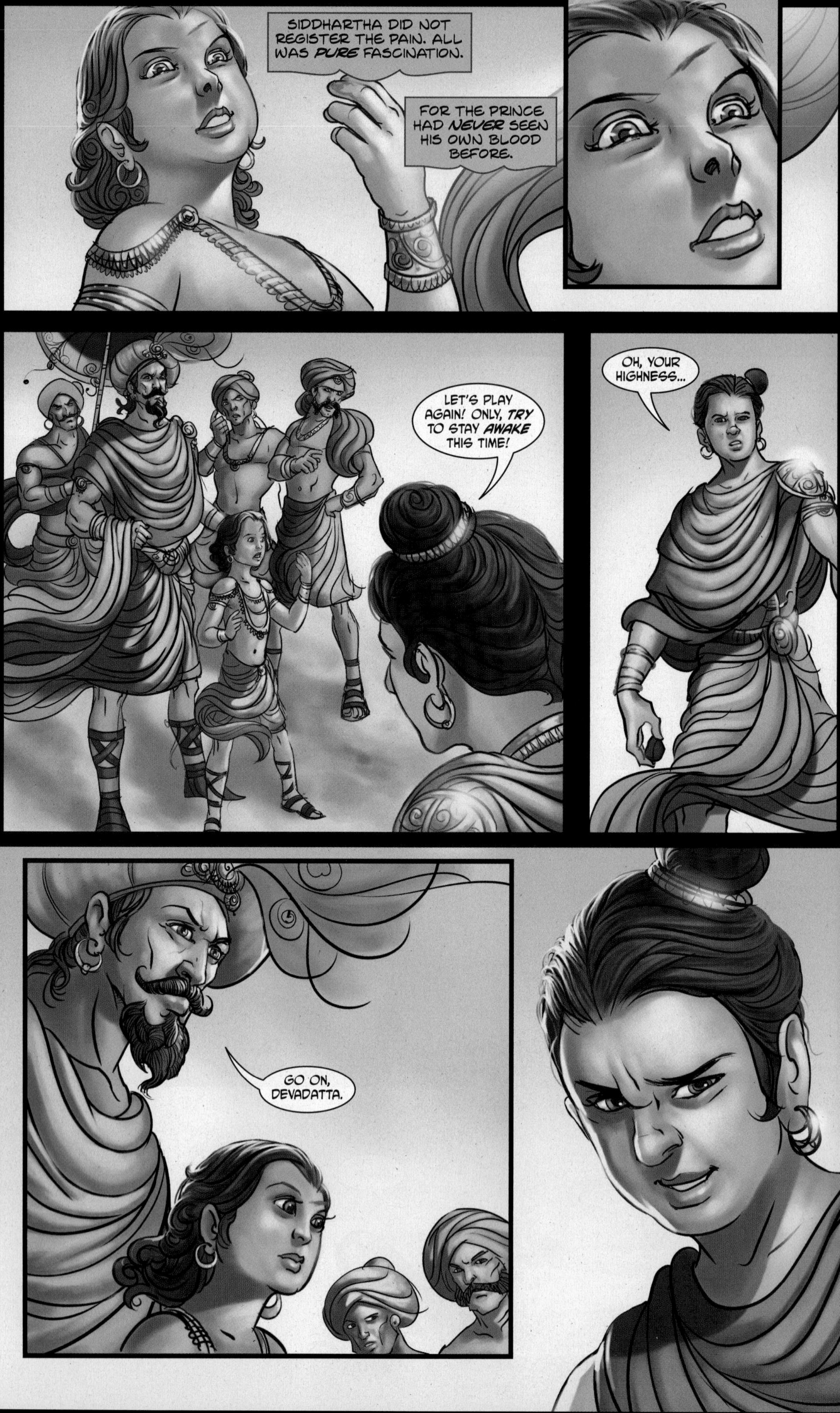
SIDDHARTHA DID NOT REGISTER THE PAIN. ALL WAS PURE FASCINATION.
FOR THE PRINCE HAD NEVER SEEN HIS OWN BLOOD BEFORE.
LET'S PLAY AGAIN! ONLY, TRY TO STAY AWAKE THIS TIME!
OH, YOUR HIGHNESS...
GO ON, DEVADATTA.

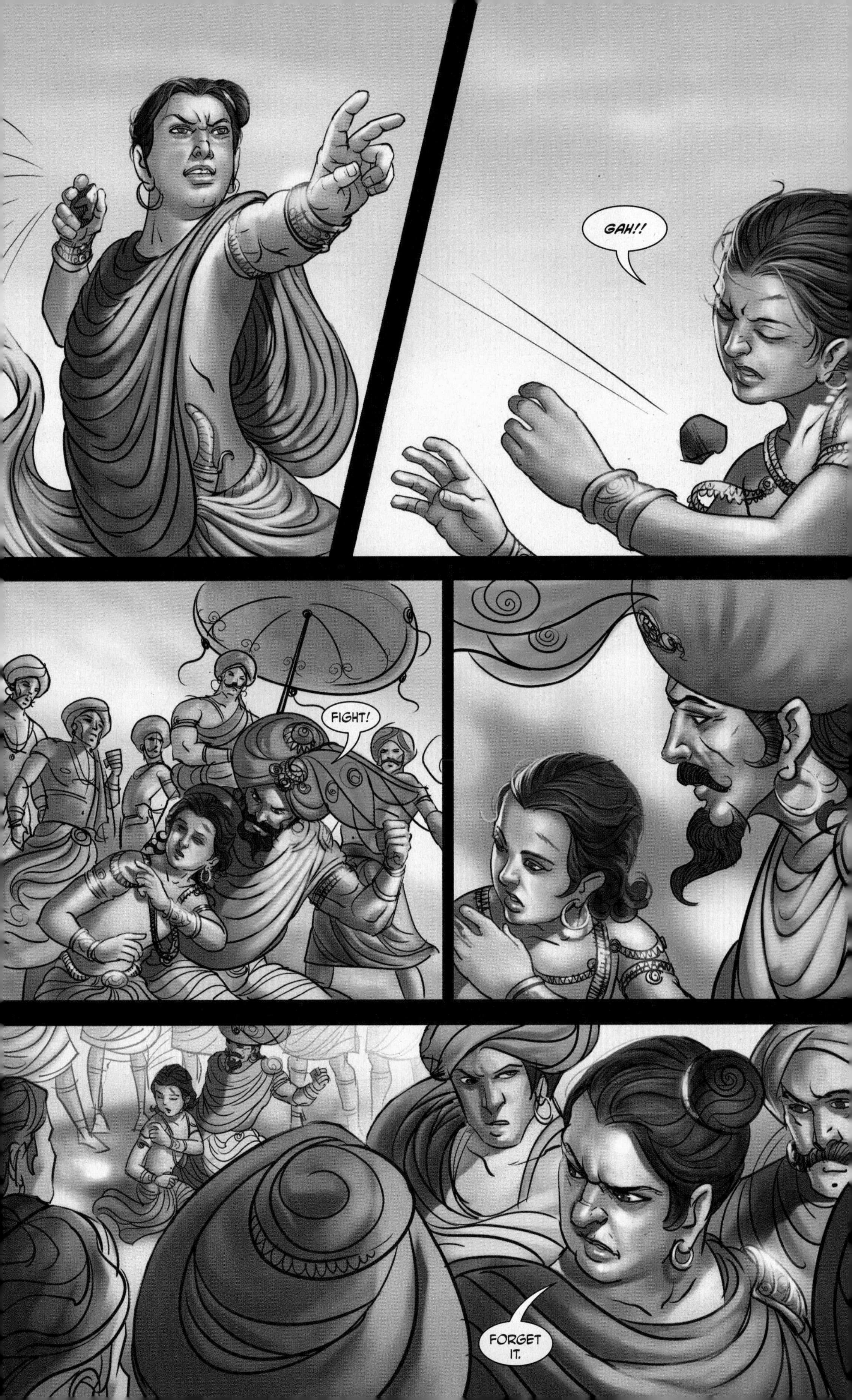
GAH!!
FIGHT!
FORGET IT.

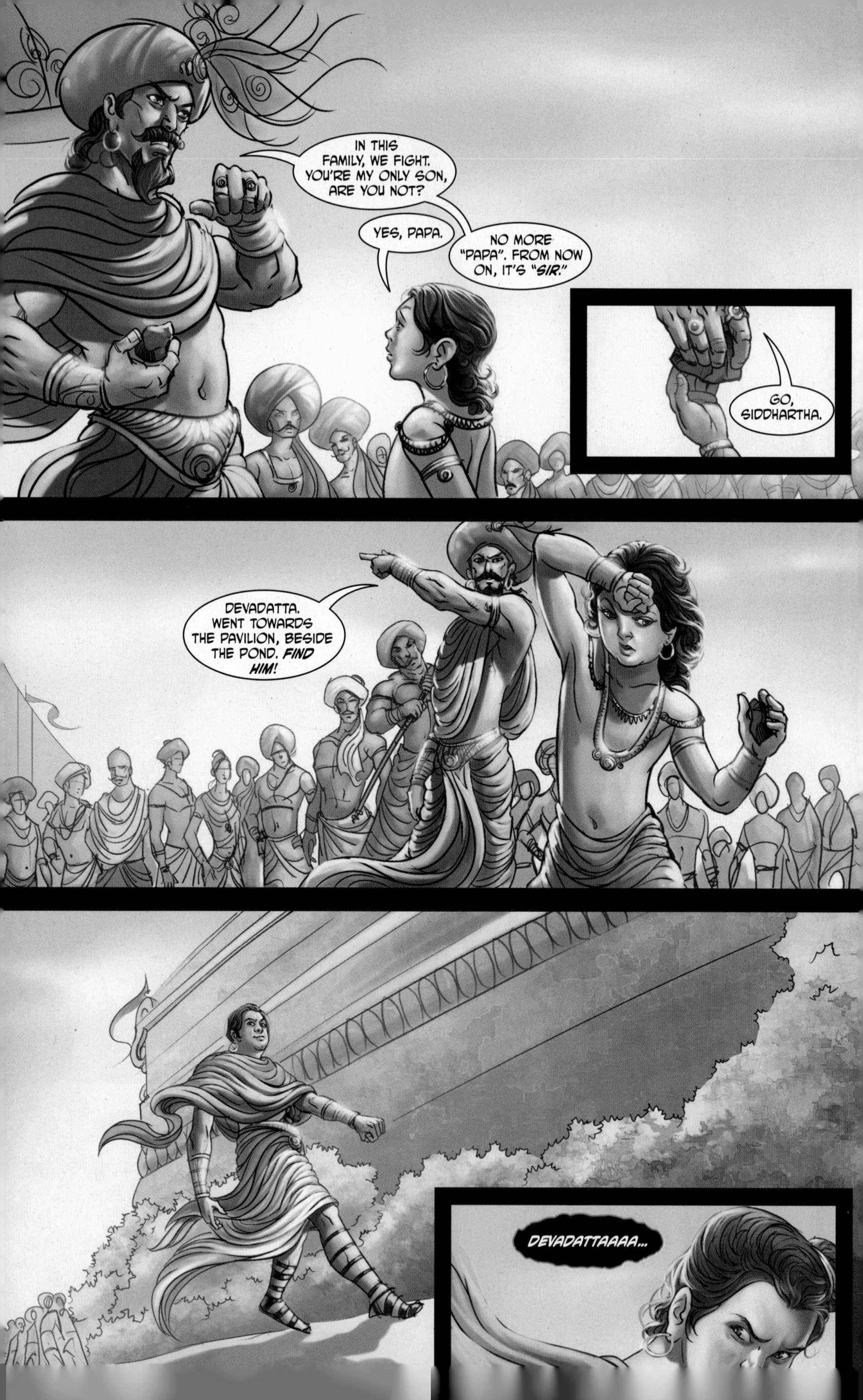
IN THIS FAMILY, WE FIGHT. YOU'RE MY ONLY SON, ARE YOU NOT?
YES, PAPA.
NO MORE "PAPA". FROM NOW ON, IT'S "*SIR.*"
GO, SIDDHARTHA.
DEVADATTA. WENT TOWARDS THE PAVILION, BESIDE THE POND. *FIND HIM!*
DEVADATTAAAA...

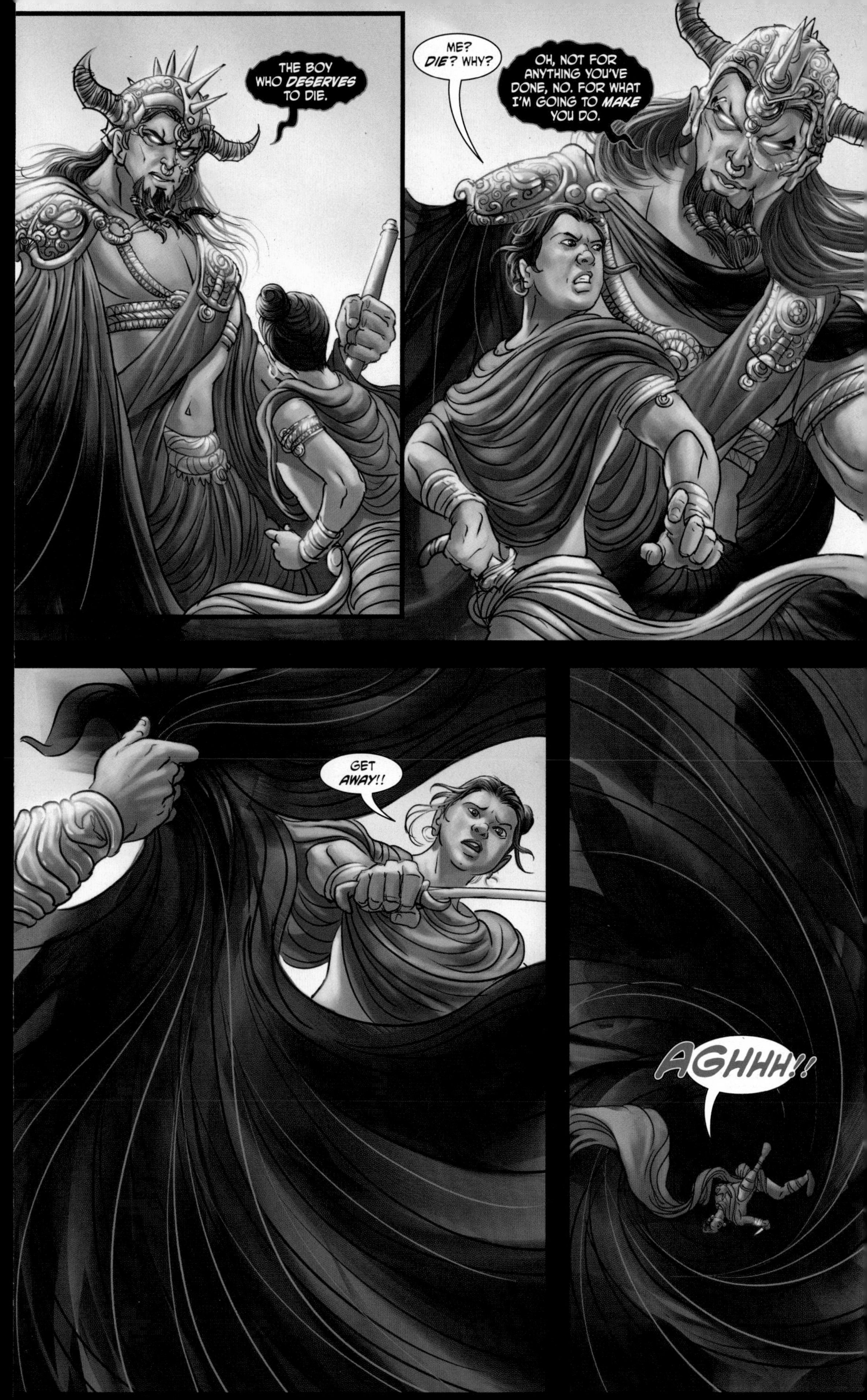
THE BOY WHO DESERVES TO DIE.
ME? DIE? WHY?
OH, NOT FOR ANYTHING YOU'VE DONE, NO. FOR WHAT I'M GOING TO MAKE YOU DO.
GET AWAY!!
AGHHH!!

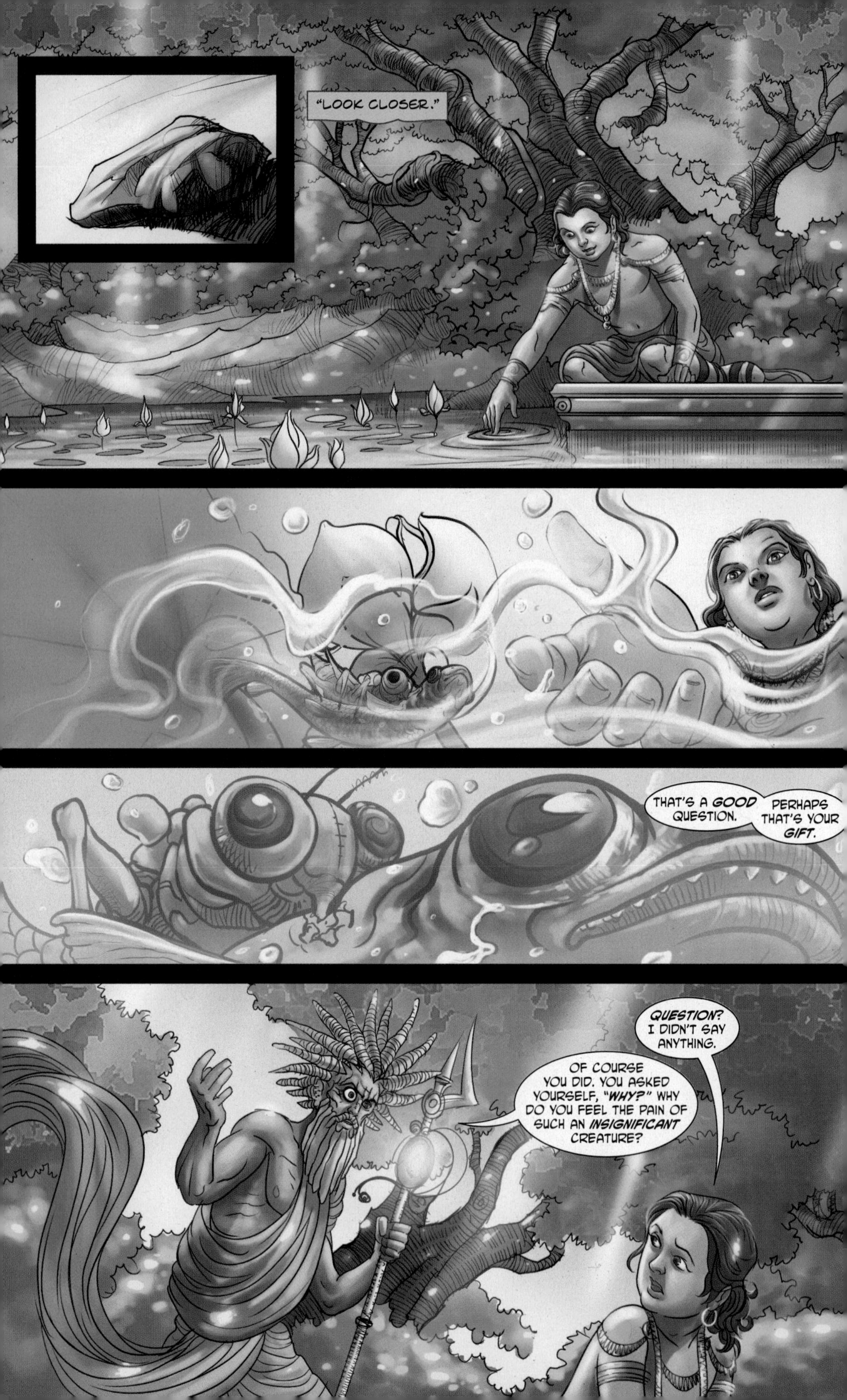
"LOOK CLOSER."
THAT'S A GOOD QUESTION.
PERHAPS THAT'S YOUR GIFT.
QUESTION? I DIDN'T SAY ANYTHING.
OF COURSE YOU DID. YOU ASKED YOURSELF, "WHY?" WHY DO YOU FEEL THE PAIN OF SUCH AN INSIGNIFICANT CREATURE?

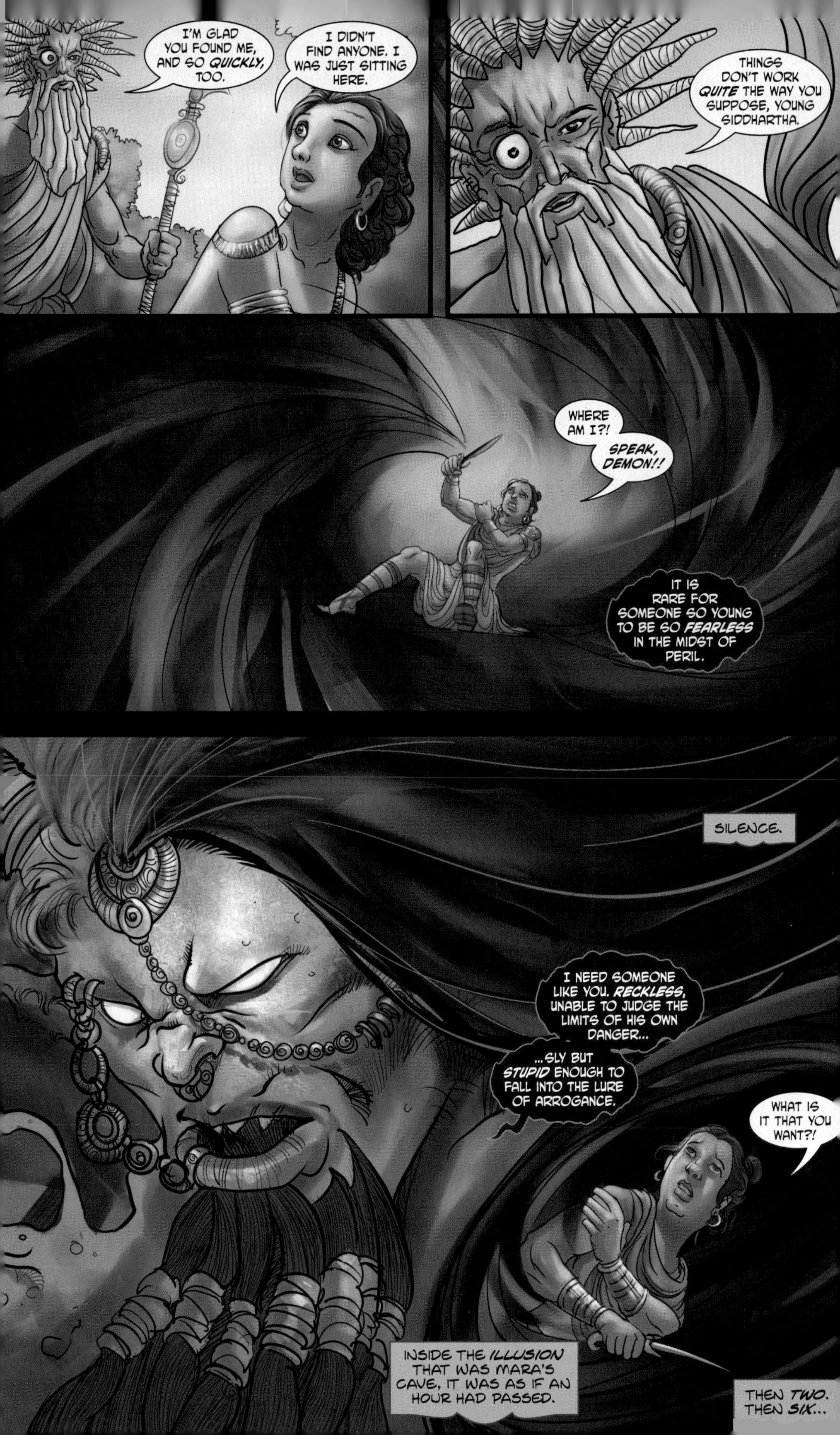
I'M GLAD YOU FOUND ME, AND SO QUICKLY, TOO.
I DIDN'T FIND ANYONE. I WAS JUST SITTING HERE.
THINGS DON'T WORK QUITE THE WAY YOU SUPPOSE, YOUNG SIDDHARTHA.
WHERE AM I?! SPEAK, DEMON!!
IT IS RARE FOR SOMEONE SO YOUNG TO BE SO FEARLESS IN THE MIDST OF PERIL.
SILENCE.
I NEED SOMEONE LIKE YOU. RECKLESS, UNABLE TO JUDGE THE LIMITS OF HIS OWN DANGER...
...SLY BUT STUPID ENOUGH TO FALL INTO THE LURE OF ARROGANCE.
WHAT IS IT THAT YOU WANT?!
INSIDE THE ILLUSION THAT WAS MARA'S CAVE, IT WAS AS IF AN HOUR HAD PASSED.
THEN TWO. THEN SIX...

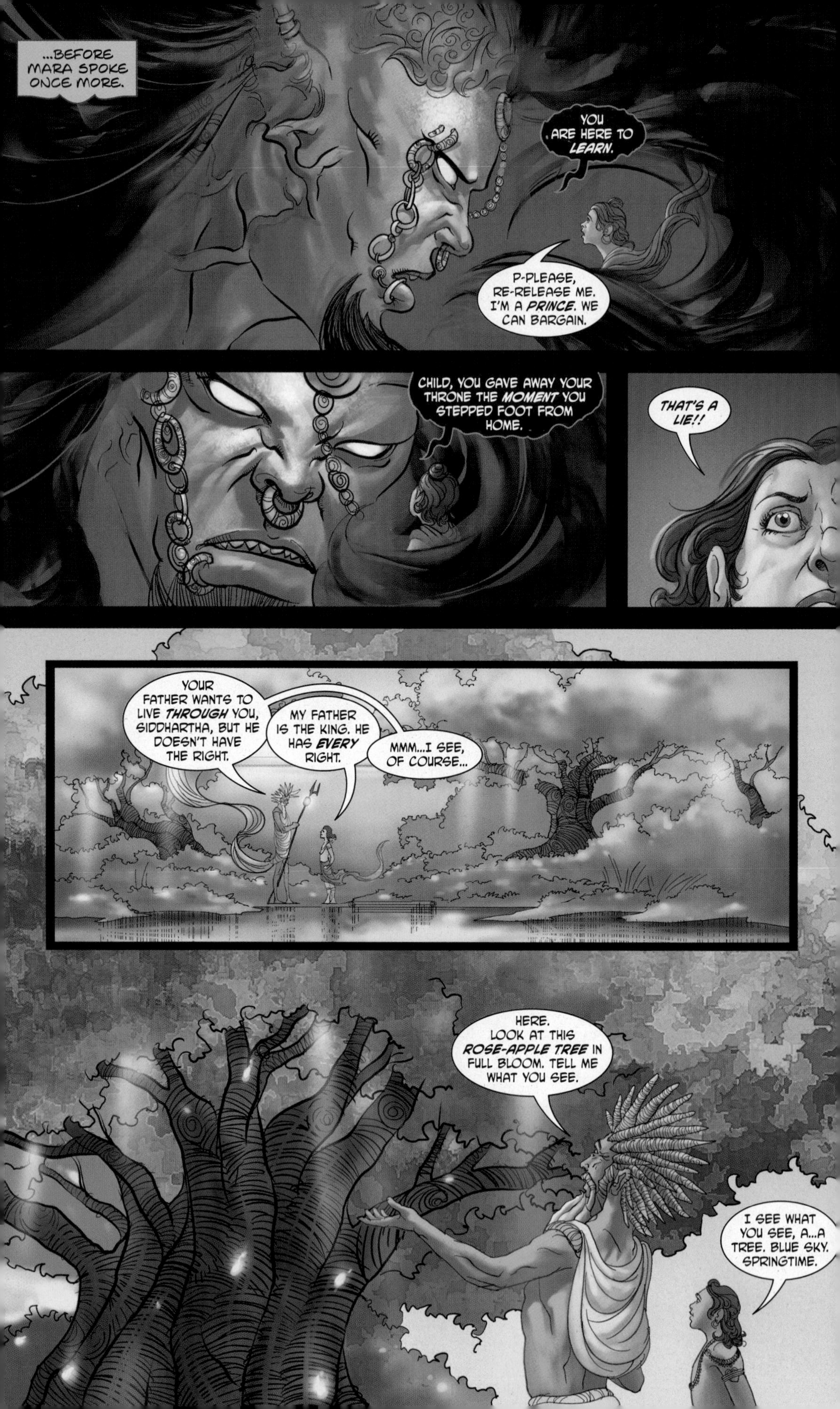
...BEFORE MARA SPOKE ONCE MORE.
YOU ARE HERE TO *LEARN*.
P-PLEASE, RE-RELEASE ME. I'M A *PRINCE*. WE CAN BARGAIN.
CHILD, YOU GAVE AWAY YOUR THRONE THE *MOMENT* YOU STEPPED FOOT FROM HOME.
THAT'S A LIE!!
YOUR FATHER WANTS TO LIVE *THROUGH* YOU, SIDDHARTHA, BUT HE DOESN'T HAVE THE RIGHT.
MY FATHER IS THE KING. HE HAS *EVERY* RIGHT.
MMM...I SEE, OF COURSE...
HERE. LOOK AT THIS *ROSE-APPLE TREE* IN FULL BLOOM. TELL ME WHAT YOU SEE.
I SEE WHAT YOU SEE, A...A TREE. BLUE SKY. SPRINGTIME.

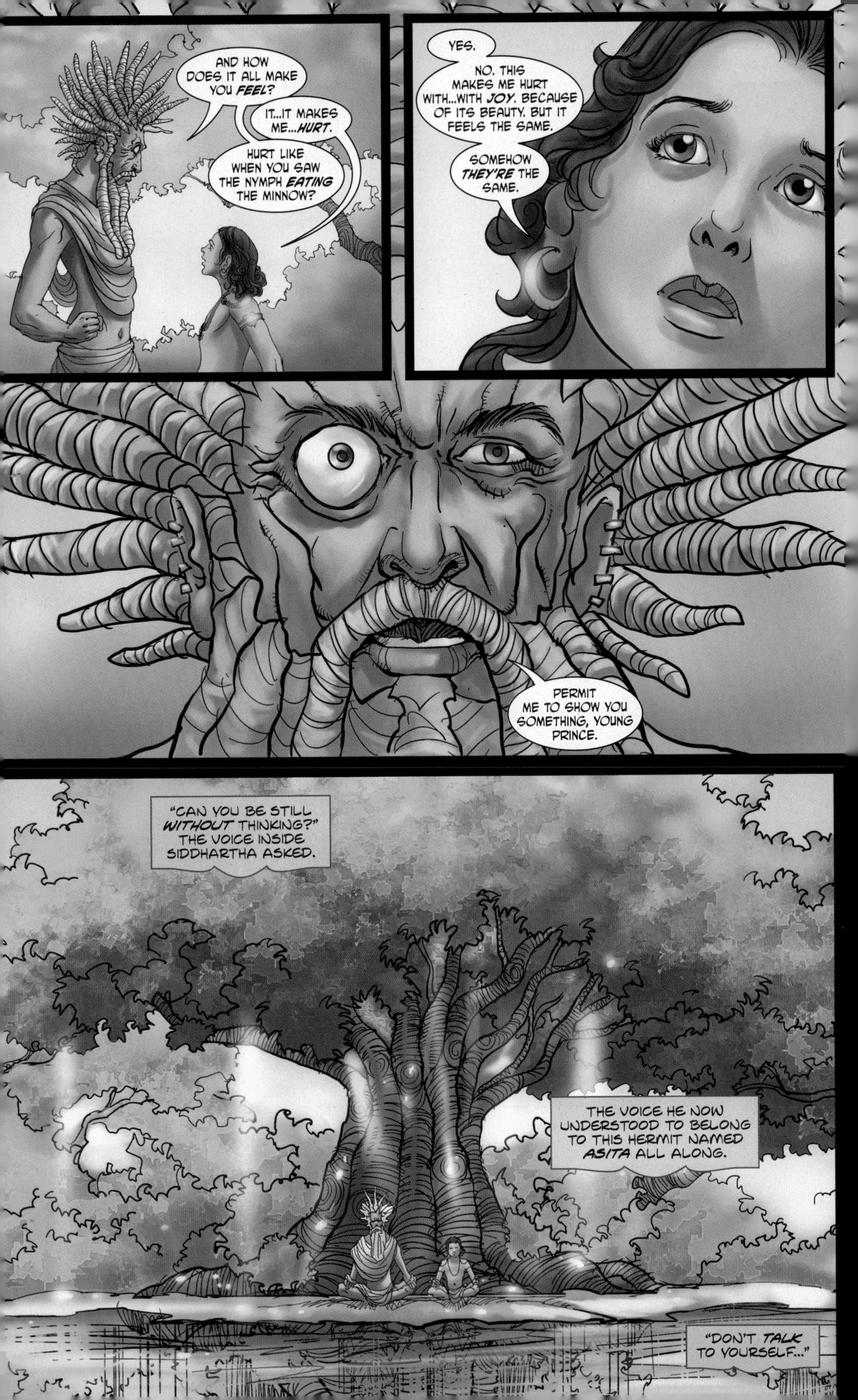
AND HOW DOES IT ALL MAKE YOU *FEEL*?
IT...IT MAKES ME...*HURT*.
HURT LIKE WHEN YOU SAW THE NYMPH *EATING* THE MINNOW?
YES.
NO. THIS MAKES ME HURT WITH...WITH *JOY*. BECAUSE OF ITS BEAUTY. BUT IT FEELS THE SAME.
SOMEHOW *THEY'RE* THE SAME.
PERMIT ME TO SHOW YOU SOMETHING, YOUNG PRINCE.
"CAN YOU BE STILL *WITHOUT* THINKING?" THE VOICE INSIDE SIDDHARTHA ASKED.
THE VOICE HE NOW UNDERSTOOD TO BELONG TO THIS HERMIT NAMED *ASITA* ALL ALONG.
"DON'T *TALK* TO YOURSELF..."

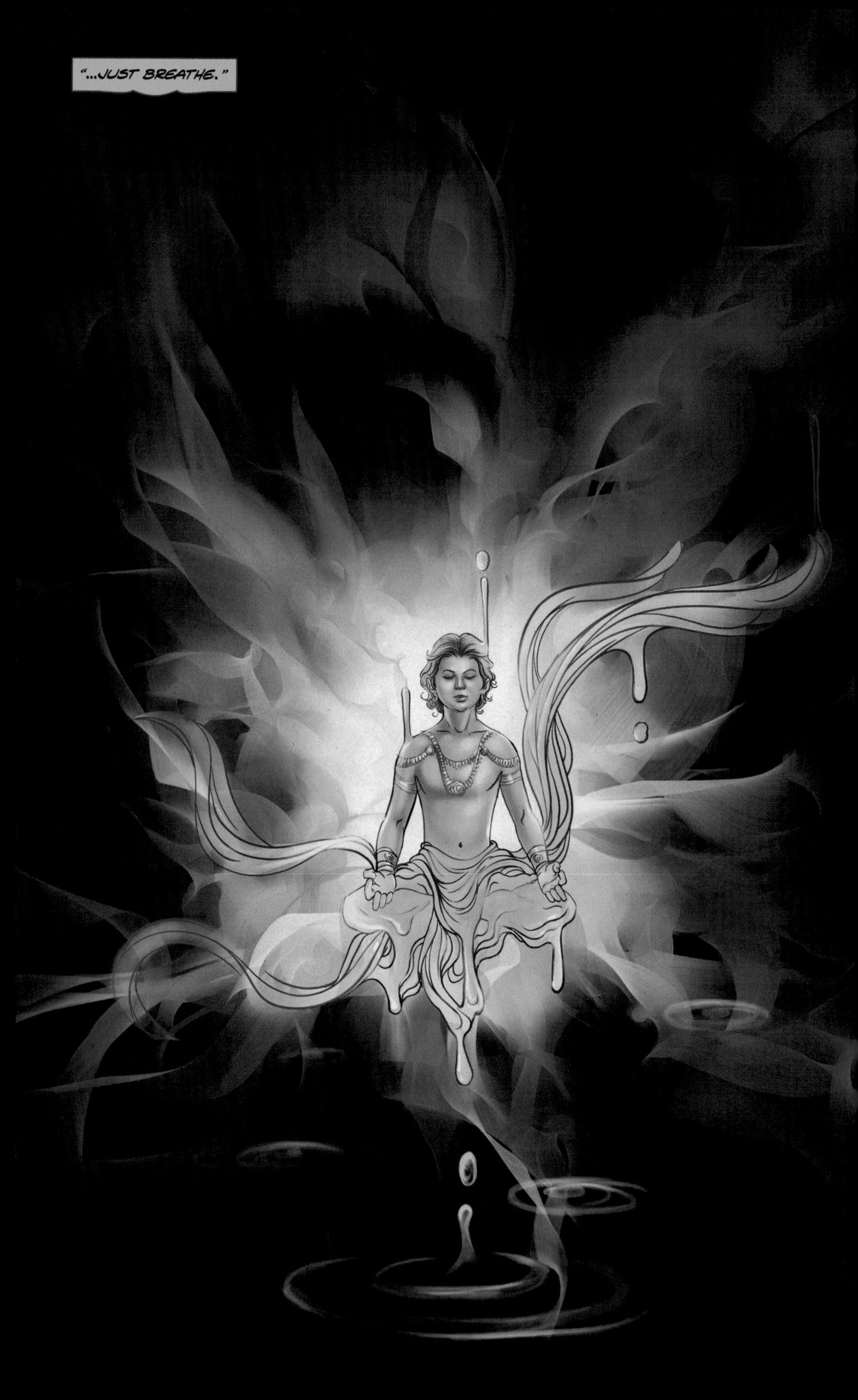
"...JUST BREATHE."

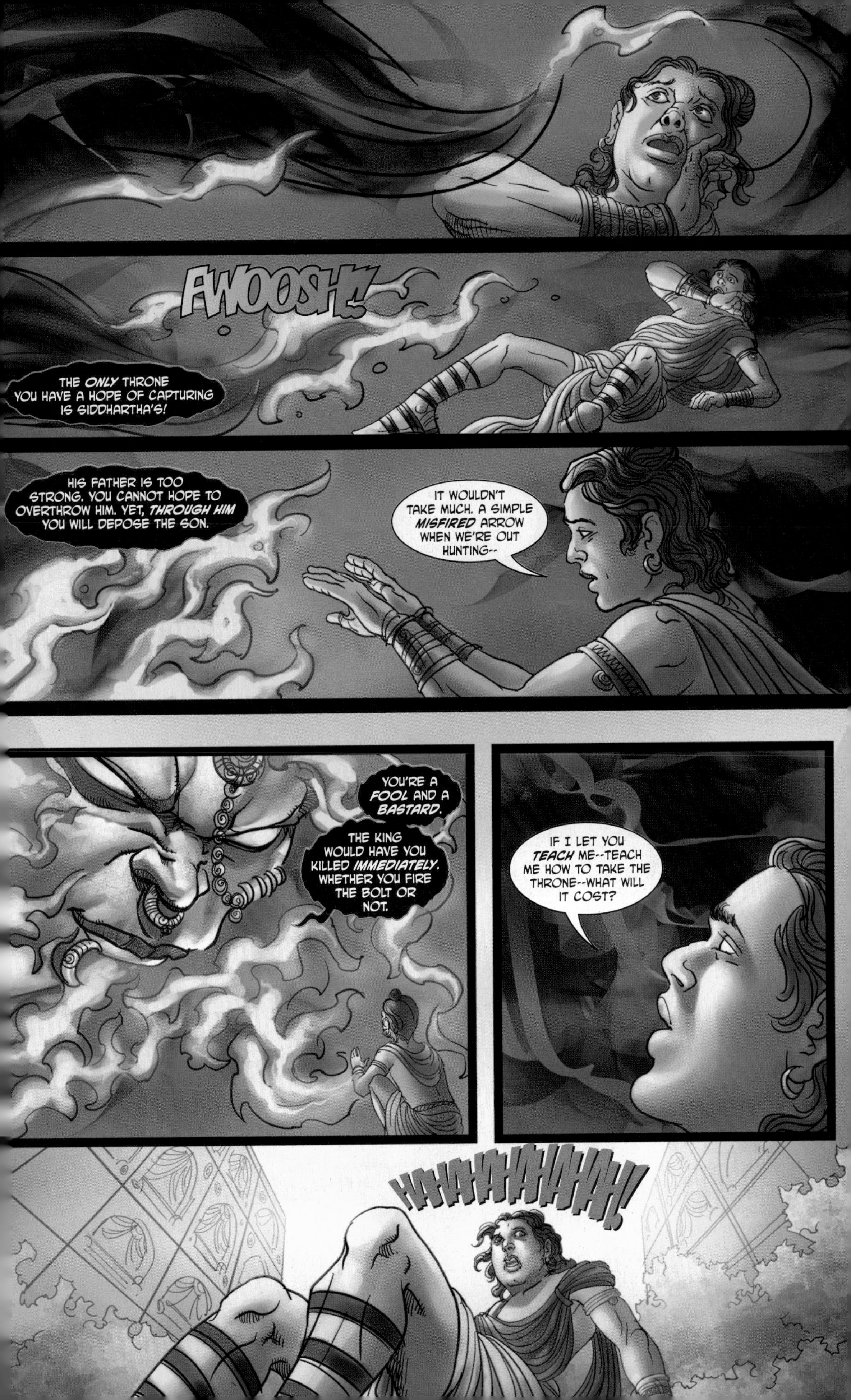
FWOOSH!
THE ONLY THRONE YOU HAVE A HOPE OF CAPTURING IS SIDDHARTHA'S!
HIS FATHER IS TOO STRONG. YOU CANNOT HOPE TO OVERTHROW HIM. YET, THROUGH HIM YOU WILL DEPOSE THE SON.
IT WOULDN'T TAKE MUCH. A SIMPLE MISFIRED ARROW WHEN WE'RE OUT HUNTING--
YOU'RE A FOOL AND A BASTARD.
THE KING WOULD HAVE YOU KILLED IMMEDIATELY. WHETHER YOU FIRE THE BOLT OR NOT.
IF I LET YOU TEACH ME--TEACH ME HOW TO TAKE THE THRONE--WHAT WILL IT COST?
HAHAHAHAHAHAH!!

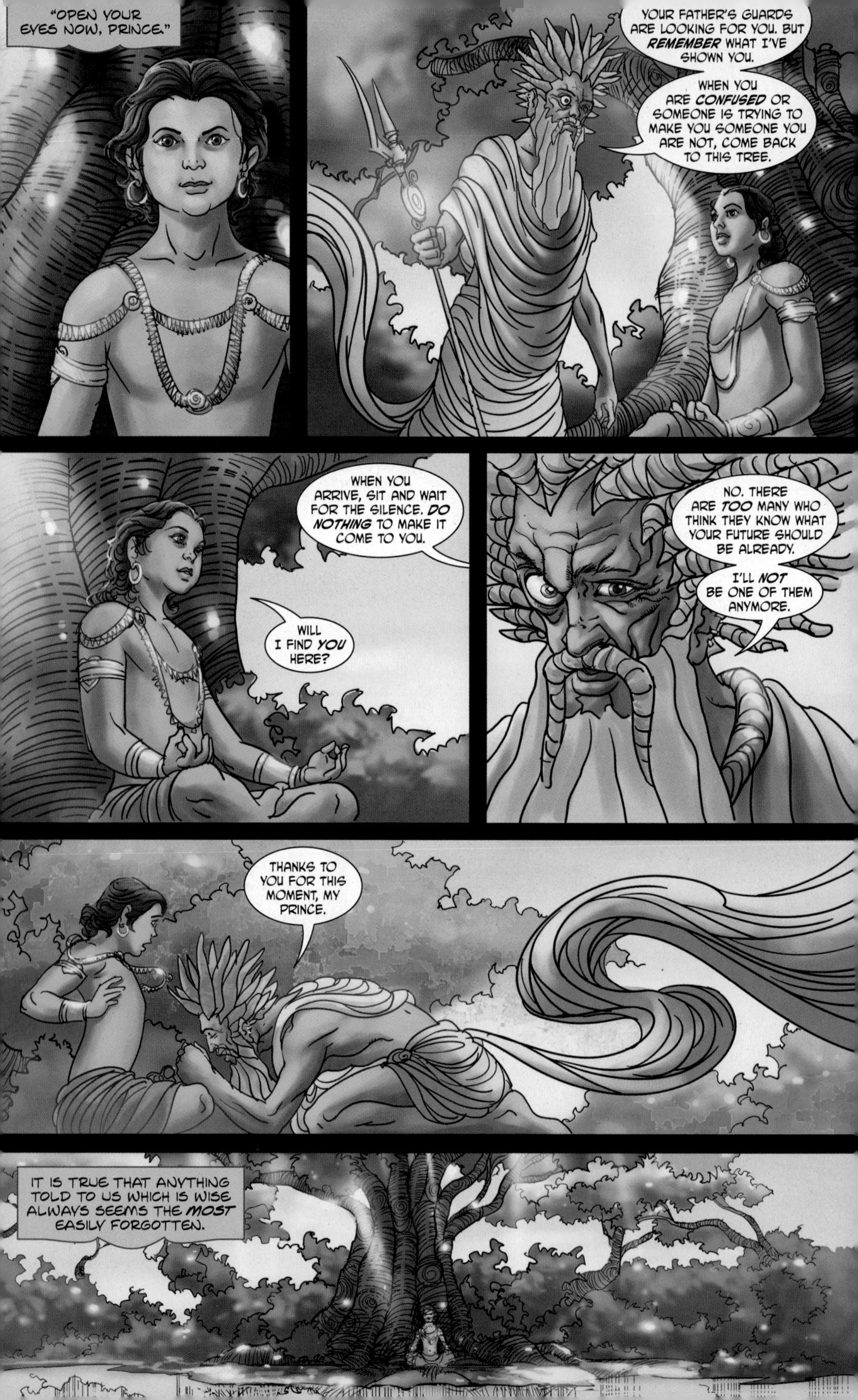
"OPEN YOUR EYES NOW, PRINCE."
YOUR FATHER'S GUARDS ARE LOOKING FOR YOU. BUT *REMEMBER* WHAT I'VE SHOWN YOU.
WHEN YOU ARE *CONFUSED* OR SOMEONE IS TRYING TO MAKE YOU SOMEONE YOU ARE NOT, COME BACK TO THIS TREE.
WHEN YOU ARRIVE, SIT AND WAIT FOR THE SILENCE. *DO NOTHING* TO MAKE IT COME TO YOU.
WILL I FIND *YOU* HERE?
NO. THERE ARE *TOO* MANY WHO THINK THEY KNOW WHAT YOUR FUTURE SHOULD BE ALREADY.
I'LL *NOT* BE ONE OF THEM ANYMORE.
THANKS TO YOU FOR THIS MOMENT, MY PRINCE.
IT IS TRUE THAT ANYTHING TOLD TO US WHICH IS WISE ALWAYS SEEMS THE *MOST* EASILY FORGOTTEN.

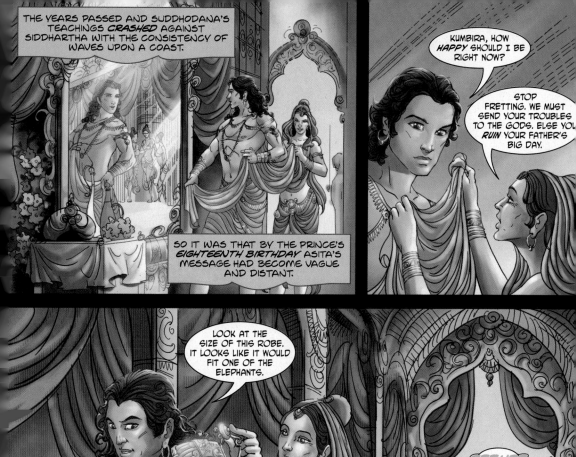

THE YEARS PASSED AND SUDDHODANA'S TEACHINGS *CRASHED* AGAINST SIDDHARTHA WITH THE CONSISTENCY OF WAVES UPON A COAST.

SO IT WAS THAT BY THE PRINCE'S *EIGHTEENTH BIRTHDAY* ASITA'S MESSAGE HAD BECOME VAGUE AND DISTANT.

KUMBIRA, HOW *HAPPY* SHOULD I BE RIGHT NOW?

STOP FRETTING. WE MUST SEND YOUR TROUBLES TO THE GODS. ELSE YOU *RUIN* YOUR FATHER'S BIG DAY.

LOOK AT THE SIZE OF THIS ROBE. IT LOOKS LIKE IT WOULD FIT ONE OF THE ELEPHANTS.

TEE HEE

YOU'RE NOT HERE TO GAWK, SUJATA!

I WASN'T, M'LADY

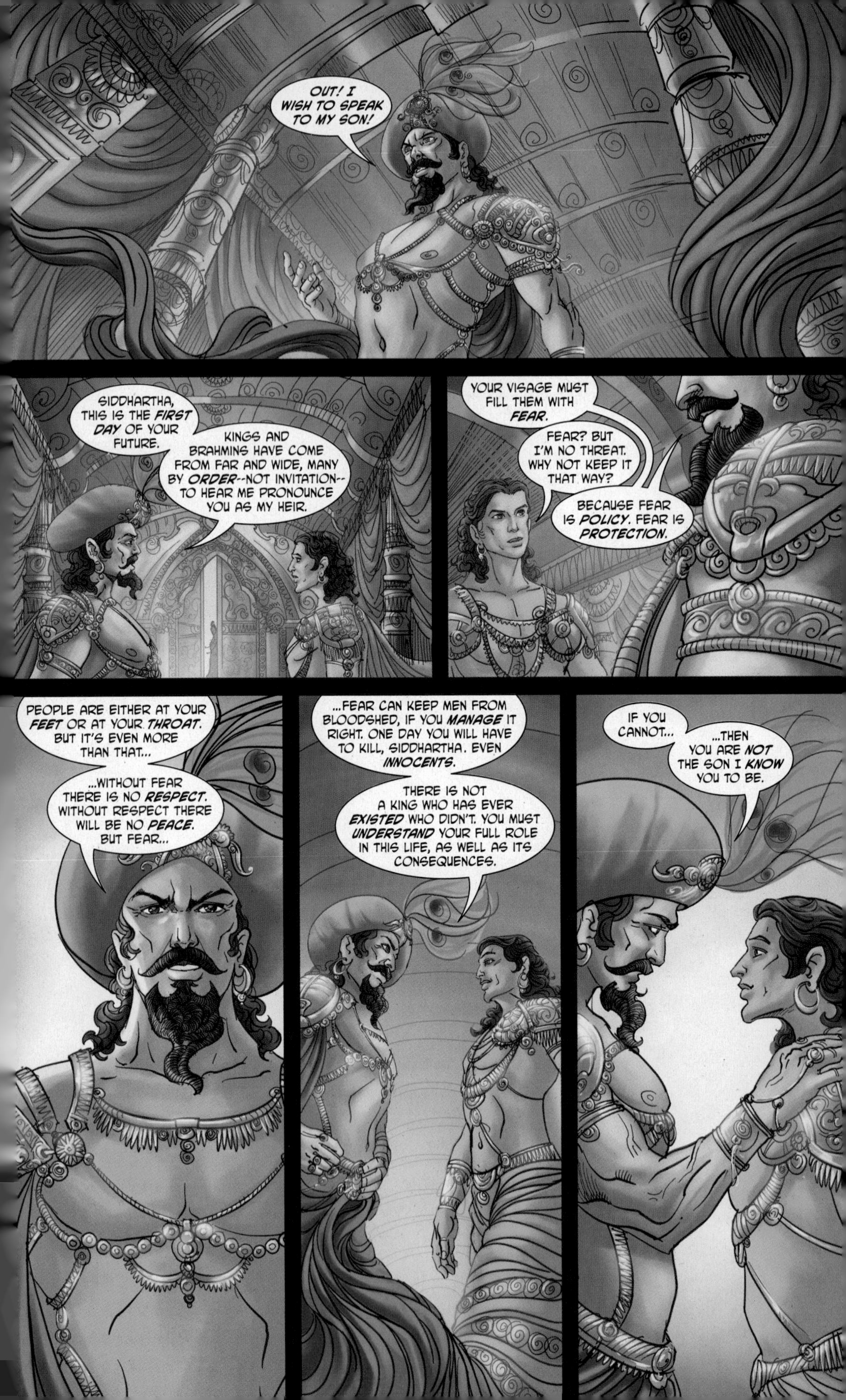

OUT! I WISH TO SPEAK TO MY SON!
SIDDHARTHA, THIS IS THE FIRST DAY OF YOUR FUTURE.
KINGS AND BRAHMINS HAVE COME FROM FAR AND WIDE, MANY BY ORDER--NOT INVITATION--TO HEAR ME PRONOUNCE YOU AS MY HEIR.
YOUR VISAGE MUST FILL THEM WITH FEAR.
FEAR? BUT I'M NO THREAT. WHY NOT KEEP IT THAT WAY?
BECAUSE FEAR IS POLICY. FEAR IS PROTECTION.
PEOPLE ARE EITHER AT YOUR FEET OR AT YOUR THROAT. BUT IT'S EVEN MORE THAN THAT...
...WITHOUT FEAR THERE IS NO RESPECT. WITHOUT RESPECT THERE WILL BE NO PEACE. BUT FEAR...
...FEAR CAN KEEP MEN FROM BLOODSHED, IF YOU MANAGE IT RIGHT. ONE DAY YOU WILL HAVE TO KILL, SIDDHARTHA. EVEN INNOCENTS.
THERE IS NOT A KING WHO HAS EVER EXISTED WHO DIDN'T. YOU MUST UNDERSTAND YOUR FULL ROLE IN THIS LIFE, AS WELL AS ITS CONSEQUENCES.
IF YOU CANNOT...
...THEN YOU ARE NOT THE SON I KNOW YOU TO BE.

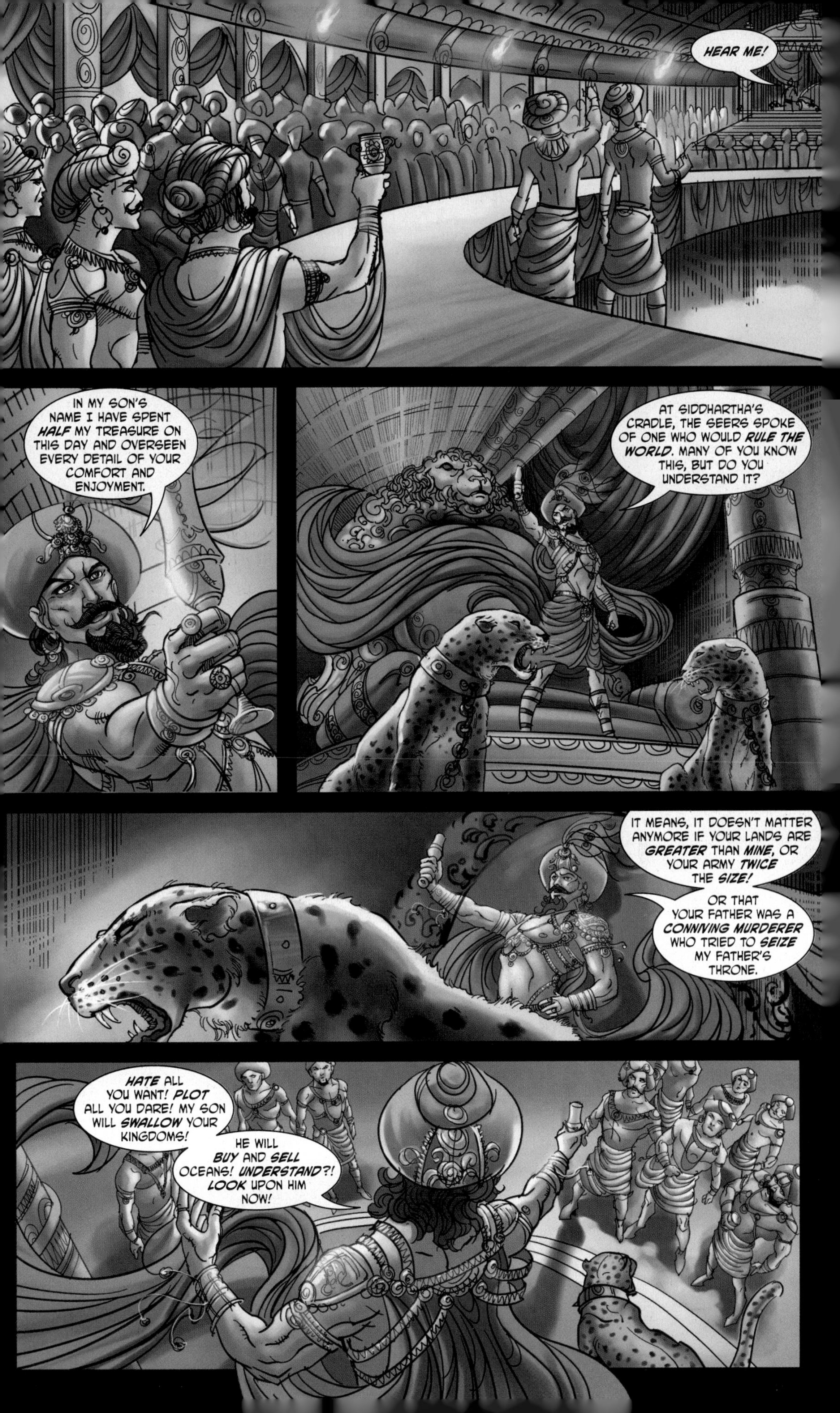
HEAR ME!
IN MY SON'S NAME I HAVE SPENT HALF MY TREASURE ON THIS DAY AND OVERSEEN EVERY DETAIL OF YOUR COMFORT AND ENJOYMENT.
AT SIDDHARTHA'S CRADLE, THE SEERS SPOKE OF ONE WHO WOULD RULE THE WORLD. MANY OF YOU KNOW THIS, BUT DO YOU UNDERSTAND IT?
IT MEANS, IT DOESN'T MATTER ANYMORE IF YOUR LANDS ARE GREATER THAN MINE, OR YOUR ARMY TWICE THE SIZE!
OR THAT YOUR FATHER WAS A CONNIVING MURDERER WHO TRIED TO SEIZE MY FATHER'S THRONE.
HATE ALL YOU WANT! PLOT ALL YOU DARE! MY SON WILL SWALLOW YOUR KINGDOMS!
HE WILL BUY AND SELL OCEANS! UNDERSTAND?! LOOK UPON HIM NOW!

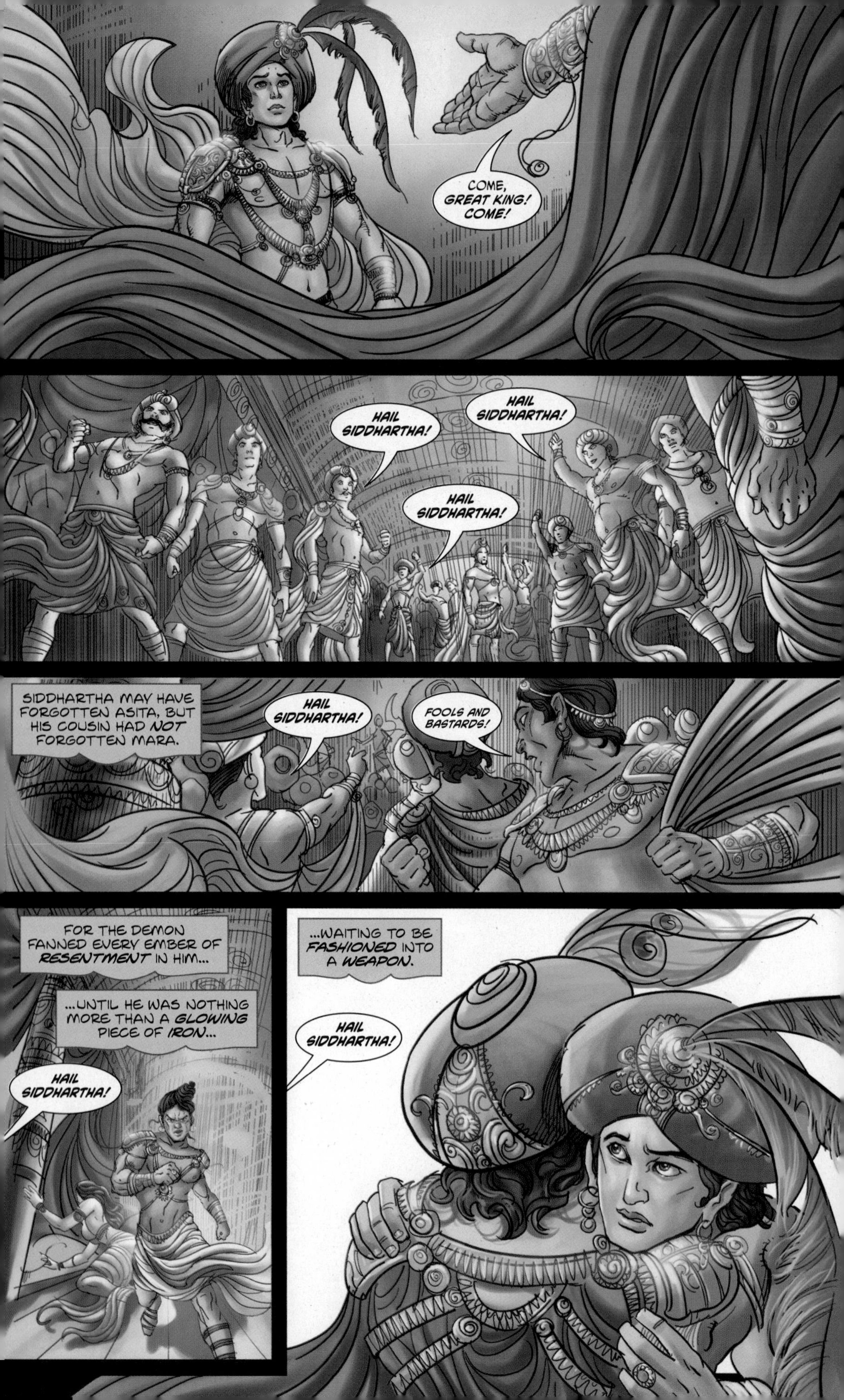
COME, GREAT KING! COME!
HAIL SIDDHARTHA!
HAIL SIDDHARTHA!
HAIL SIDDHARTHA!
SIDDHARTHA MAY HAVE FORGOTTEN ASITA, BUT HIS COUSIN HAD NOT FORGOTTEN MARA.
HAIL SIDDHARTHA!
FOOLS AND BASTARDS!
FOR THE DEMON FANNED EVERY EMBER OF RESENTMENT IN HIM...
...UNTIL HE WAS NOTHING MORE THAN A GLOWING PIECE OF IRON...
HAIL SIDDHARTHA!
...WAITING TO BE FASHIONED INTO A WEAPON.
HAIL SIDDHARTHA!

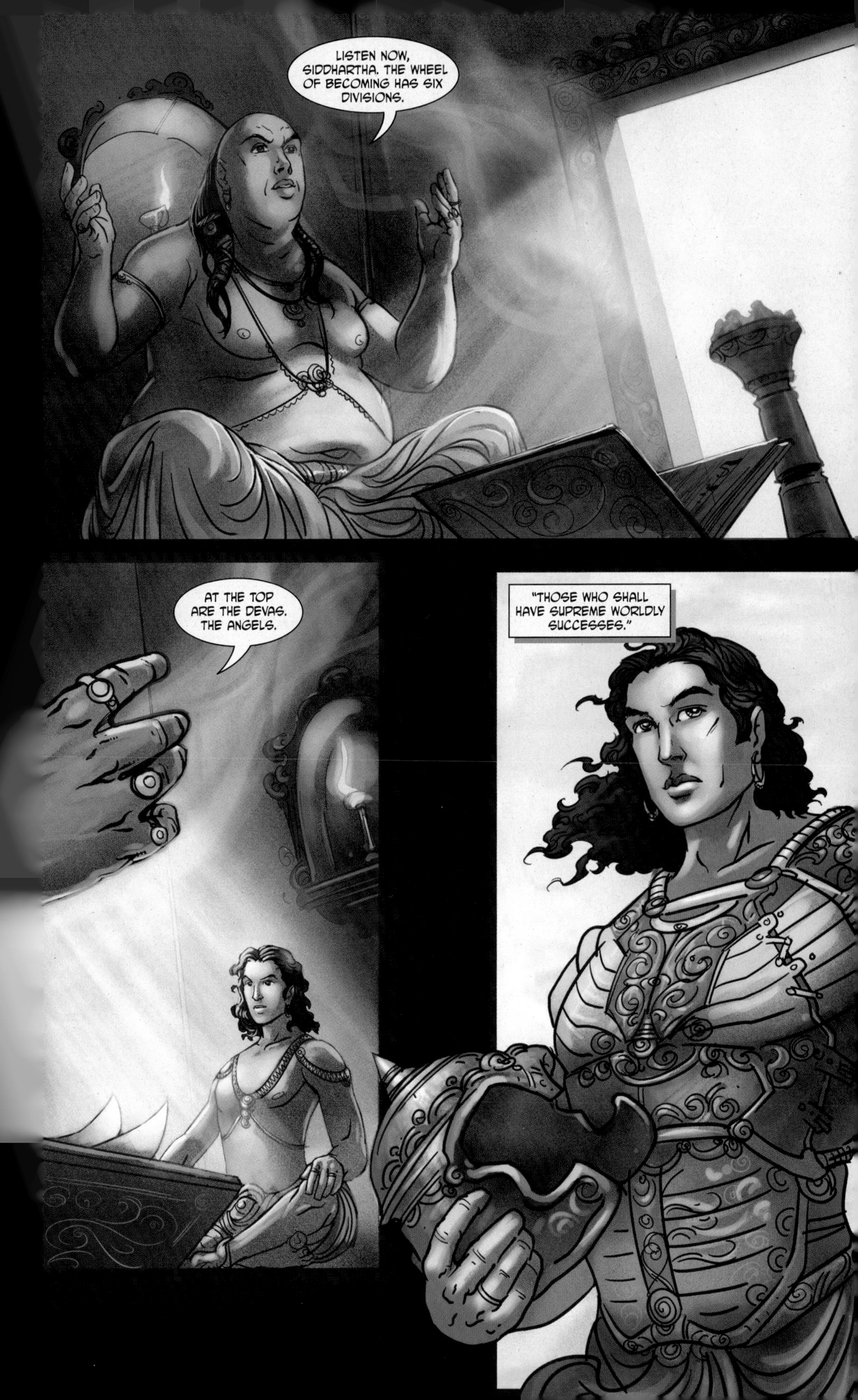
LISTEN NOW, SIDDHARTHA. THE WHEEL OF BECOMING HAS SIX DIVISIONS.
AT THE TOP ARE THE DEVAS. THE ANGELS.
"THOSE WHO SHALL HAVE SUPREME WORLDLY SUCCESSES."

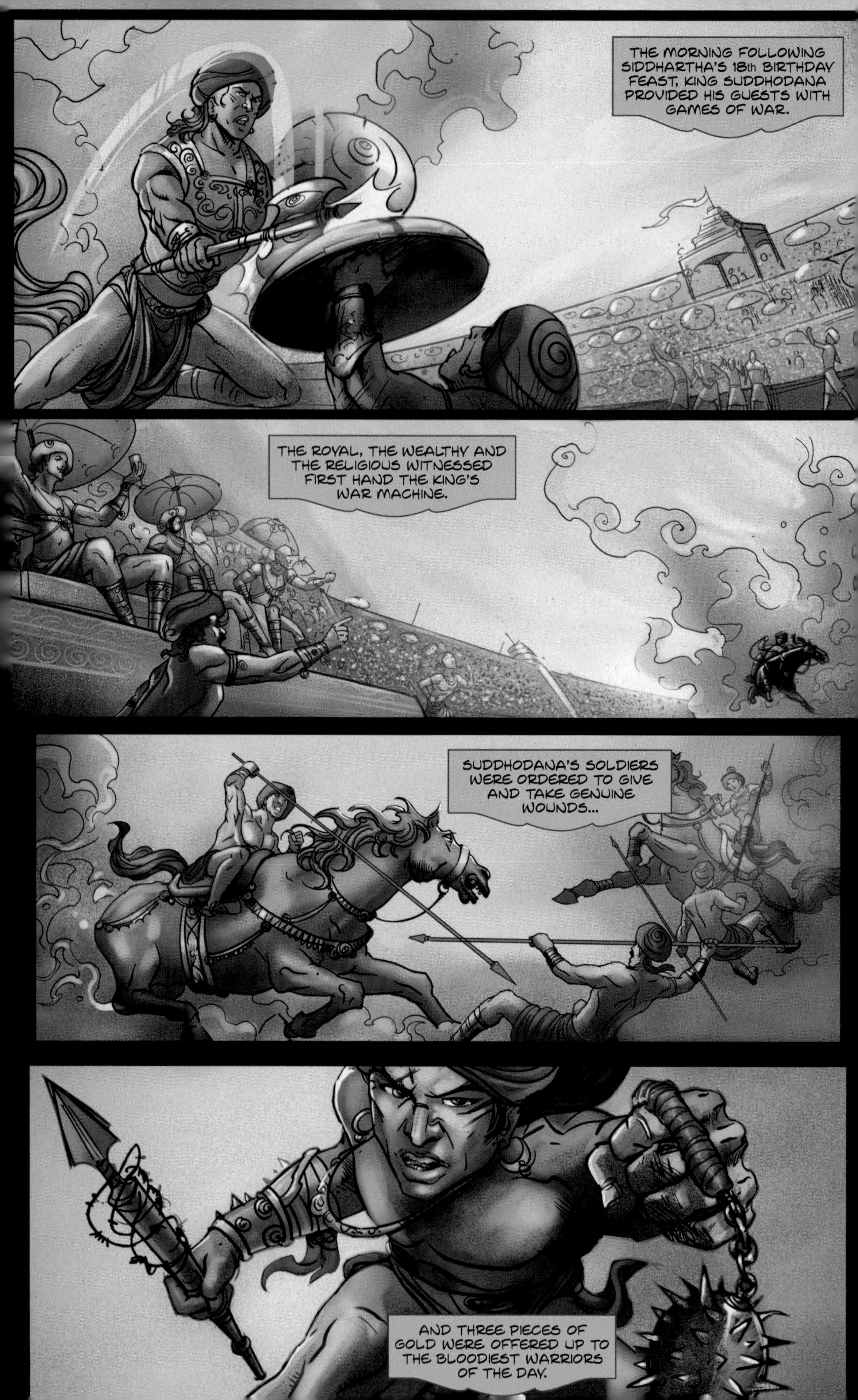
THE MORNING FOLLOWING SIDDHARTHA'S 18th BIRTHDAY FEAST, KING SUDDHODANA PROVIDED HIS GUESTS WITH GAMES OF WAR.
THE ROYAL, THE WEALTHY AND THE RELIGIOUS WITNESSED FIRST HAND THE KING'S WAR MACHINE.
SUDDHODANA'S SOLDIERS WERE ORDERED TO GIVE AND TAKE GENUINE WOUNDS...
AND THREE PIECES OF GOLD WERE OFFERED UP TO THE BLOODIEST WARRIORS OF THE DAY.

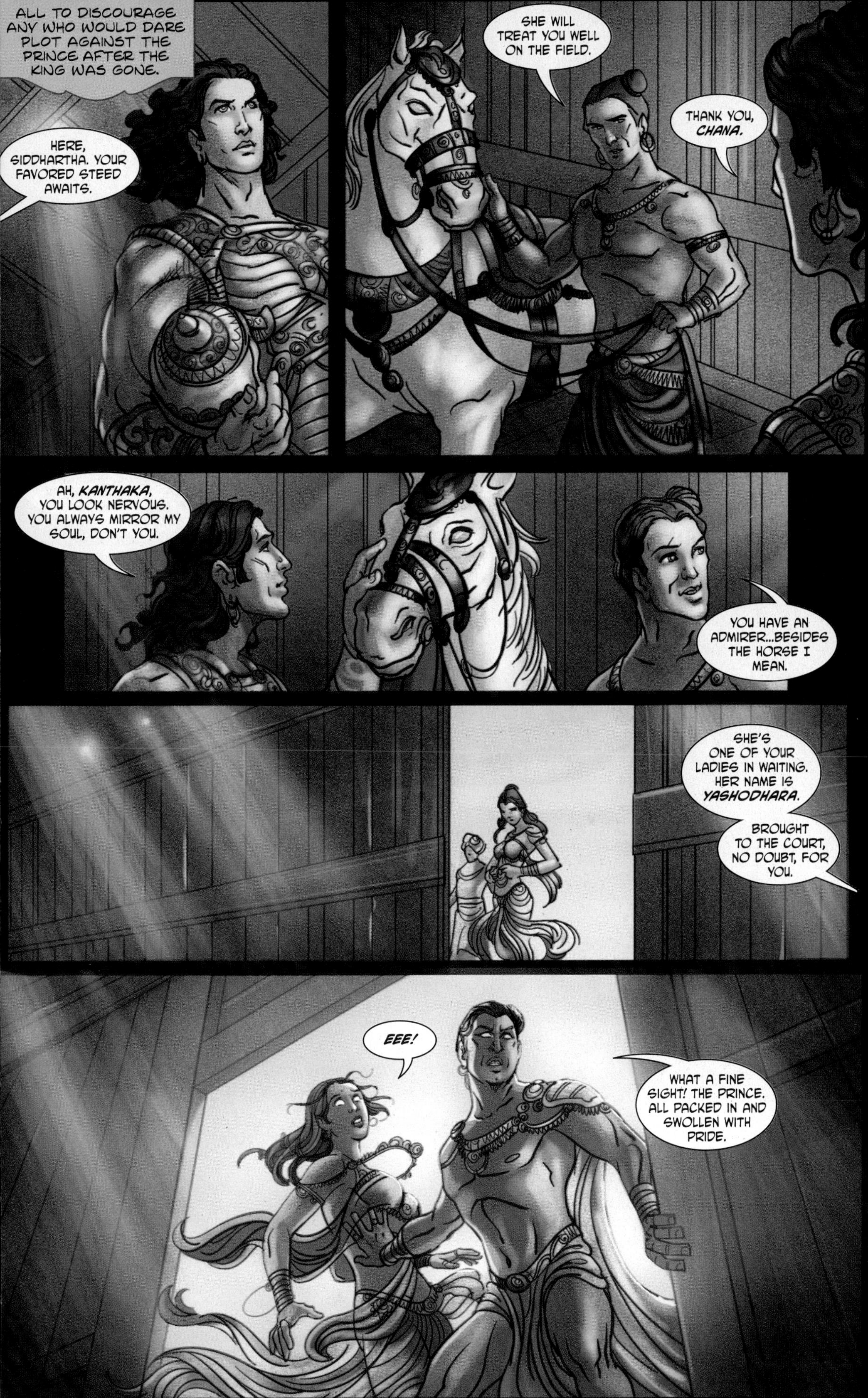
ALL TO DISCOURAGE ANY WHO WOULD DARE PLOT AGAINST THE PRINCE AFTER THE KING WAS GONE.
HERE, SIDDHARTHA. YOUR FAVORED STEED AWAITS.
SHE WILL TREAT YOU WELL ON THE FIELD.
THANK YOU, CHANA.
AH, KANTHAKA, YOU LOOK NERVOUS. YOU ALWAYS MIRROR MY SOUL, DON'T YOU.
YOU HAVE AN ADMIRER...BESIDES THE HORSE I MEAN.
SHE'S ONE OF YOUR LADIES IN WAITING. HER NAME IS YASHODHARA.
BROUGHT TO THE COURT, NO DOUBT, FOR YOU.
EEE!
WHAT A FINE SIGHT! THE PRINCE. ALL PACKED IN AND SWOLLEN WITH PRIDE.

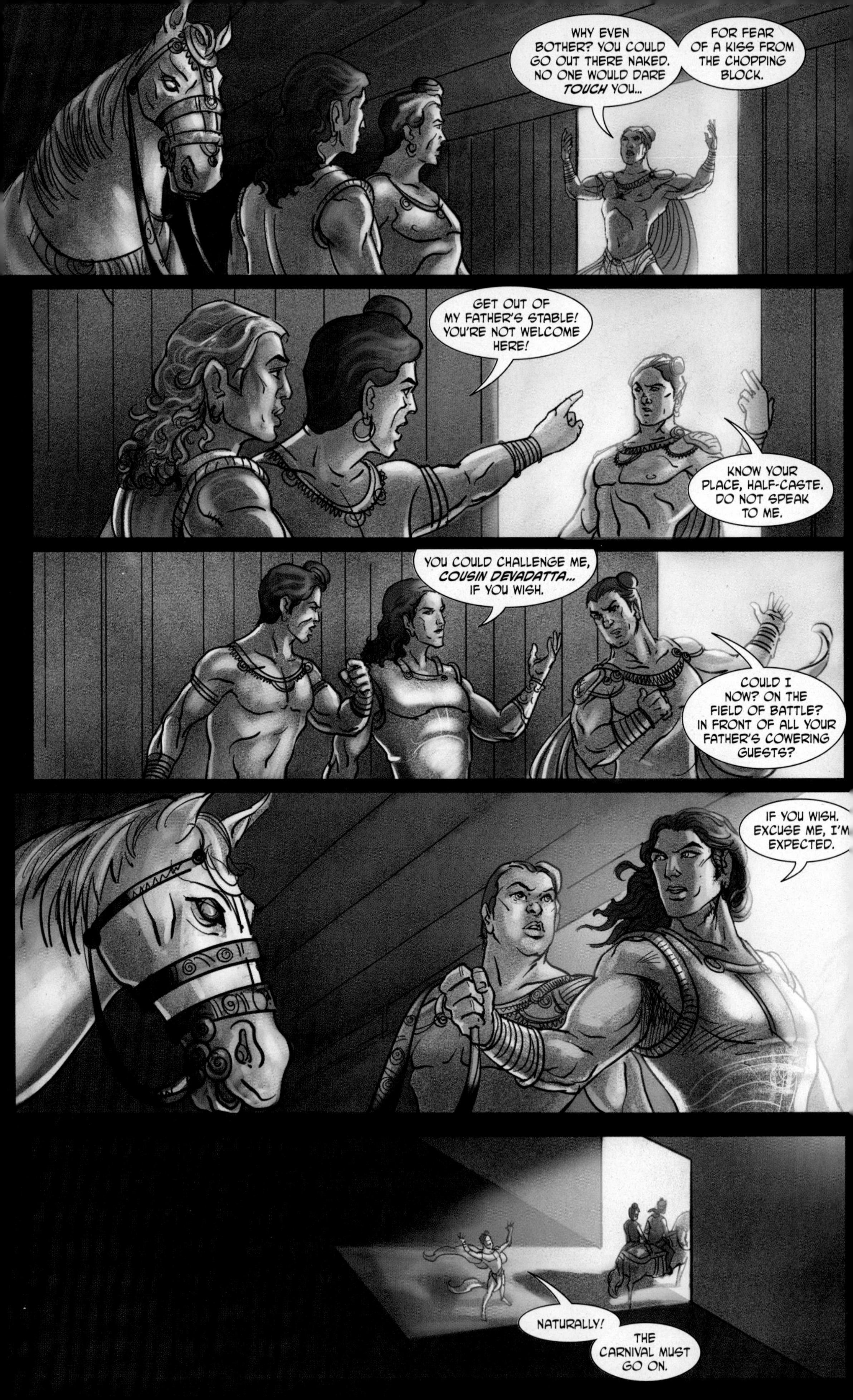
WHY EVEN BOTHER? YOU COULD GO OUT THERE NAKED. NO ONE WOULD DARE *TOUCH* YOU...
FOR FEAR OF A KISS FROM THE CHOPPING BLOCK.
GET OUT OF MY FATHER'S STABLE! YOU'RE NOT WELCOME HERE!
KNOW YOUR PLACE, HALF-CASTE. DO NOT SPEAK TO ME.
YOU COULD CHALLENGE ME, *COUSIN DEVADATTA*... IF YOU WISH.
COULD I NOW? ON THE FIELD OF BATTLE? IN FRONT OF ALL YOUR FATHER'S COWERING GUESTS?
IF YOU WISH. EXCUSE ME, I'M EXPECTED.
NATURALLY!
THE CARNIVAL MUST GO ON.

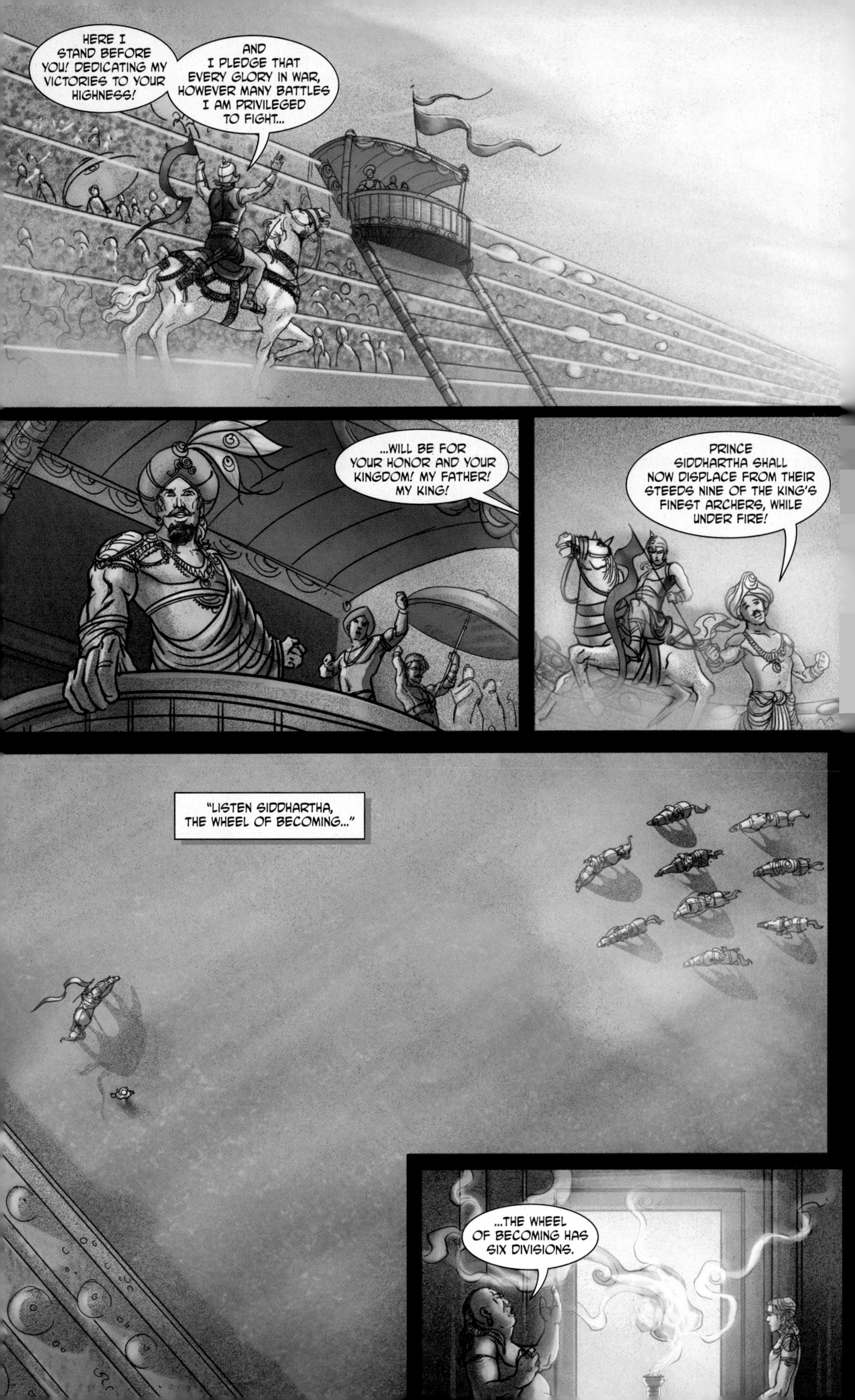
HERE I STAND BEFORE YOU! DEDICATING MY VICTORIES TO YOUR HIGHNESS!
AND I PLEDGE THAT EVERY GLORY IN WAR, HOWEVER MANY BATTLES I AM PRIVILEGED TO FIGHT...
...WILL BE FOR YOUR HONOR AND YOUR KINGDOM! MY FATHER! MY KING!
PRINCE SIDDHARTHA SHALL NOW DISPLACE FROM THEIR STEEDS NINE OF THE KING'S FINEST ARCHERS, WHILE UNDER FIRE!
"LISTEN SIDDHARTHA, THE WHEEL OF BECOMING..."
...THE WHEEL OF BECOMING HAS SIX DIVISIONS.

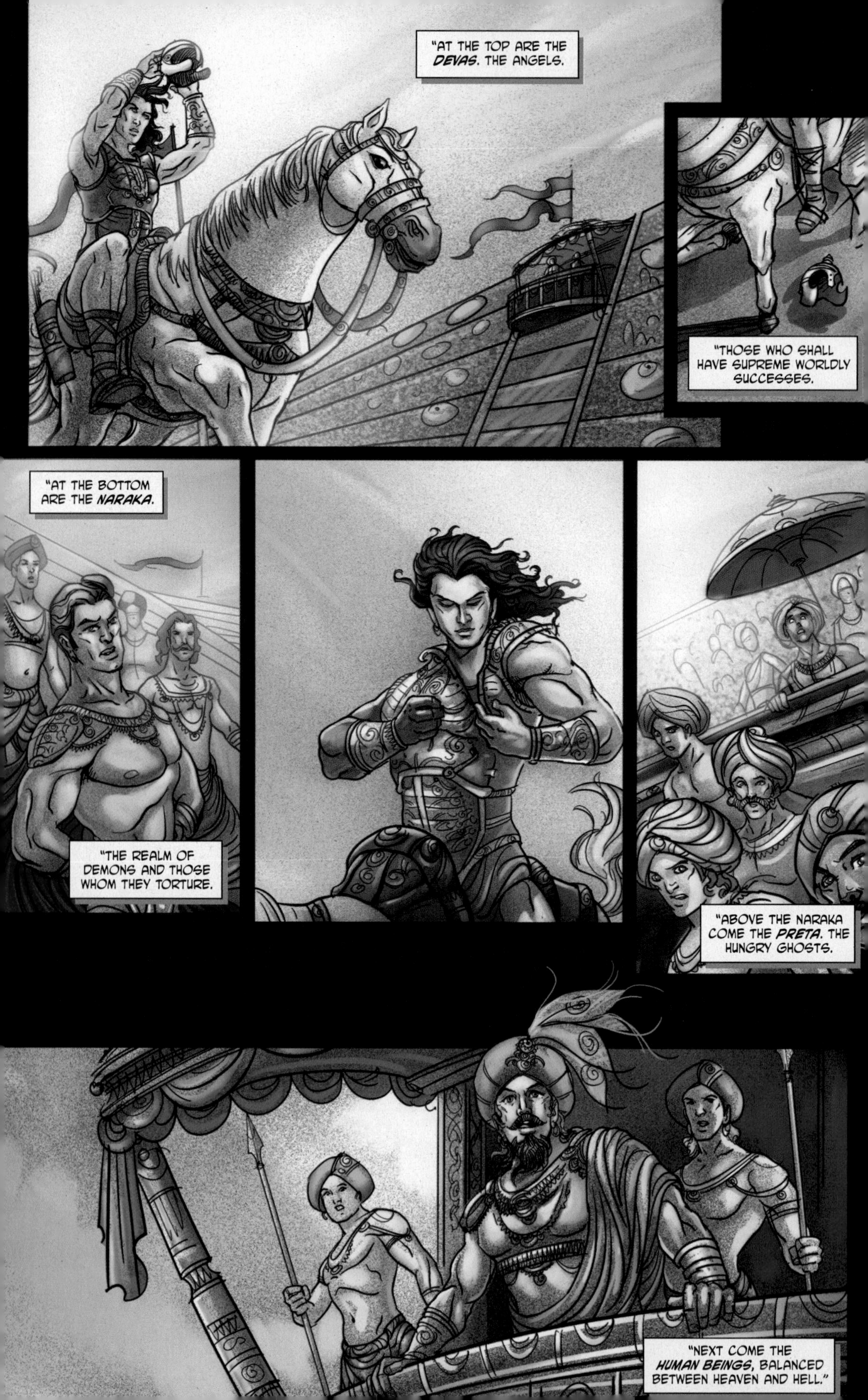
"AT THE TOP ARE THE *DEVAS*. THE ANGELS.
"THOSE WHO SHALL HAVE SUPREME WORLDLY SUCCESSES.
"AT THE BOTTOM ARE THE *NARAKA*.
"THE REALM OF DEMONS AND THOSE WHOM THEY TORTURE.
"ABOVE THE NARAKA COME THE *PRETA*. THE HUNGRY GHOSTS.
"NEXT COME THE *HUMAN BEINGS*, BALANCED BETWEEN HEAVEN AND HELL."

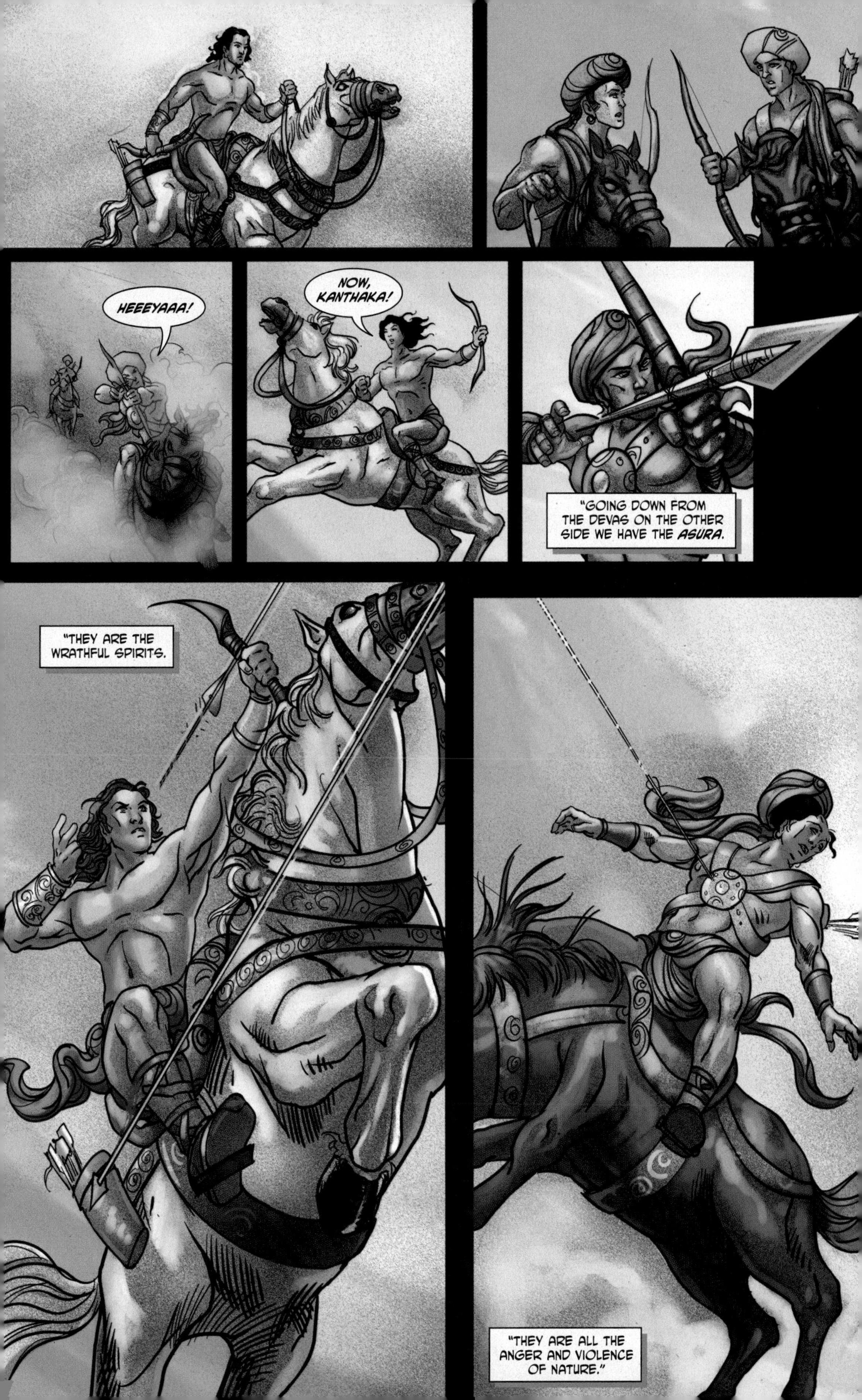

HEEEYAAA!
NOW, KANTHAKA!
"GOING DOWN FROM THE DEVAS ON THE OTHER SIDE WE HAVE THE ASURA.
"THEY ARE THE WRATHFUL SPIRITS.
"THEY ARE ALL THE ANGER AND VIOLENCE OF NATURE."

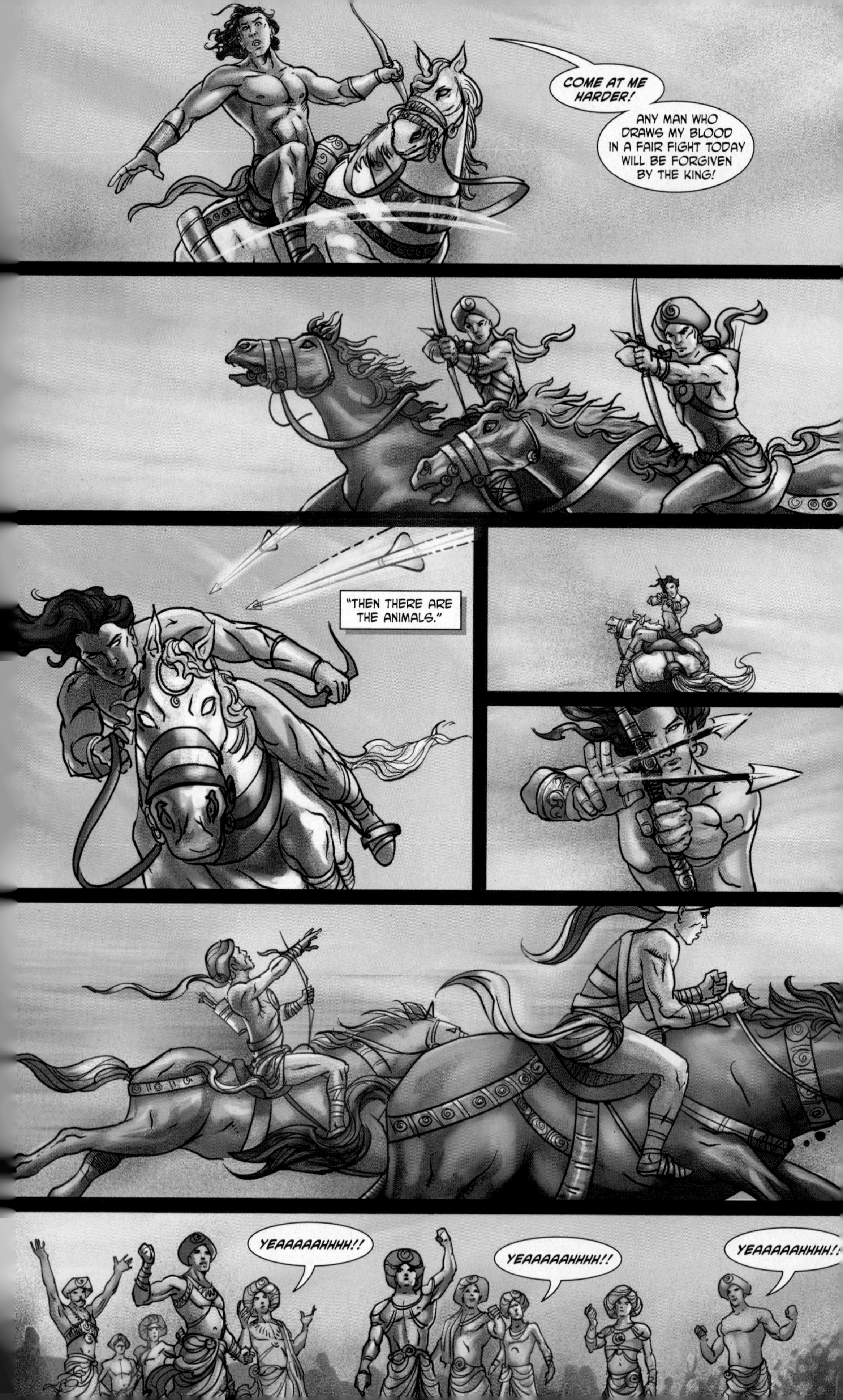
COME AT ME HARDER!
ANY MAN WHO DRAWS MY BLOOD IN A FAIR FIGHT TODAY WILL BE FORGIVEN BY THE KING!
"THEN THERE ARE THE ANIMALS."
YEAAAAAHHHH!!
YEAAAAAHHHH!!

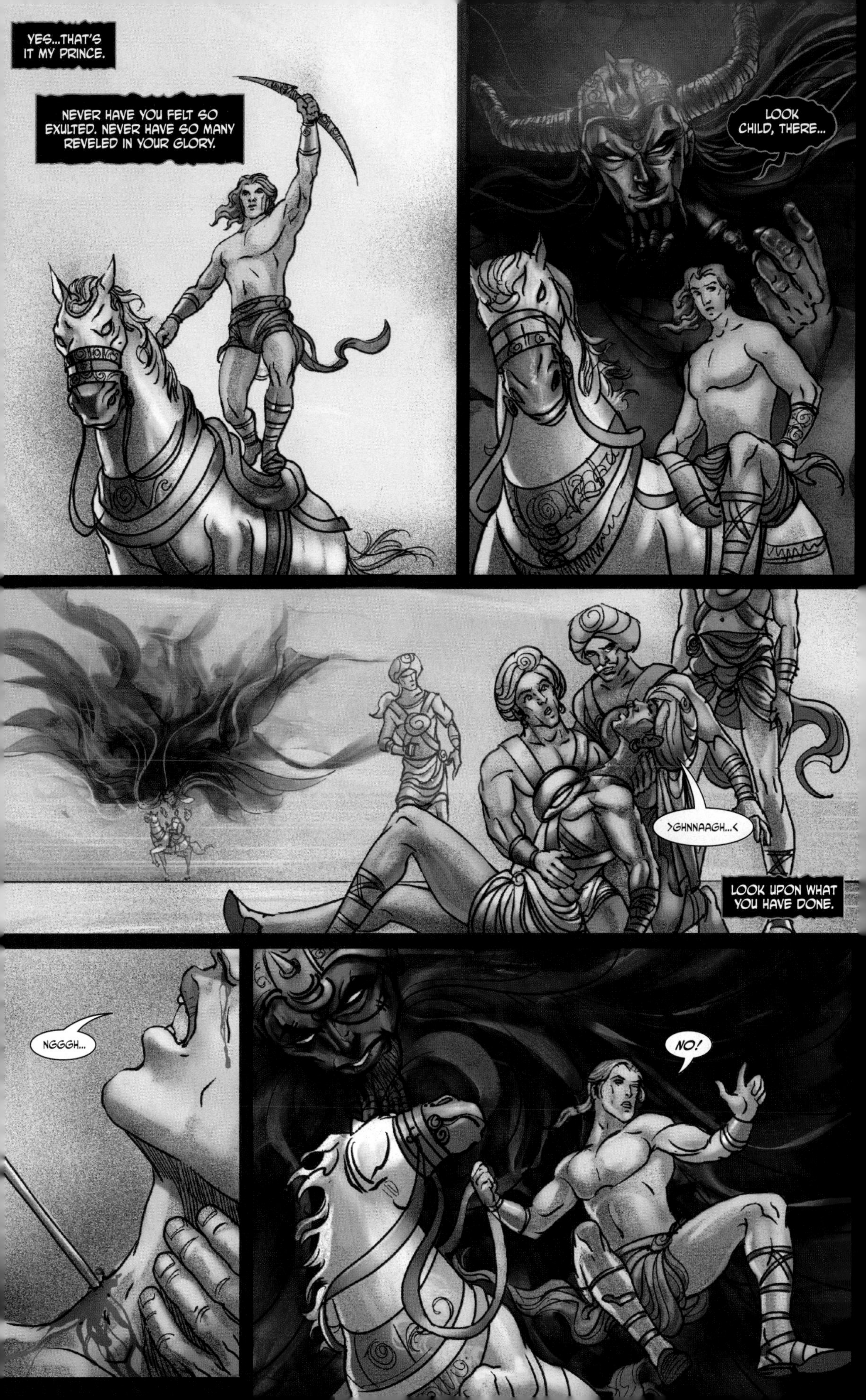
YES...THAT'S IT MY PRINCE.
NEVER HAVE YOU FELT SO EXULTED. NEVER HAVE SO MANY REVELED IN YOUR GLORY.
LOOK CHILD, THERE...
>GHNNAAGH...<
LOOK UPON WHAT YOU HAVE DONE.
NGGGH...
NO!

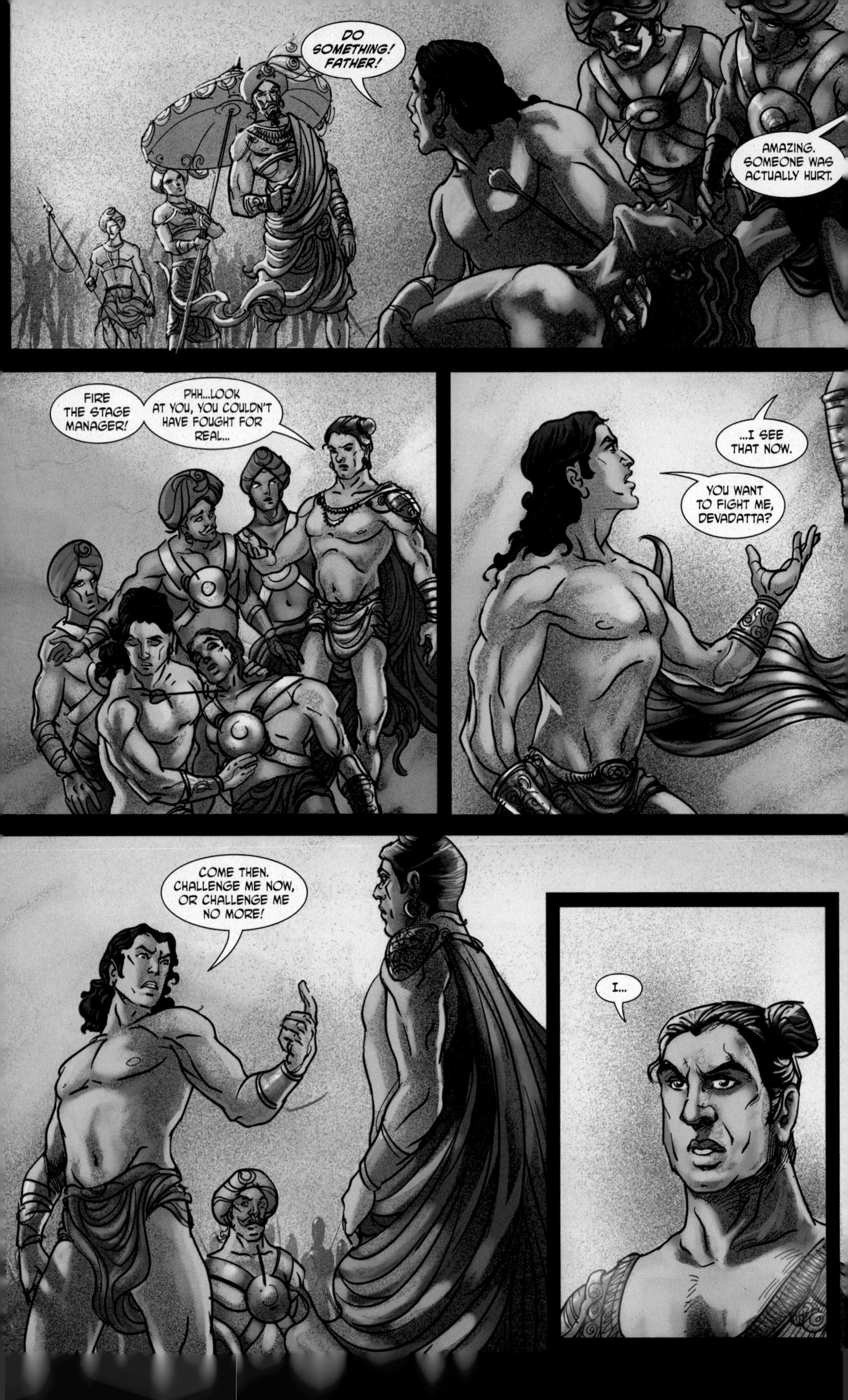
DO SOMETHING! FATHER!
AMAZING. SOMEONE WAS ACTUALLY HURT.
FIRE THE STAGE MANAGER!
PHH...LOOK AT YOU, YOU COULDN'T HAVE FOUGHT FOR REAL...
...I SEE THAT NOW.
YOU WANT TO FIGHT ME, DEVADATTA?
COME THEN. CHALLENGE ME NOW, OR CHALLENGE ME NO MORE!
I...

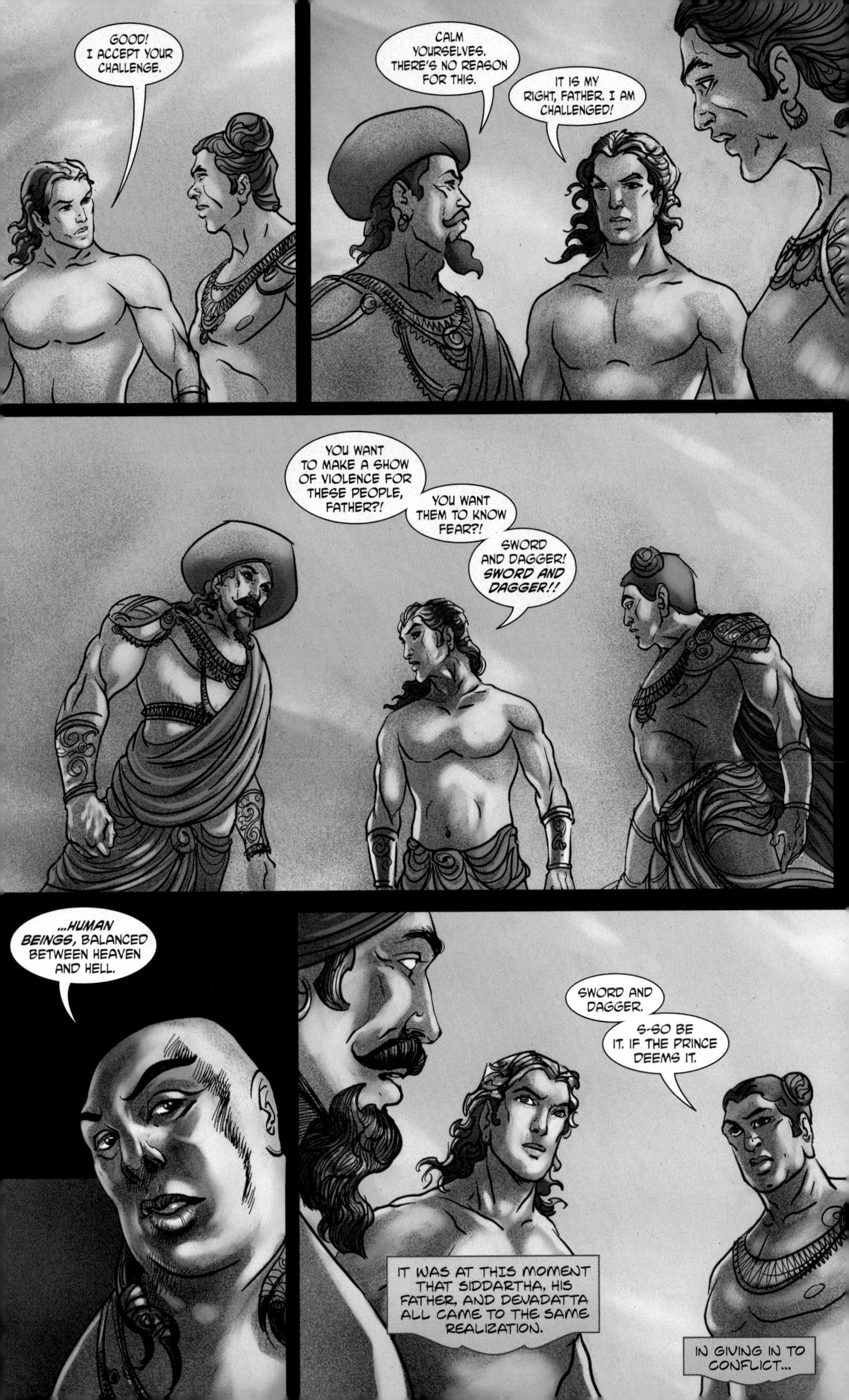
GOOD! I ACCEPT YOUR CHALLENGE.
CALM YOURSELVES. THERE'S NO REASON FOR THIS.
IT IS MY RIGHT, FATHER. I AM CHALLENGED!
YOU WANT TO MAKE A SHOW OF VIOLENCE FOR THESE PEOPLE, FATHER?!
YOU WANT THEM TO KNOW FEAR?!
SWORD AND DAGGER! SWORD AND DAGGER!!
...HUMAN BEINGS, BALANCED BETWEEN HEAVEN AND HELL.
SWORD AND DAGGER.
S-SO BE IT. IF THE PRINCE DEEMS IT.
IT WAS AT THIS MOMENT THAT SIDDARTHA, HIS FATHER, AND DEVADATTA ALL CAME TO THE SAME REALIZATION.
IN GIVING IN TO CONFLICT...

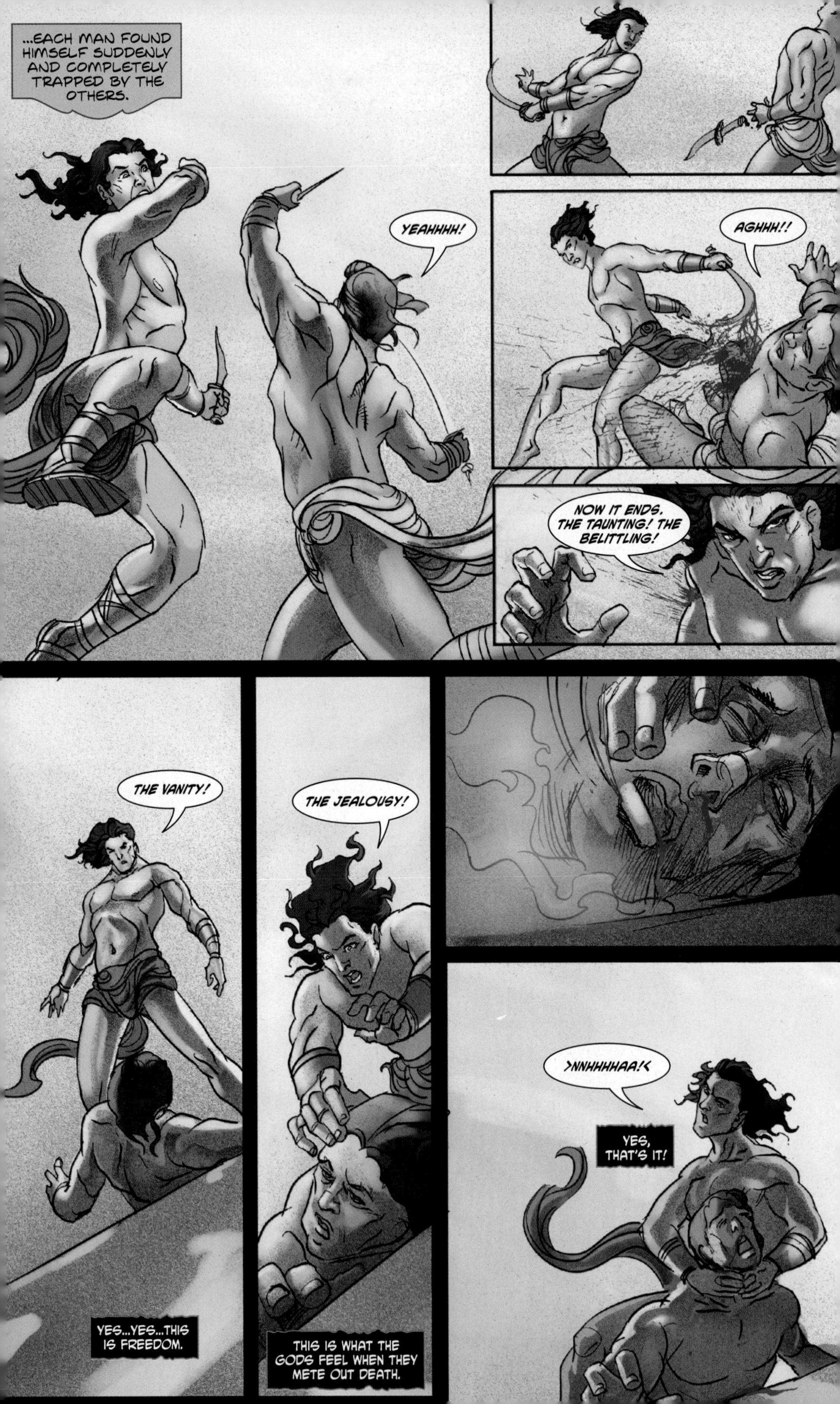
...EACH MAN FOUND HIMSELF SUDDENLY AND COMPLETELY TRAPPED BY THE OTHERS.
YEAHHHH!
AGHHH!!
NOW IT ENDS. THE TAUNTING! THE BELITTLING!
THE VANITY!
YES...YES...THIS IS FREEDOM.
THE JEALOUSY!
THIS IS WHAT THE GODS FEEL WHEN THEY METE OUT DEATH.
>NNHHHHAA!<
YES, THAT'S IT!

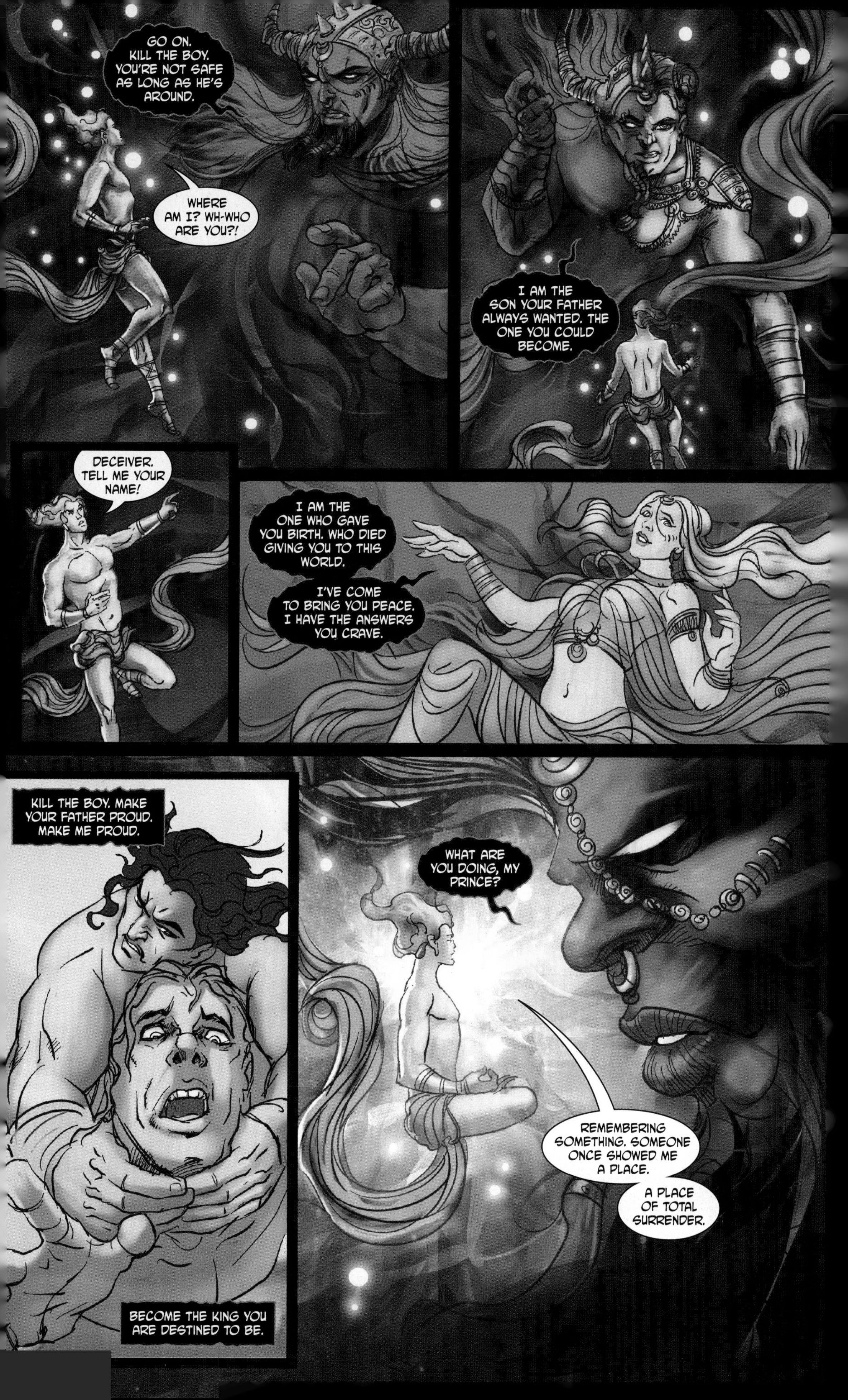
GO ON. KILL THE BOY. YOU'RE NOT SAFE AS LONG AS HE'S AROUND.
WHERE AM I? WH-WHO ARE YOU?!
I AM THE SON YOUR FATHER ALWAYS WANTED. THE ONE YOU COULD BECOME.
DECEIVER. TELL ME YOUR NAME!
I AM THE ONE WHO GAVE YOU BIRTH. WHO DIED GIVING YOU TO THIS WORLD.
I'VE COME TO BRING YOU PEACE. I HAVE THE ANSWERS YOU CRAVE.
KILL THE BOY. MAKE YOUR FATHER PROUD. MAKE ME PROUD.
BECOME THE KING YOU ARE DESTINED TO BE.
WHAT ARE YOU DOING, MY PRINCE?
REMEMBERING SOMETHING. SOMEONE ONCE SHOWED ME A PLACE.
A PLACE OF TOTAL SURRENDER.

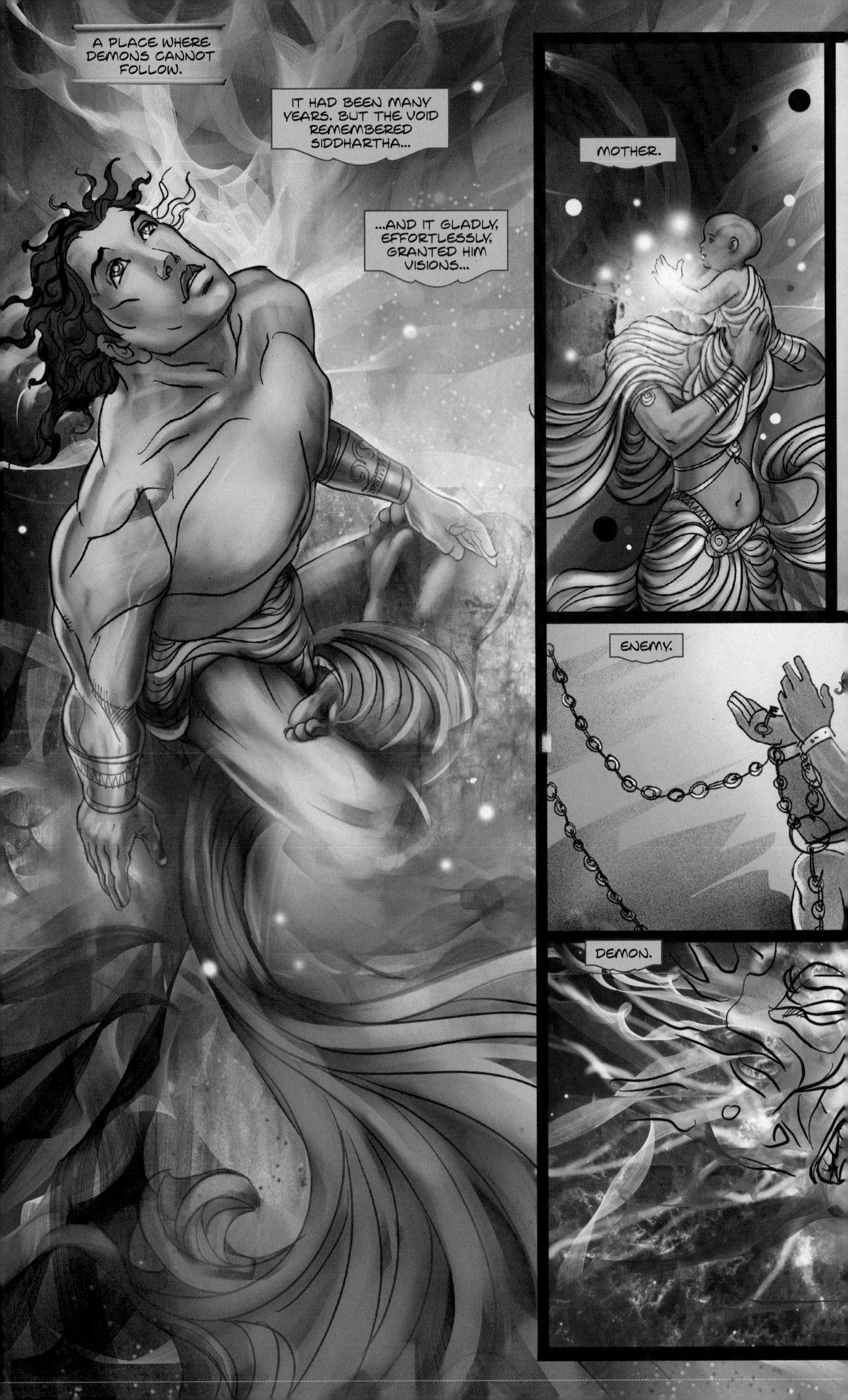
A PLACE WHERE DEMONS CANNOT FOLLOW.
IT HAD BEEN MANY YEARS. BUT THE VOID REMEMBERED SIDDHARTHA...
...AND IT GLADLY, EFFORTLESSLY, GRANTED HIM VISIONS...
MOTHER.
ENEMY.
DEMON.

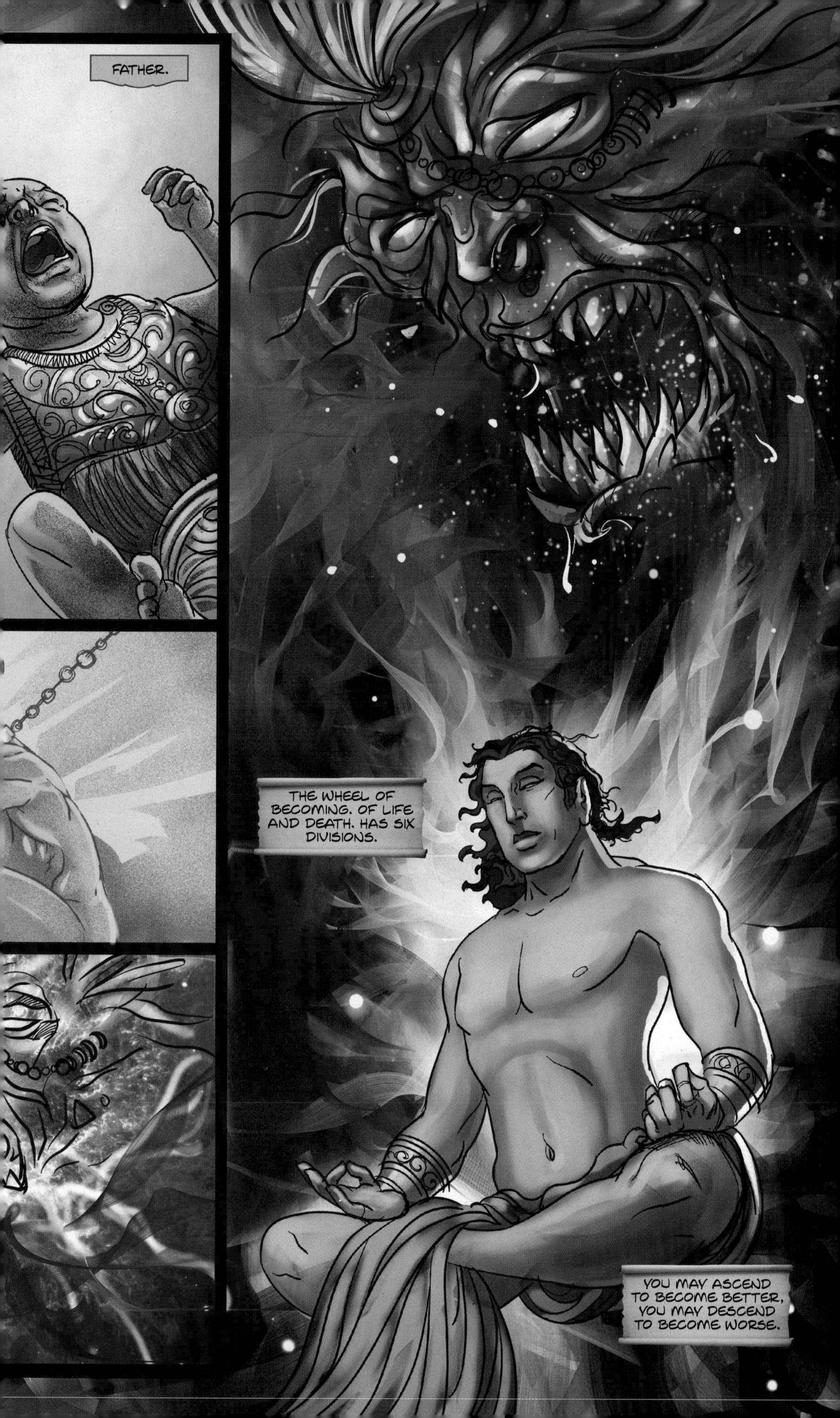
FATHER.
THE WHEEL OF BECOMING, OF LIFE AND DEATH, HAS SIX DIVISIONS.
YOU MAY ASCEND TO BECOME BETTER, YOU MAY DESCEND TO BECOME WORSE.

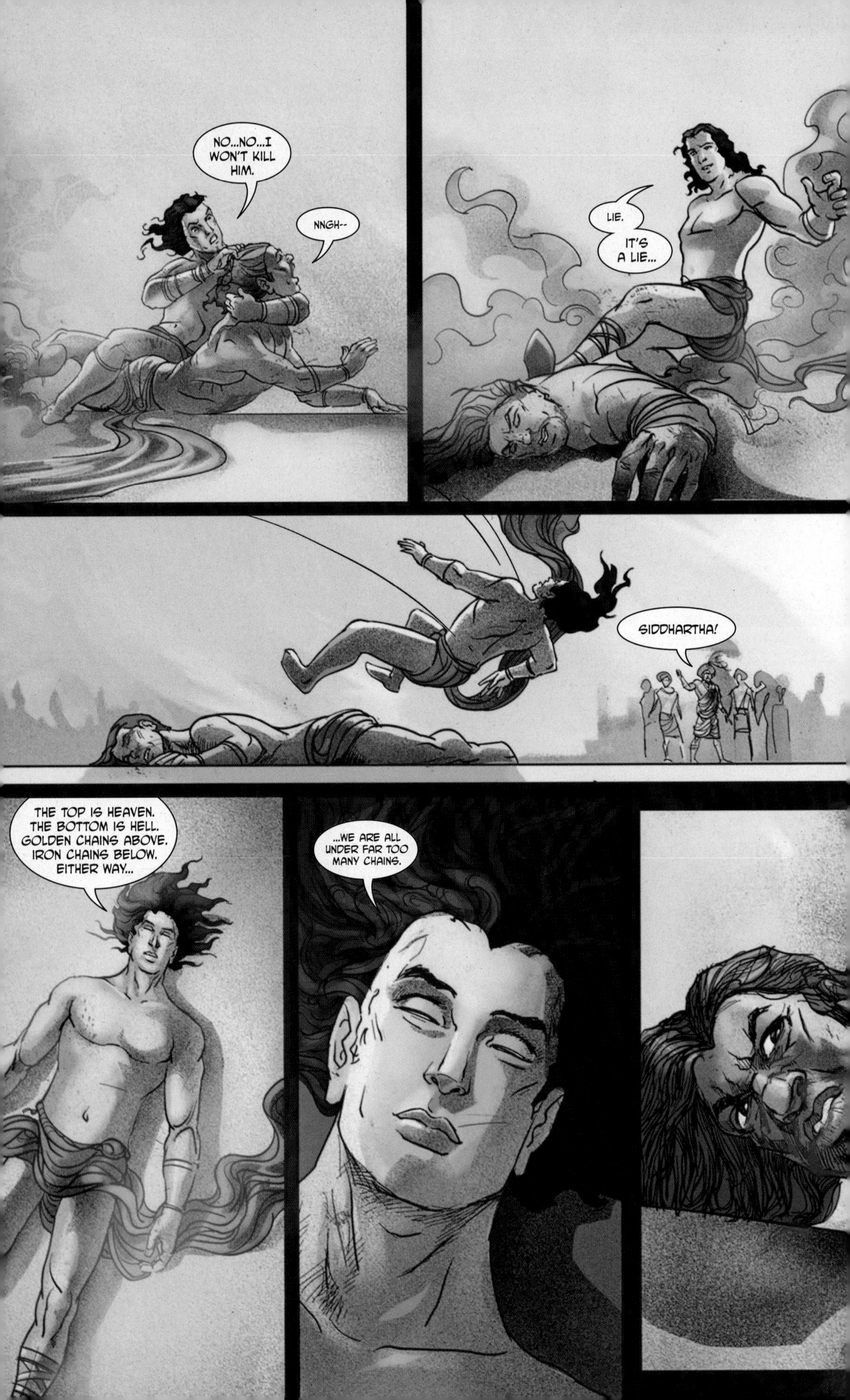
NO...NO...I WON'T KILL HIM.
NNGH--
LIE.
IT'S A LIE...
SIDDHARTHA!
THE TOP IS HEAVEN. THE BOTTOM IS HELL. GOLDEN CHAINS ABOVE. IRON CHAINS BELOW. EITHER WAY...
...WE ARE ALL UNDER FAR TOO MANY CHAINS.

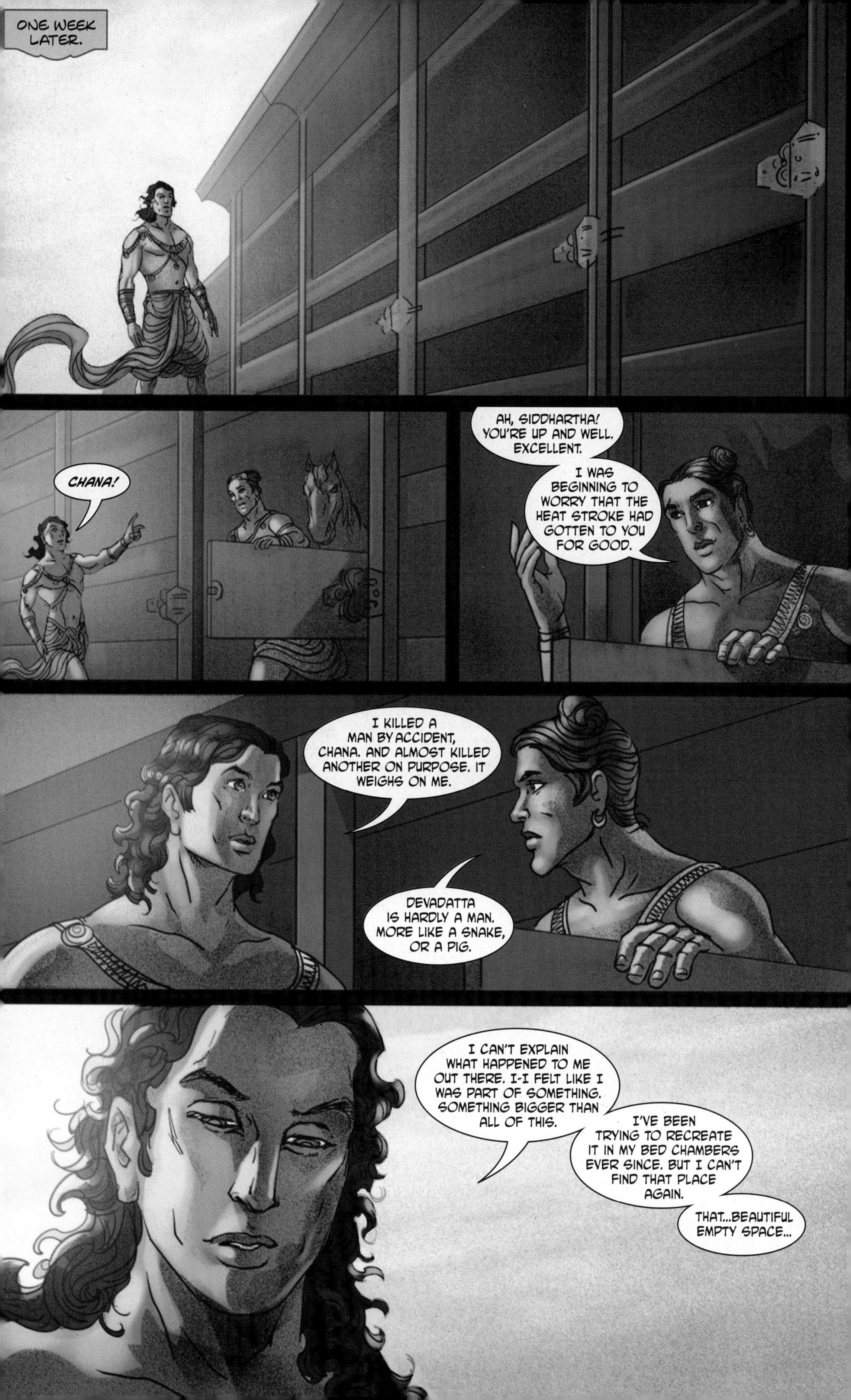
ONE WEEK LATER.
CHANA!
AH, SIDDHARTHA! YOU'RE UP AND WELL. EXCELLENT.
I WAS BEGINNING TO WORRY THAT THE HEAT STROKE HAD GOTTEN TO YOU FOR GOOD.
I KILLED A MAN BY ACCIDENT, CHANA. AND ALMOST KILLED ANOTHER ON PURPOSE. IT WEIGHS ON ME.
DEVADATTA IS HARDLY A MAN. MORE LIKE A SNAKE, OR A PIG.
I CAN'T EXPLAIN WHAT HAPPENED TO ME OUT THERE. I-I FELT LIKE I WAS PART OF SOMETHING. SOMETHING BIGGER THAN ALL OF THIS.
I'VE BEEN TRYING TO RECREATE IT IN MY BED CHAMBERS EVER SINCE. BUT I CAN'T FIND THAT PLACE AGAIN.
THAT...BEAUTIFUL EMPTY SPACE...

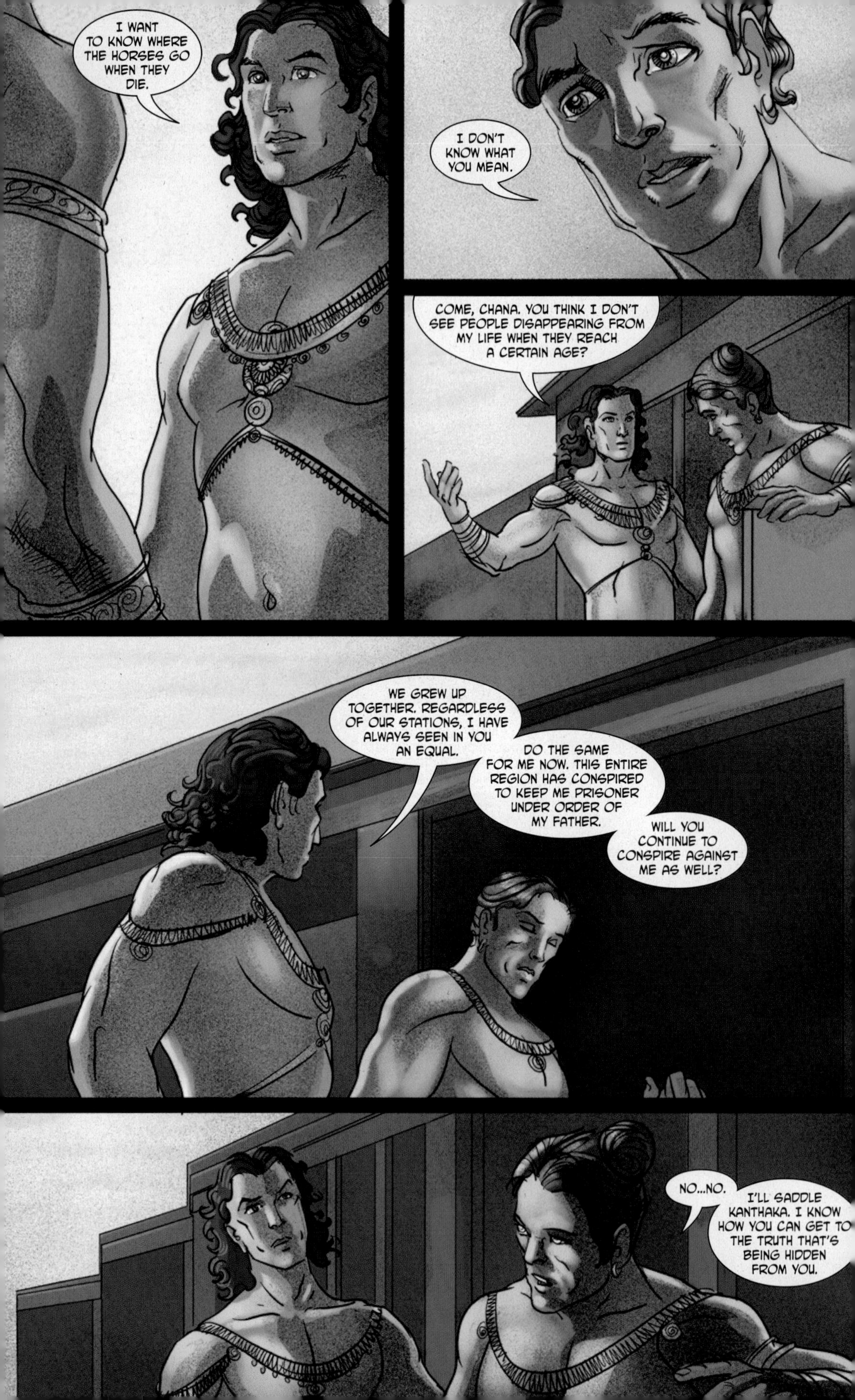
I WANT TO KNOW WHERE THE HORSES GO WHEN THEY DIE.
I DON'T KNOW WHAT YOU MEAN.
COME, CHANA. YOU THINK I DON'T SEE PEOPLE DISAPPEARING FROM MY LIFE WHEN THEY REACH A CERTAIN AGE?
WE GREW UP TOGETHER. REGARDLESS OF OUR STATIONS, I HAVE ALWAYS SEEN IN YOU AN EQUAL.
DO THE SAME FOR ME NOW. THIS ENTIRE REGION HAS CONSPIRED TO KEEP ME PRISONER UNDER ORDER OF MY FATHER.
WILL YOU CONTINUE TO CONSPIRE AGAINST ME AS WELL?
NO...NO.
I'LL SADDLE KANTHAKA. I KNOW HOW YOU CAN GET TO THE TRUTH THAT'S BEING HIDDEN FROM YOU.

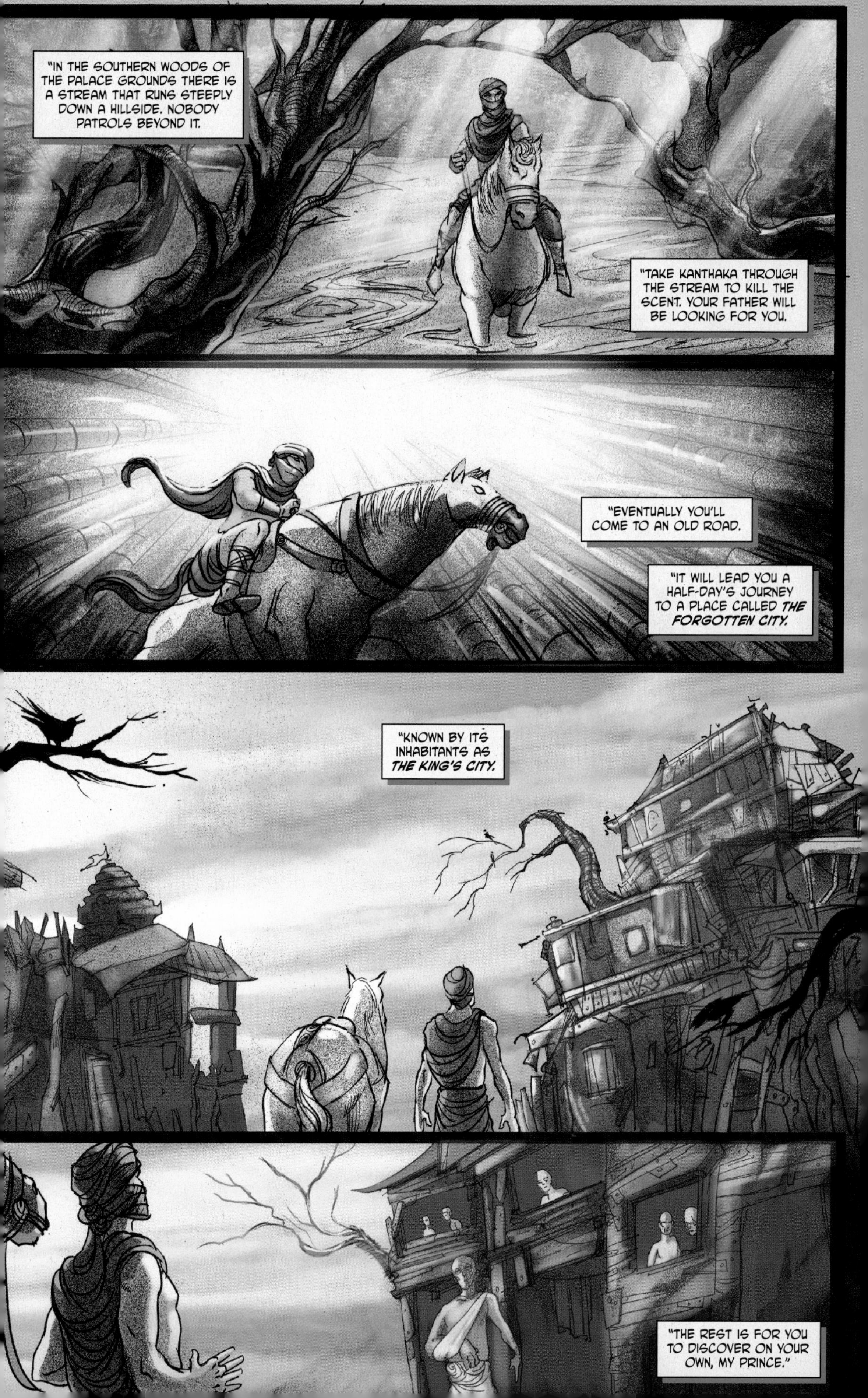
"IN THE SOUTHERN WOODS OF THE PALACE GROUNDS THERE IS A STREAM THAT RUNS STEEPLY DOWN A HILLSIDE. NOBODY PATROLS BEYOND IT.
"TAKE KANTHAKA THROUGH THE STREAM TO KILL THE SCENT. YOUR FATHER WILL BE LOOKING FOR YOU.
"EVENTUALLY YOU'LL COME TO AN OLD ROAD.
"IT WILL LEAD YOU A HALF-DAY'S JOURNEY TO A PLACE CALLED *THE FORGOTTEN CITY.*
"KNOWN BY ITS INHABITANTS AS *THE KING'S CITY.*
"THE REST IS FOR YOU TO DISCOVER ON YOUR OWN, MY PRINCE."

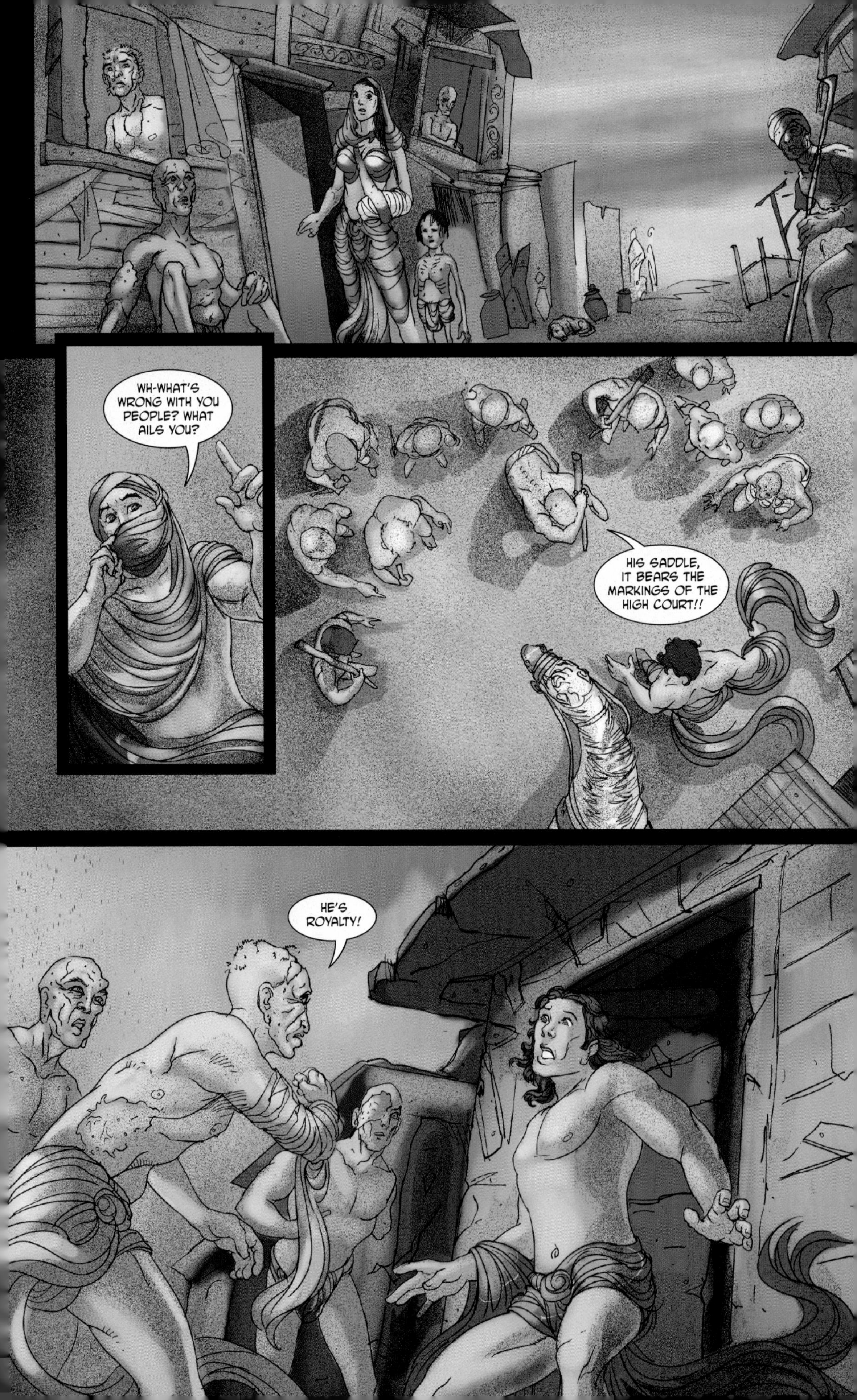
WH-WHAT'S WRONG WITH YOU PEOPLE? WHAT AILS YOU?
HIS SADDLE, IT BEARS THE MARKINGS OF THE HIGH COURT!!
HE'S ROYALTY!

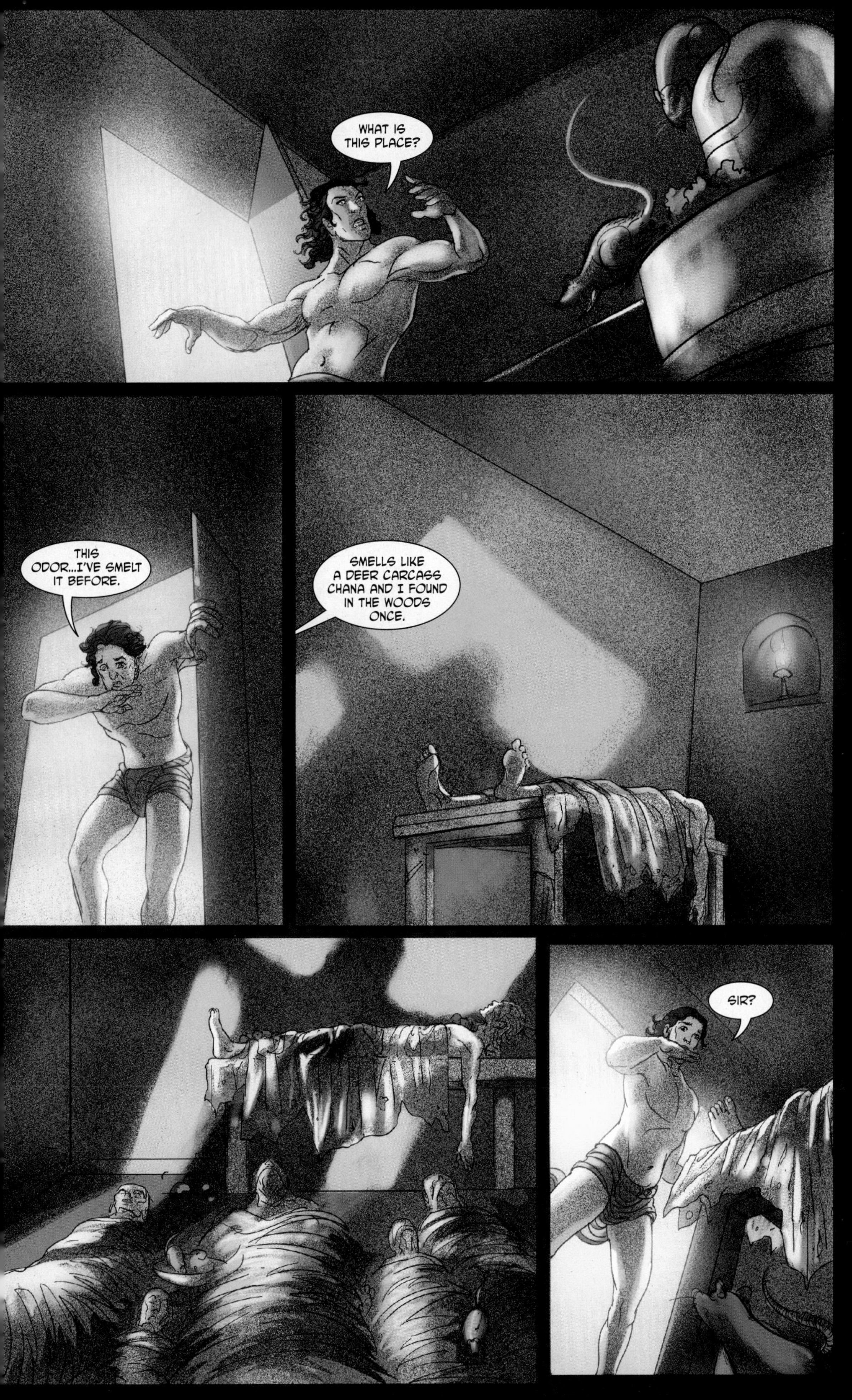
WHAT IS THIS PLACE?
THIS ODOR...I'VE SMELT IT BEFORE.
SMELLS LIKE A DEER CARCASS CHANA AND I FOUND IN THE WOODS ONCE.
SIR?

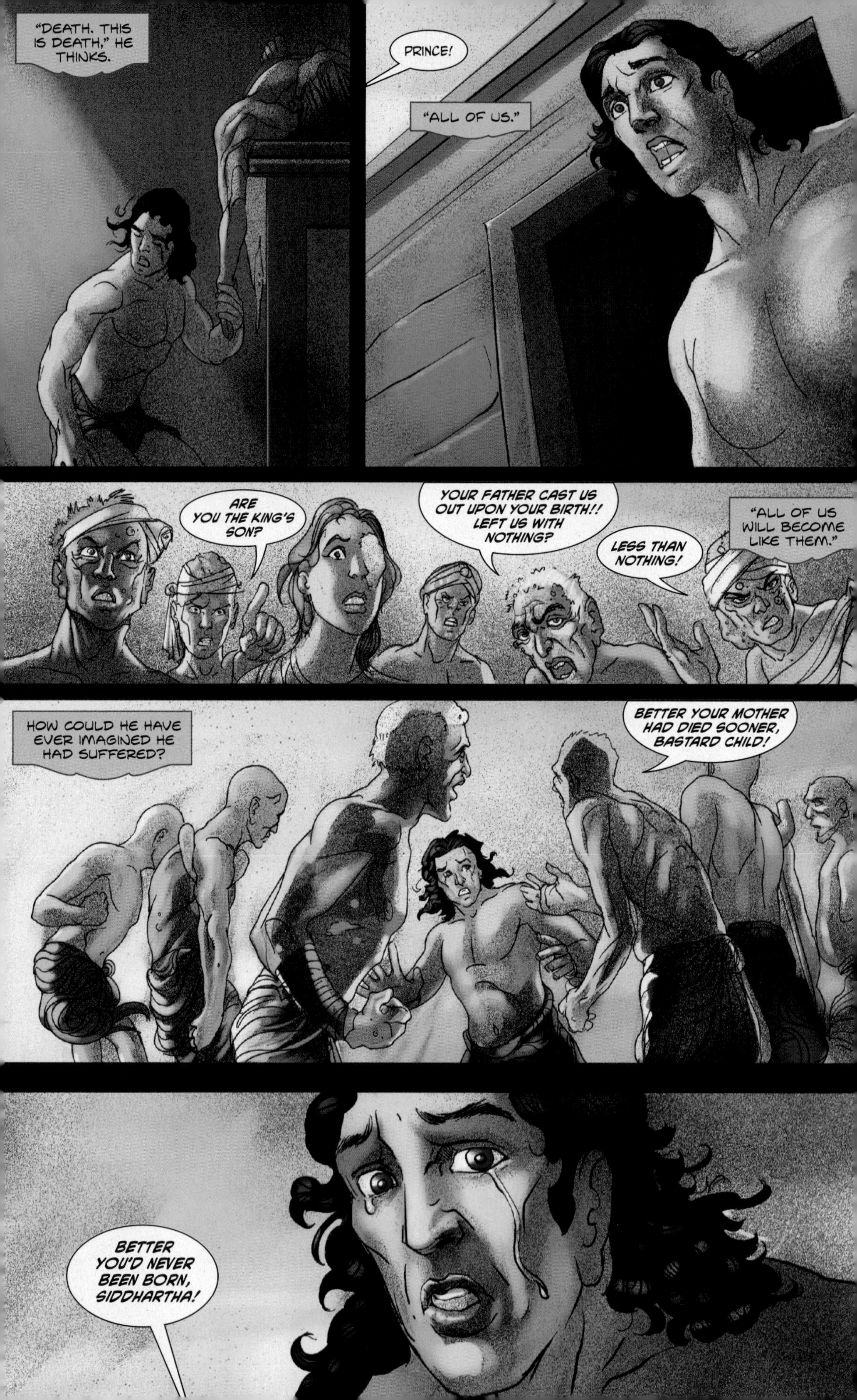
"DEATH. THIS IS DEATH," HE THINKS.
PRINCE!
"ALL OF US."
ARE YOU THE KING'S SON?
YOUR FATHER CAST US OUT UPON YOUR BIRTH!! LEFT US WITH NOTHING?
LESS THAN NOTHING!
"ALL OF US WILL BECOME LIKE THEM."
HOW COULD HE HAVE EVER IMAGINED HE HAD SUFFERED?
BETTER YOUR MOTHER HAD DIED SOONER, BASTARD CHILD!
BETTER YOU'D NEVER BEEN BORN, SIDDHARTHA!

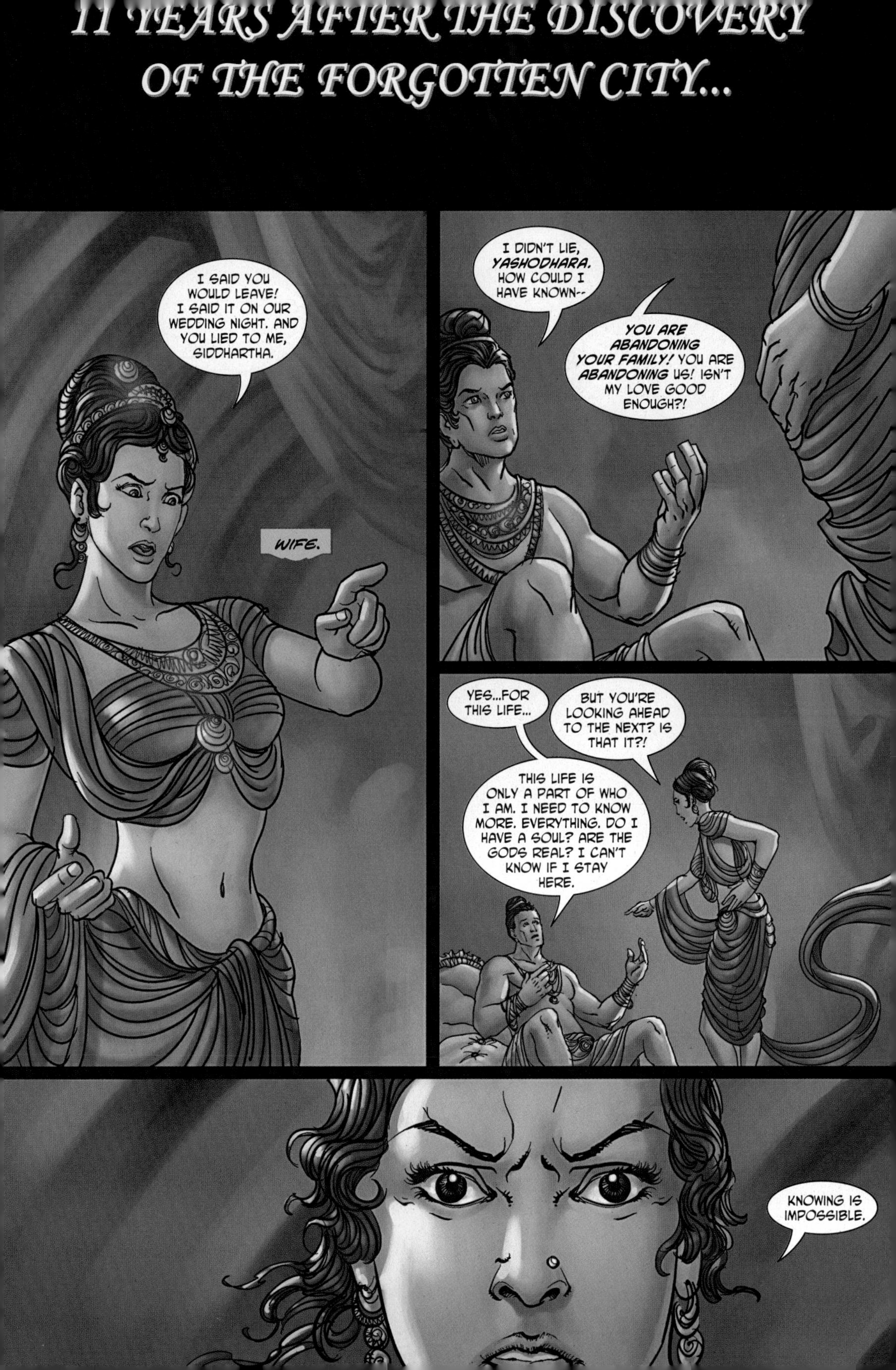
11 YEARS AFTER THE DISCOVERY OF THE FORGOTTEN CITY...
I SAID YOU WOULD LEAVE! I SAID IT ON OUR WEDDING NIGHT. AND YOU LIED TO ME, SIDDHARTHA.
WIFE.
I DIDN'T LIE, YASHODHARA. HOW COULD I HAVE KNOWN--
YOU ARE ABANDONING YOUR FAMILY! YOU ARE ABANDONING US! ISN'T MY LOVE GOOD ENOUGH?!
YES...FOR THIS LIFE...
BUT YOU'RE LOOKING AHEAD TO THE NEXT? IS THAT IT?!
THIS LIFE IS ONLY A PART OF WHO I AM. I NEED TO KNOW MORE. EVERYTHING. DO I HAVE A SOUL? ARE THE GODS REAL? I CAN'T KNOW IF I STAY HERE.
KNOWING IS IMPOSSIBLE.

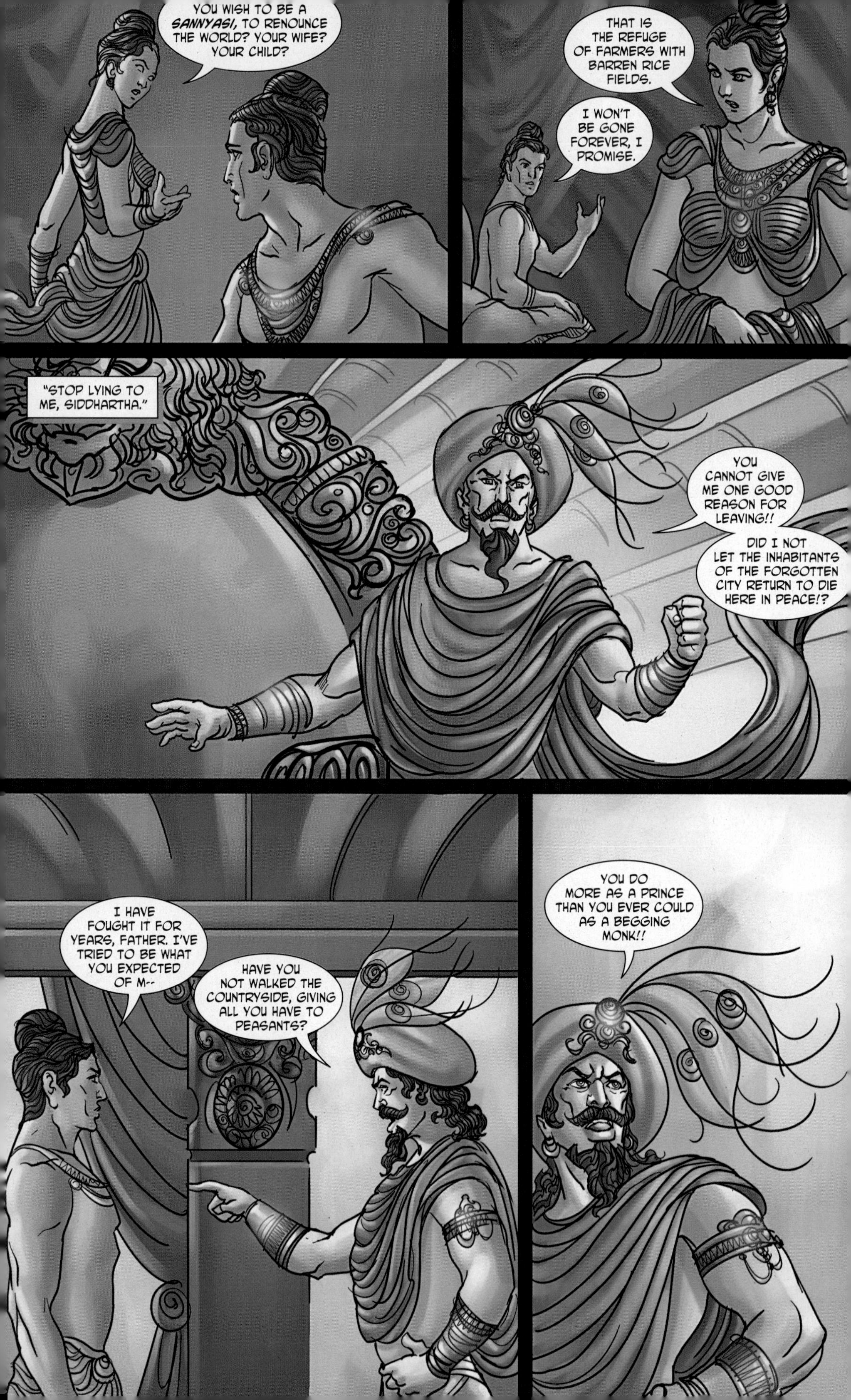
YOU WISH TO BE A *SANNYASI,* TO RENOUNCE THE WORLD? YOUR WIFE? YOUR CHILD?
THAT IS THE REFUGE OF FARMERS WITH BARREN RICE FIELDS.
I WON'T BE GONE FOREVER, I PROMISE.
"STOP LYING TO ME, SIDDHARTHA."
YOU CANNOT GIVE ME ONE GOOD REASON FOR LEAVING!!
DID I NOT LET THE INHABITANTS OF THE FORGOTTEN CITY RETURN TO DIE HERE IN PEACE!?
I HAVE FOUGHT IT FOR YEARS, FATHER. I'VE TRIED TO BE WHAT YOU EXPECTED OF M--
HAVE YOU NOT WALKED THE COUNTRYSIDE, GIVING ALL YOU HAVE TO PEASANTS?
YOU DO MORE AS A PRINCE THAN YOU EVER COULD AS A BEGGING MONK!!

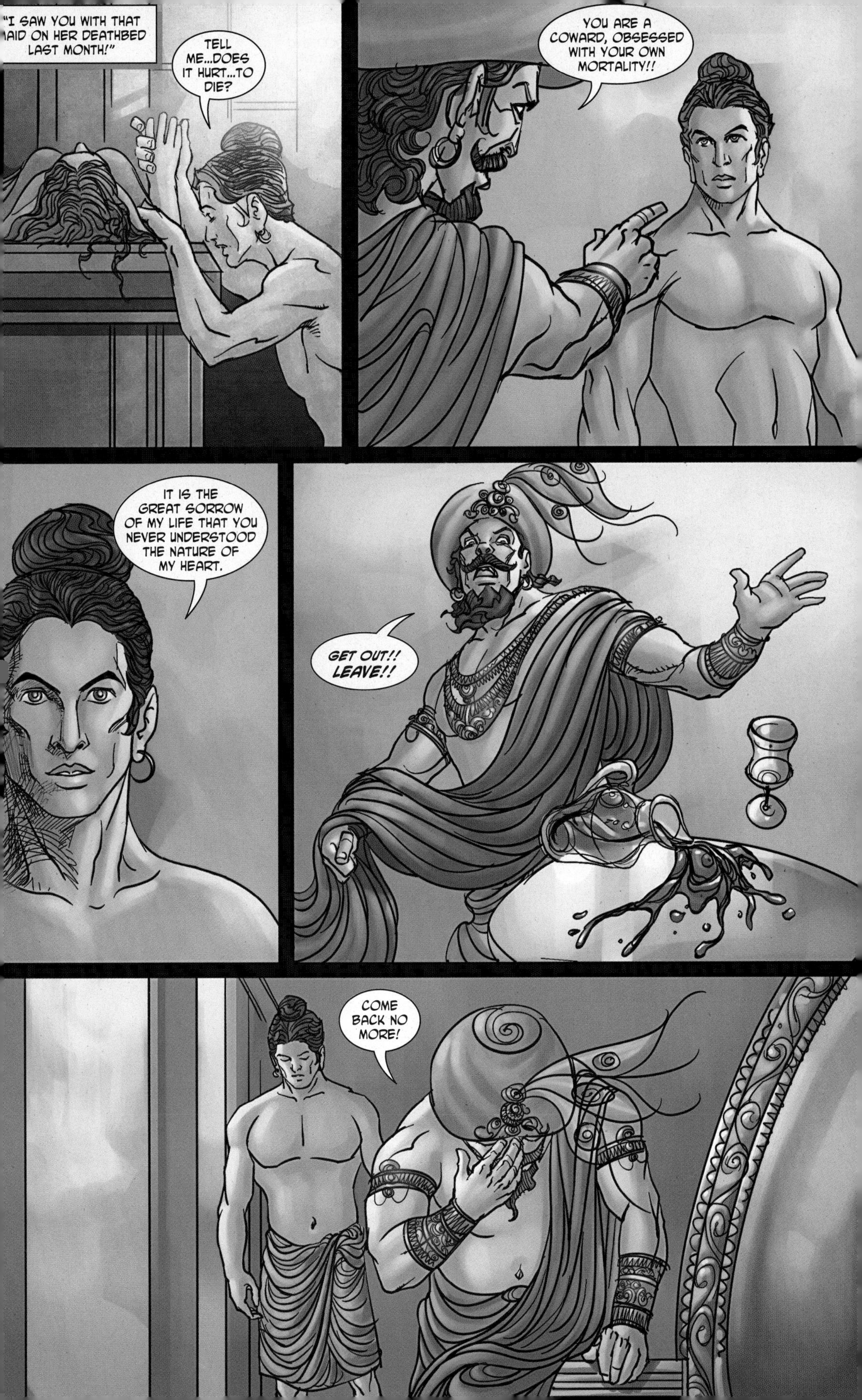
"I SAW YOU WITH THAT
MAID ON HER DEATHBED
LAST MONTH!"
TELL ME...DOES IT HURT...TO DIE?
YOU ARE A COWARD, OBSESSED WITH YOUR OWN MORTALITY!!
IT IS THE GREAT SORROW OF MY LIFE THAT YOU NEVER UNDERSTOOD THE NATURE OF MY HEART.
GET OUT!! LEAVE!!
COME BACK NO MORE!

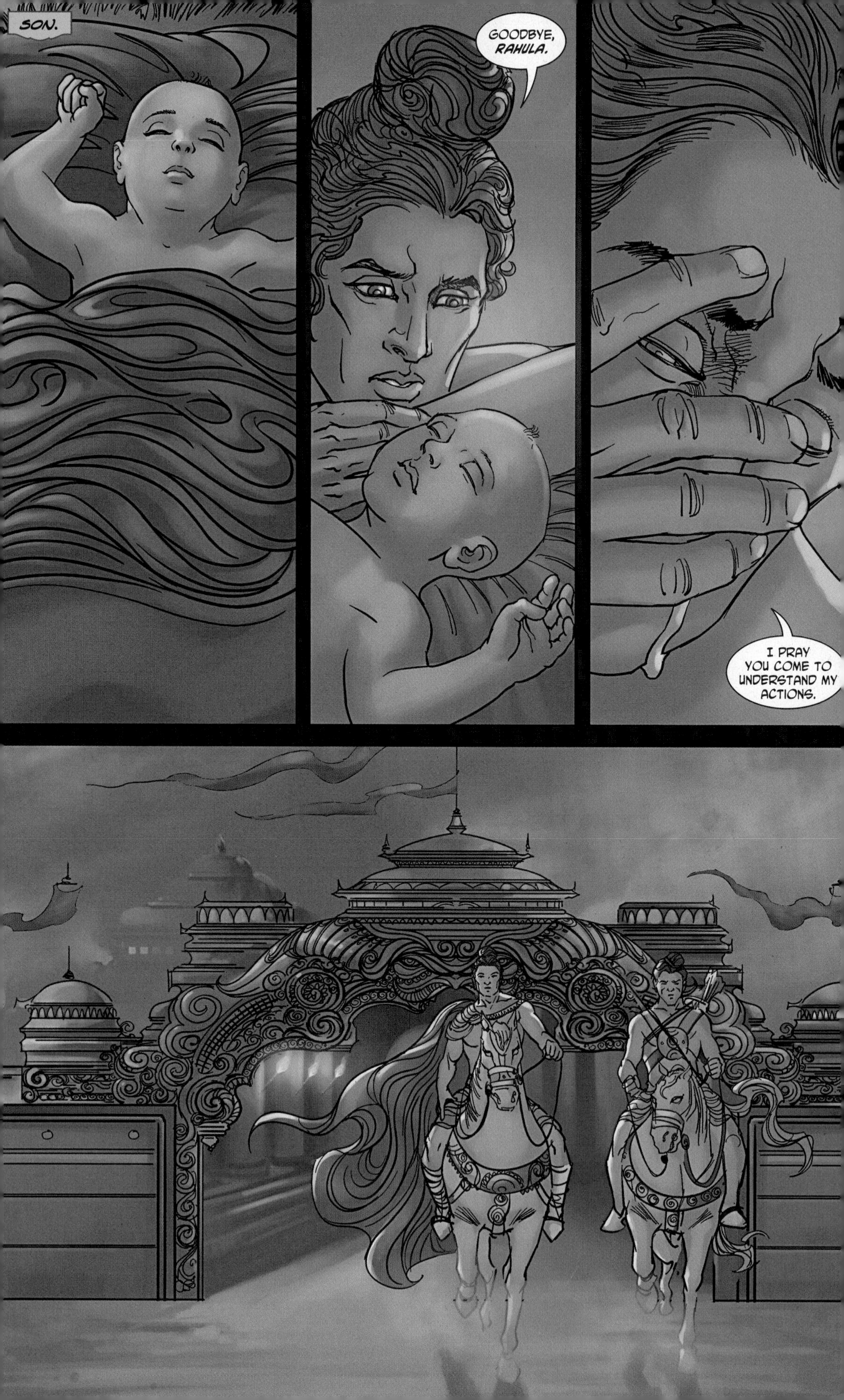
SON.
GOODBYE, RAHULA.
I PRAY YOU COME TO UNDERSTAND MY ACTIONS.

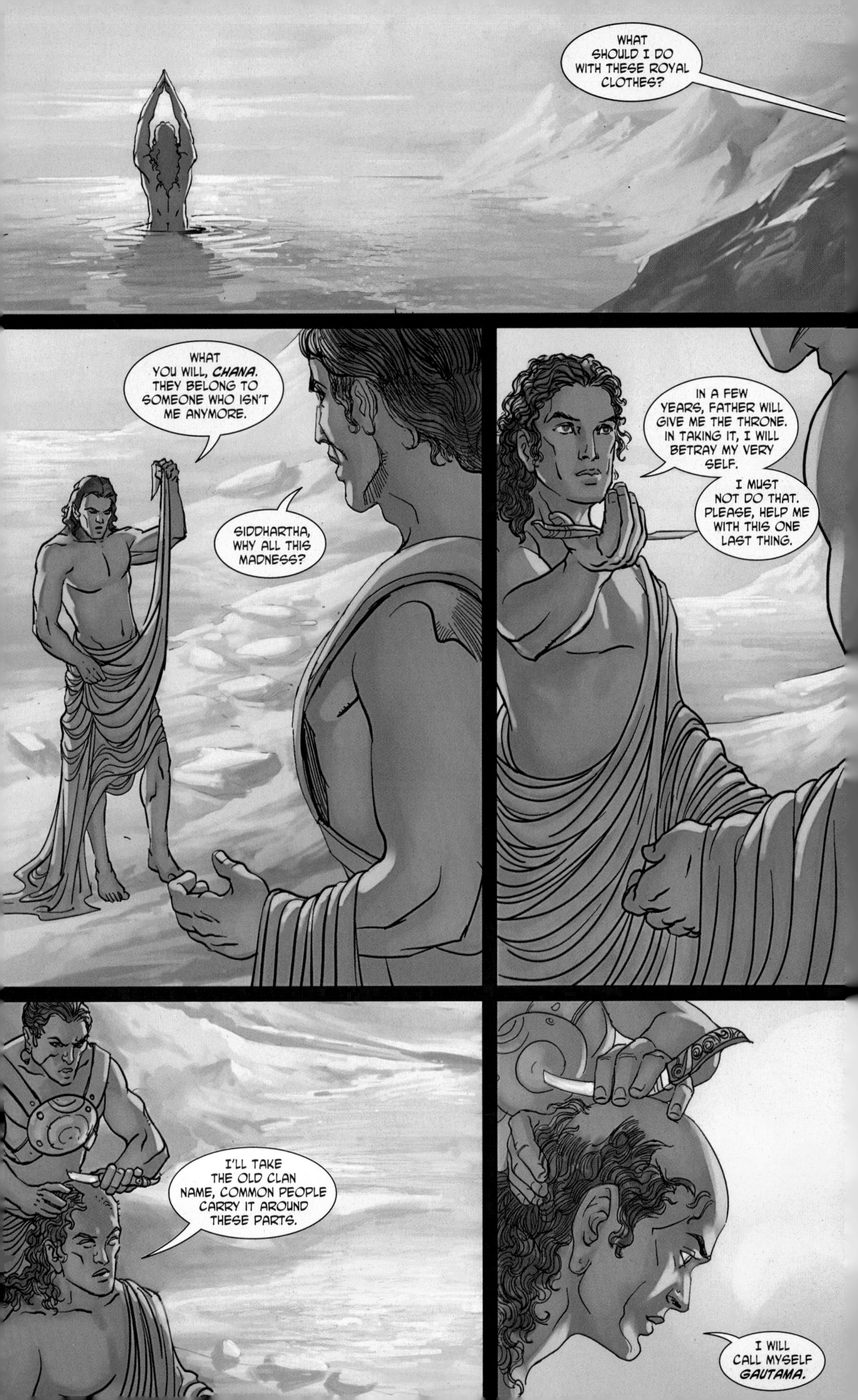
WHAT SHOULD I DO WITH THESE ROYAL CLOTHES?
WHAT YOU WILL, *CHANA*. THEY BELONG TO SOMEONE WHO ISN'T ME ANYMORE.
SIDDHARTHA, WHY ALL THIS MADNESS?
IN A FEW YEARS, FATHER WILL GIVE ME THE THRONE. IN TAKING IT, I WILL BETRAY MY VERY SELF.
I MUST NOT DO THAT. PLEASE, HELP ME WITH THIS ONE LAST THING.
I'LL TAKE THE OLD CLAN NAME, COMMON PEOPLE CARRY IT AROUND THESE PARTS.
I WILL CALL MYSELF *GAUTAMA*.

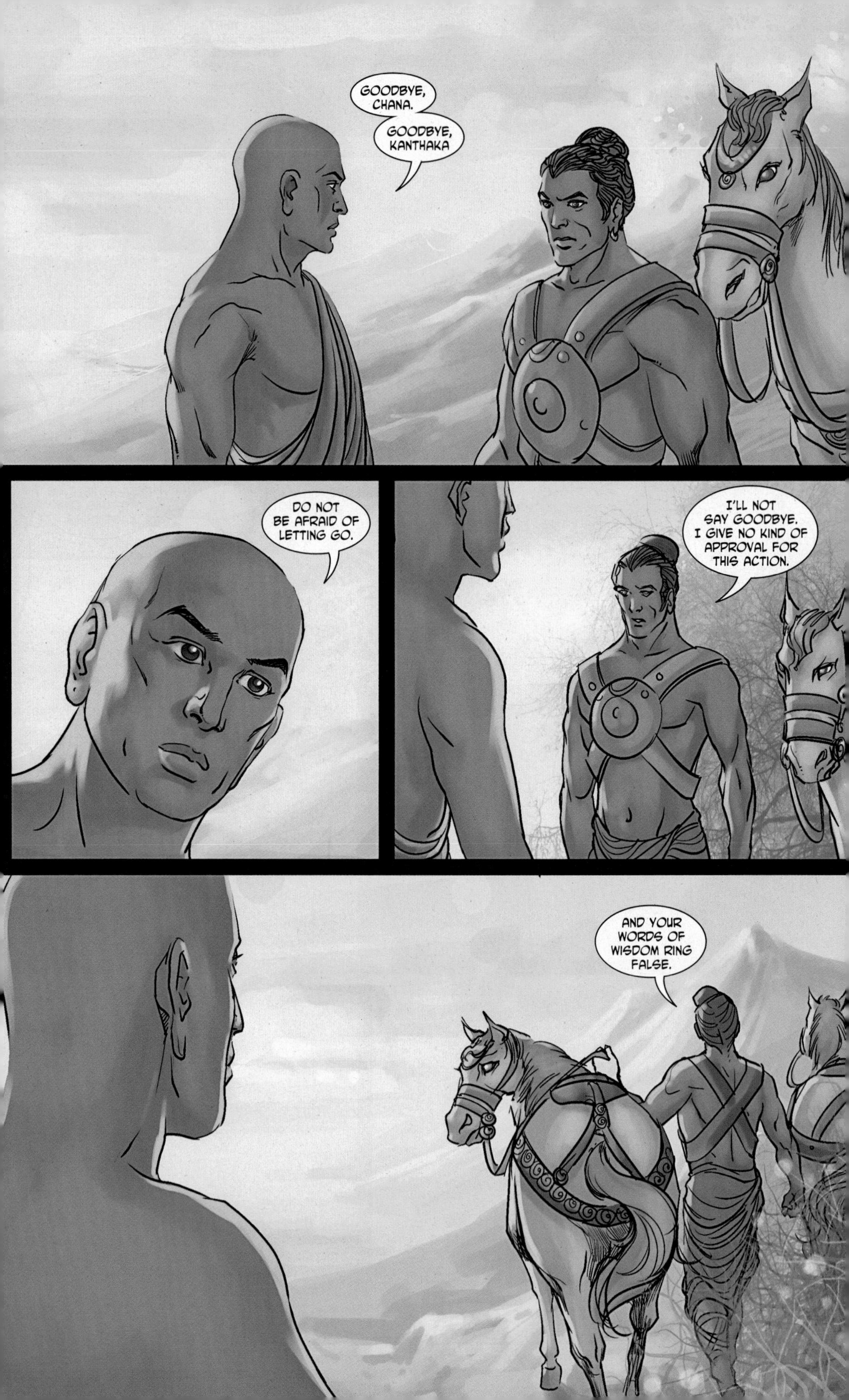
GOODBYE, CHANA.
GOODBYE, KANTHAKA
DO NOT BE AFRAID OF LETTING GO.
I'LL NOT SAY GOODBYE. I GIVE NO KIND OF APPROVAL FOR THIS ACTION.
AND YOUR WORDS OF WISDOM RING FALSE.

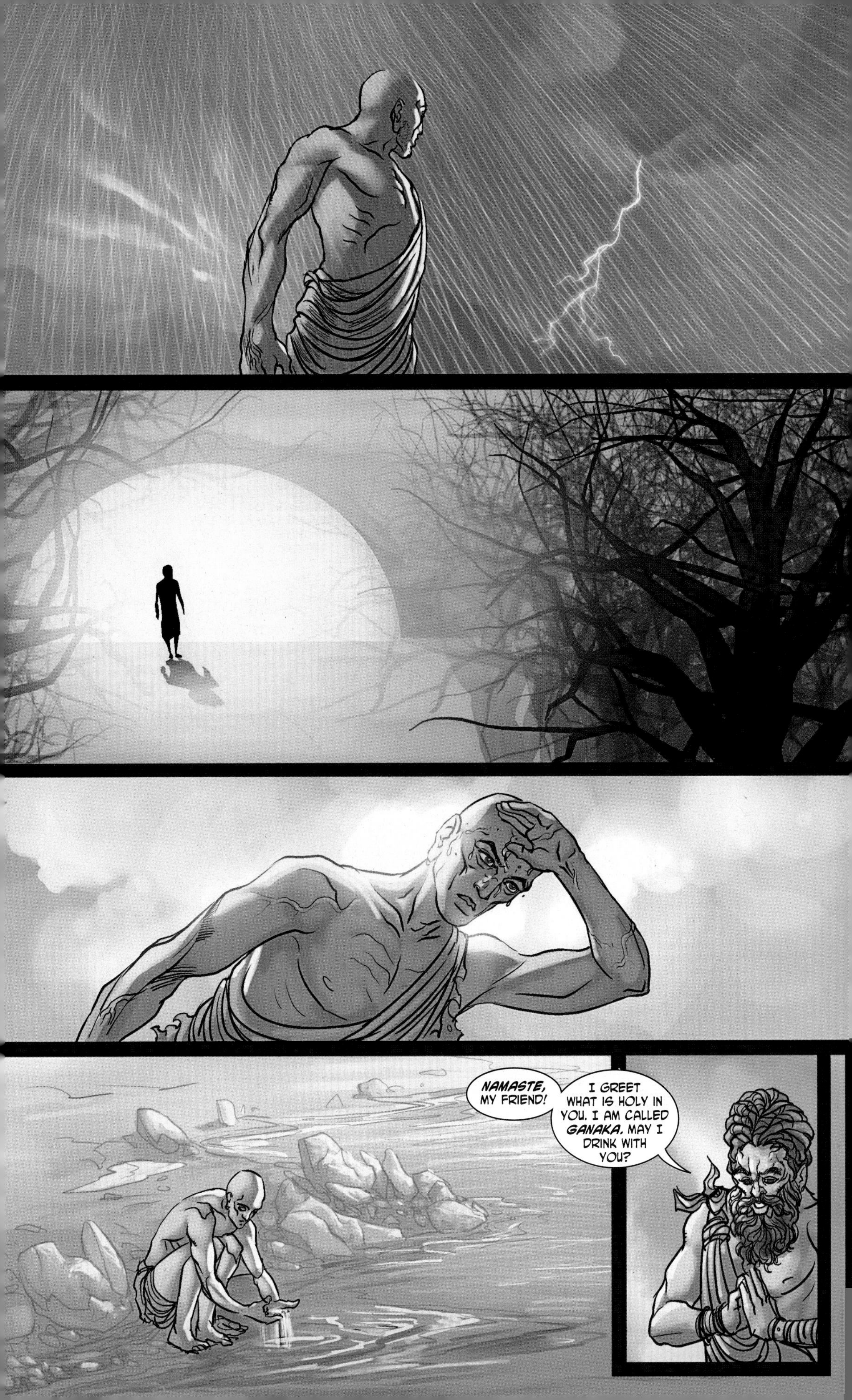
NAMASTE, MY FRIEND!
I GREET WHAT IS HOLY IN YOU. I AM CALLED GANAKA. MAY I DRINK WITH YOU?

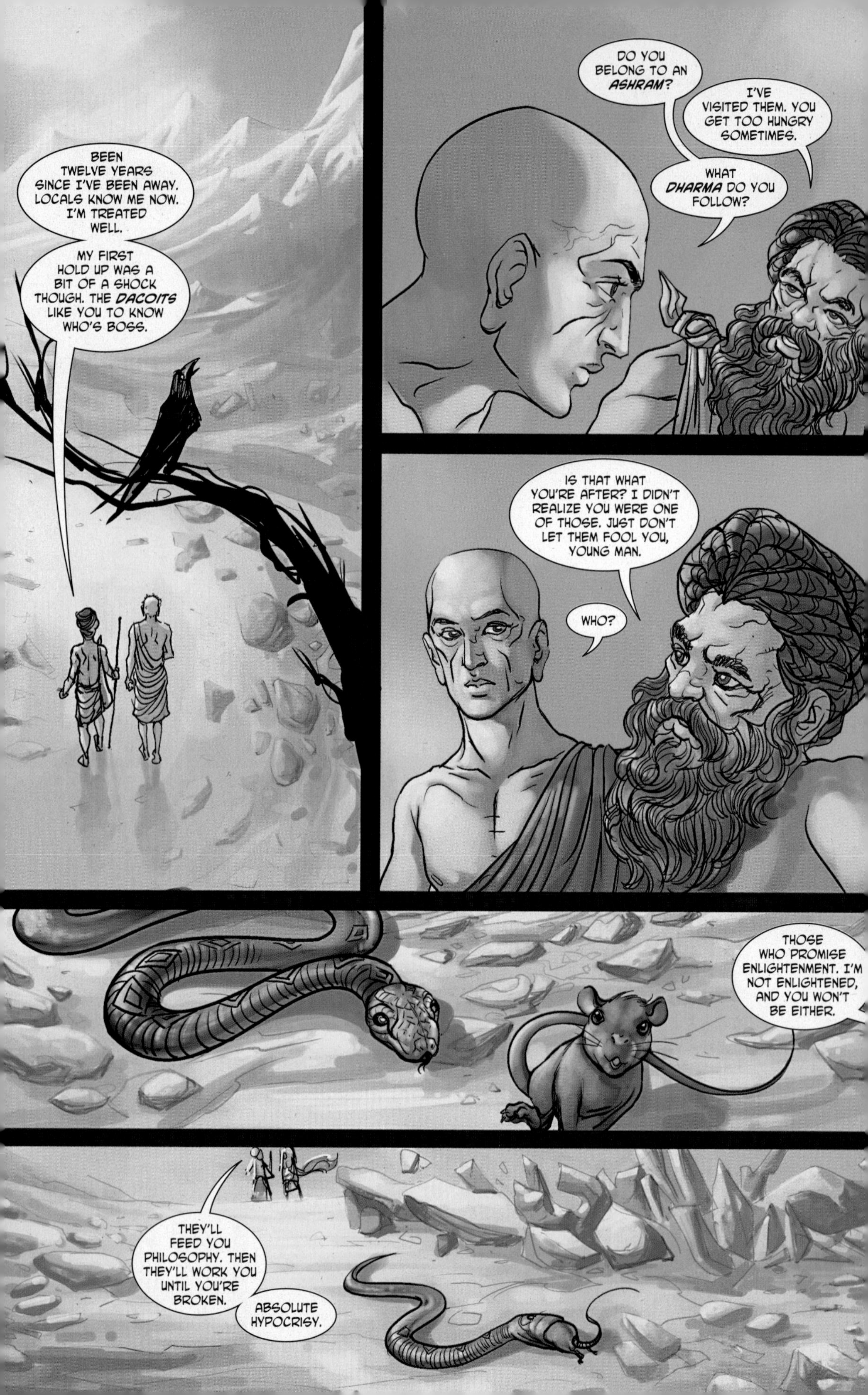
BEEN TWELVE YEARS SINCE I'VE BEEN AWAY. LOCALS KNOW ME NOW. I'M TREATED WELL.
MY FIRST HOLD UP WAS A BIT OF A SHOCK THOUGH. THE DACOITS LIKE YOU TO KNOW WHO'S BOSS.
DO YOU BELONG TO AN ASHRAM?
I'VE VISITED THEM. YOU GET TOO HUNGRY SOMETIMES.
WHAT DHARMA DO YOU FOLLOW?
IS THAT WHAT YOU'RE AFTER? I DIDN'T REALIZE YOU WERE ONE OF THOSE. JUST DON'T LET THEM FOOL YOU, YOUNG MAN.
WHO?
THOSE WHO PROMISE ENLIGHTENMENT. I'M NOT ENLIGHTENED, AND YOU WON'T BE EITHER.
THEY'LL FEED YOU PHILOSOPHY. THEN THEY'LL WORK YOU UNTIL YOU'RE BROKEN.
ABSOLUTE HYPOCRISY.

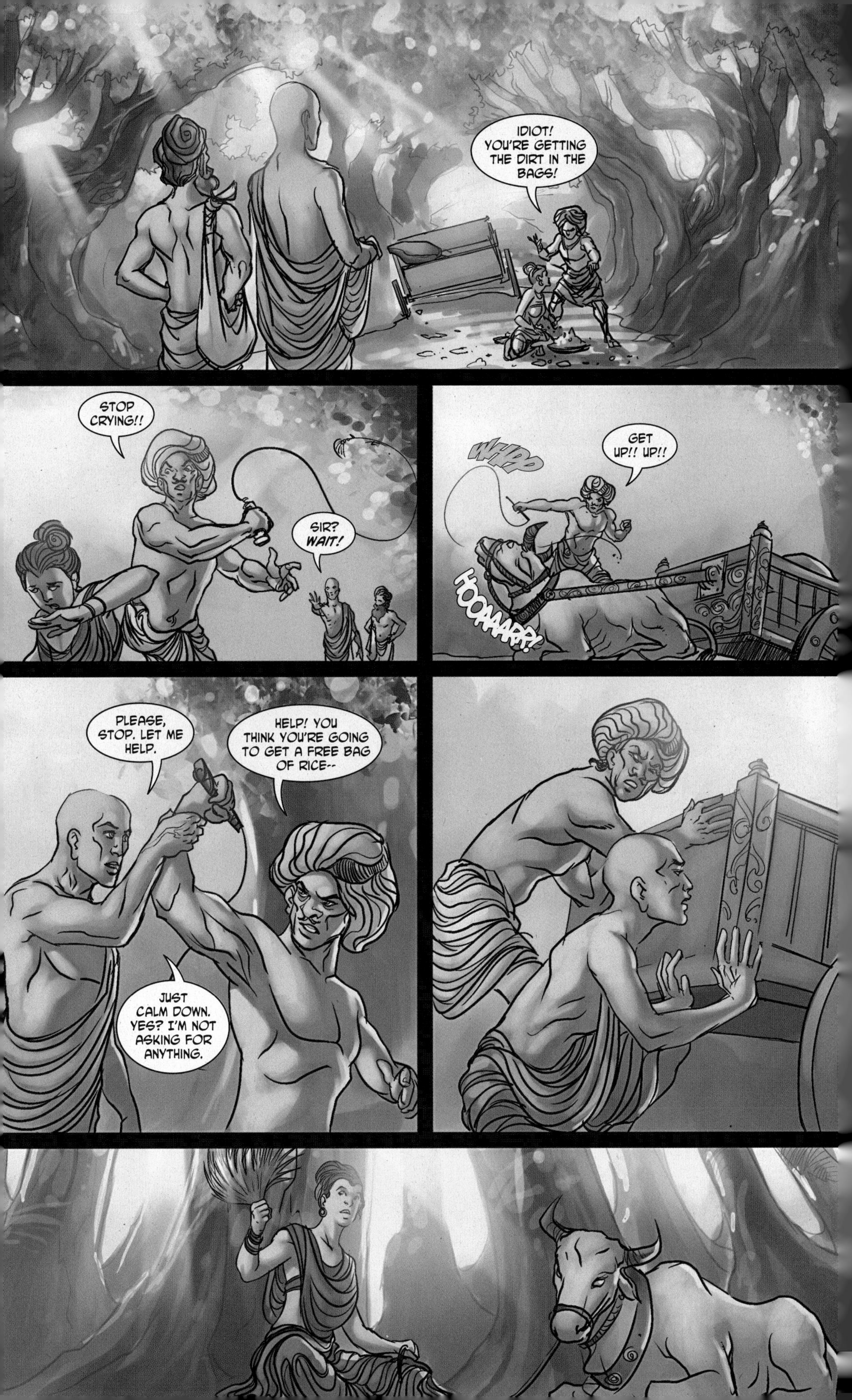
IDIOT! YOU'RE GETTING THE DIRT IN THE BAGS!
STOP CRYING!!
SIR? WAIT!
WHPP
GET UP!! UP!!
HOOAAARR!
PLEASE, STOP. LET ME HELP.
HELP! YOU THINK YOU'RE GOING TO GET A FREE BAG OF RICE--
JUST CALM DOWN. YES? I'M NOT ASKING FOR ANYTHING.

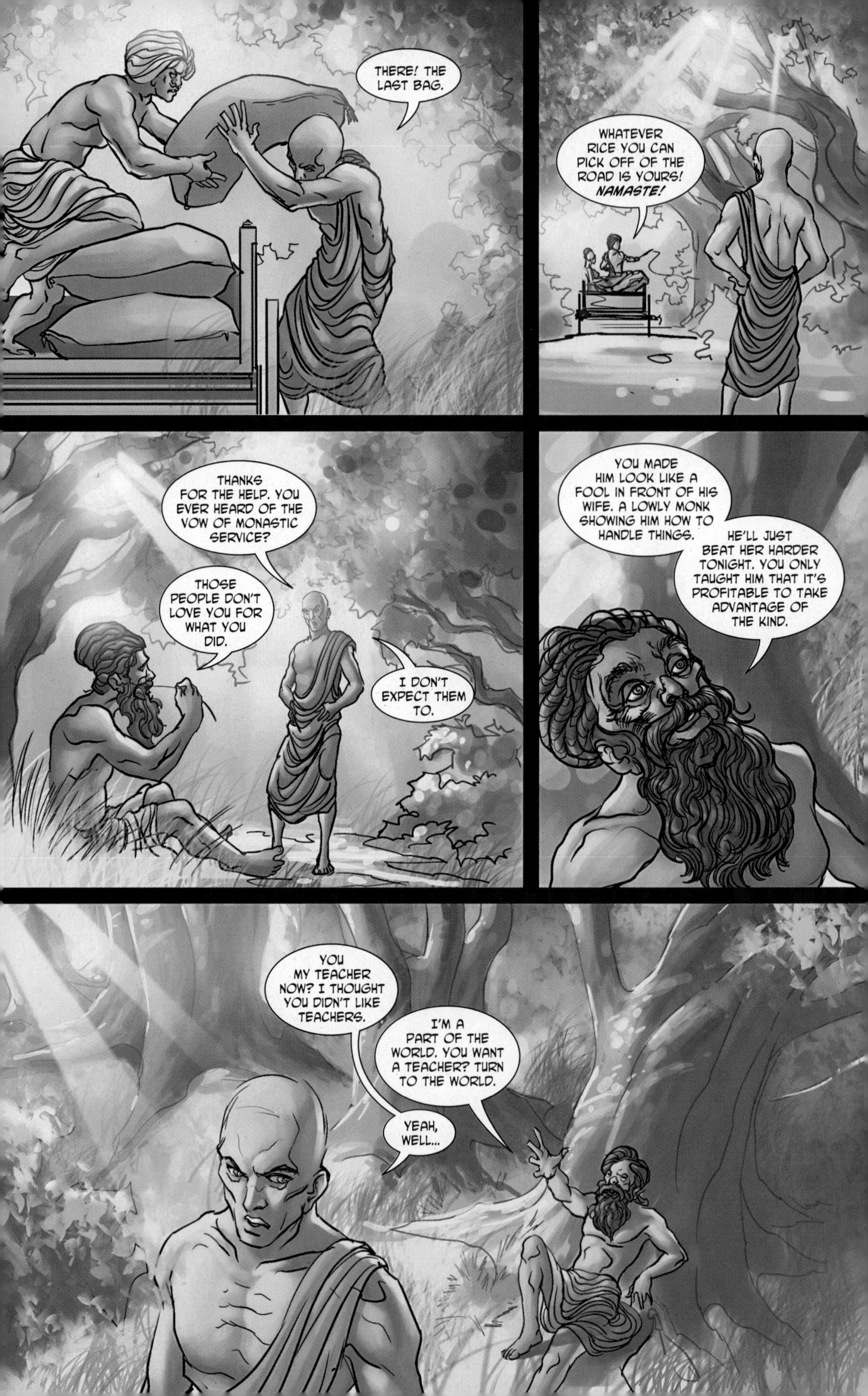
THERE! THE LAST BAG.
WHATEVER RICE YOU CAN PICK OFF OF THE ROAD IS YOURS! *NAMASTE!*
THANKS FOR THE HELP. YOU EVER HEARD OF THE VOW OF MONASTIC SERVICE?
THOSE PEOPLE DON'T LOVE YOU FOR WHAT YOU DID.
I DON'T EXPECT THEM TO.
YOU MADE HIM LOOK LIKE A FOOL IN FRONT OF HIS WIFE. A LOWLY MONK SHOWING HIM HOW TO HANDLE THINGS.
HE'LL JUST BEAT HER HARDER TONIGHT. YOU ONLY TAUGHT HIM THAT IT'S PROFITABLE TO TAKE ADVANTAGE OF THE KIND.
YOU MY TEACHER NOW? I THOUGHT YOU DIDN'T LIKE TEACHERS.
I'M A PART OF THE WORLD. YOU WANT A TEACHER? TURN TO THE WORLD.
YEAH, WELL...

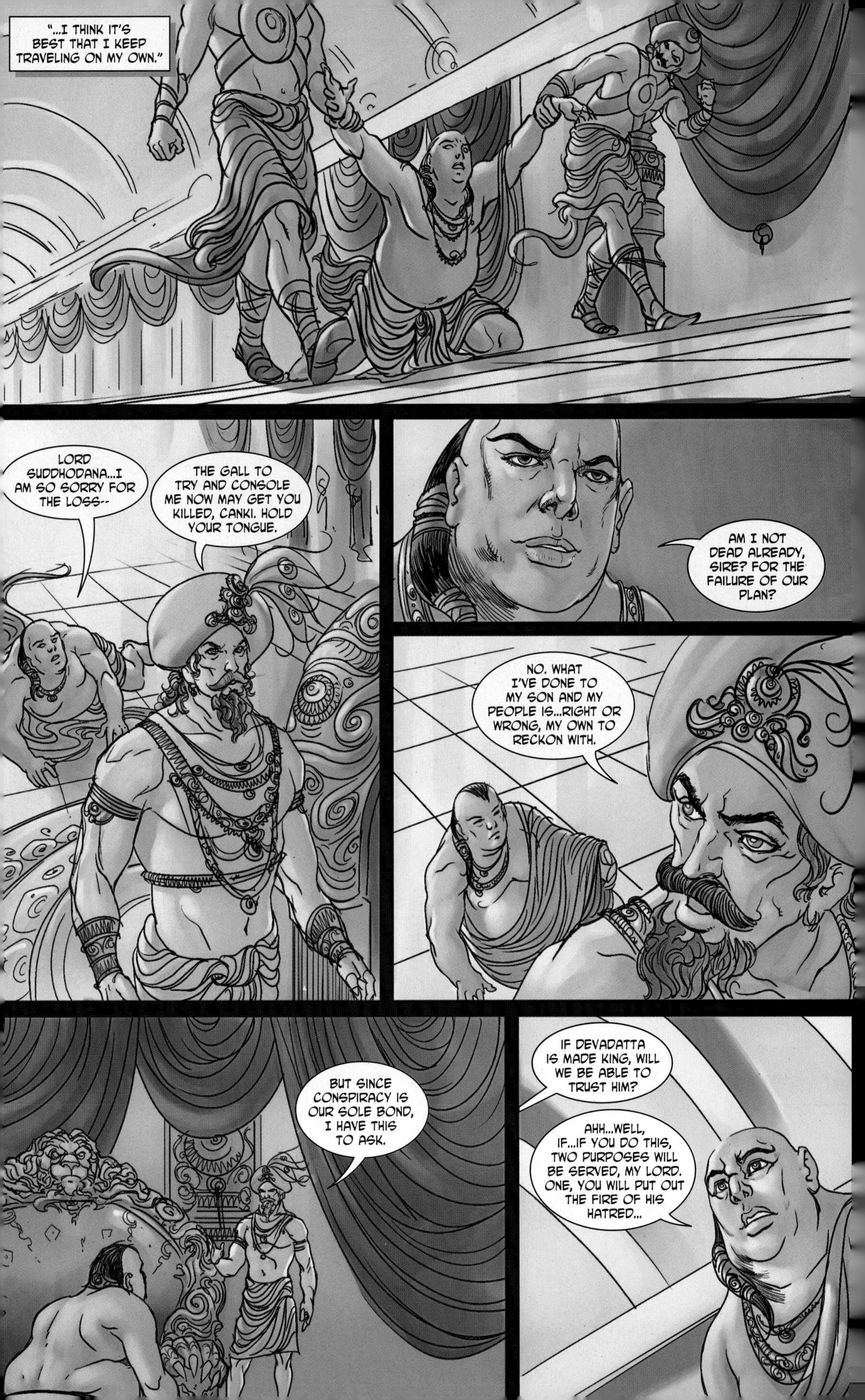
"...I THINK IT'S BEST THAT I KEEP TRAVELING ON MY OWN."
LORD SUDDHODANA...I AM SO SORRY FOR THE LOSS--
THE GALL TO TRY AND CONSOLE ME NOW MAY GET YOU KILLED, CANKI. HOLD YOUR TONGUE.
AM I NOT DEAD ALREADY, SIRE? FOR THE FAILURE OF OUR PLAN?
NO. WHAT I'VE DONE TO MY SON AND MY PEOPLE IS...RIGHT OR WRONG, MY OWN TO RECKON WITH.
BUT SINCE CONSPIRACY IS OUR SOLE BOND, I HAVE THIS TO ASK.
IF DEVADATTA IS MADE KING, WILL WE BE ABLE TO TRUST HIM?
AHH...WELL, IF...IF YOU DO THIS, TWO PURPOSES WILL BE SERVED, MY LORD. ONE, YOU WILL PUT OUT THE FIRE OF HIS HATRED...

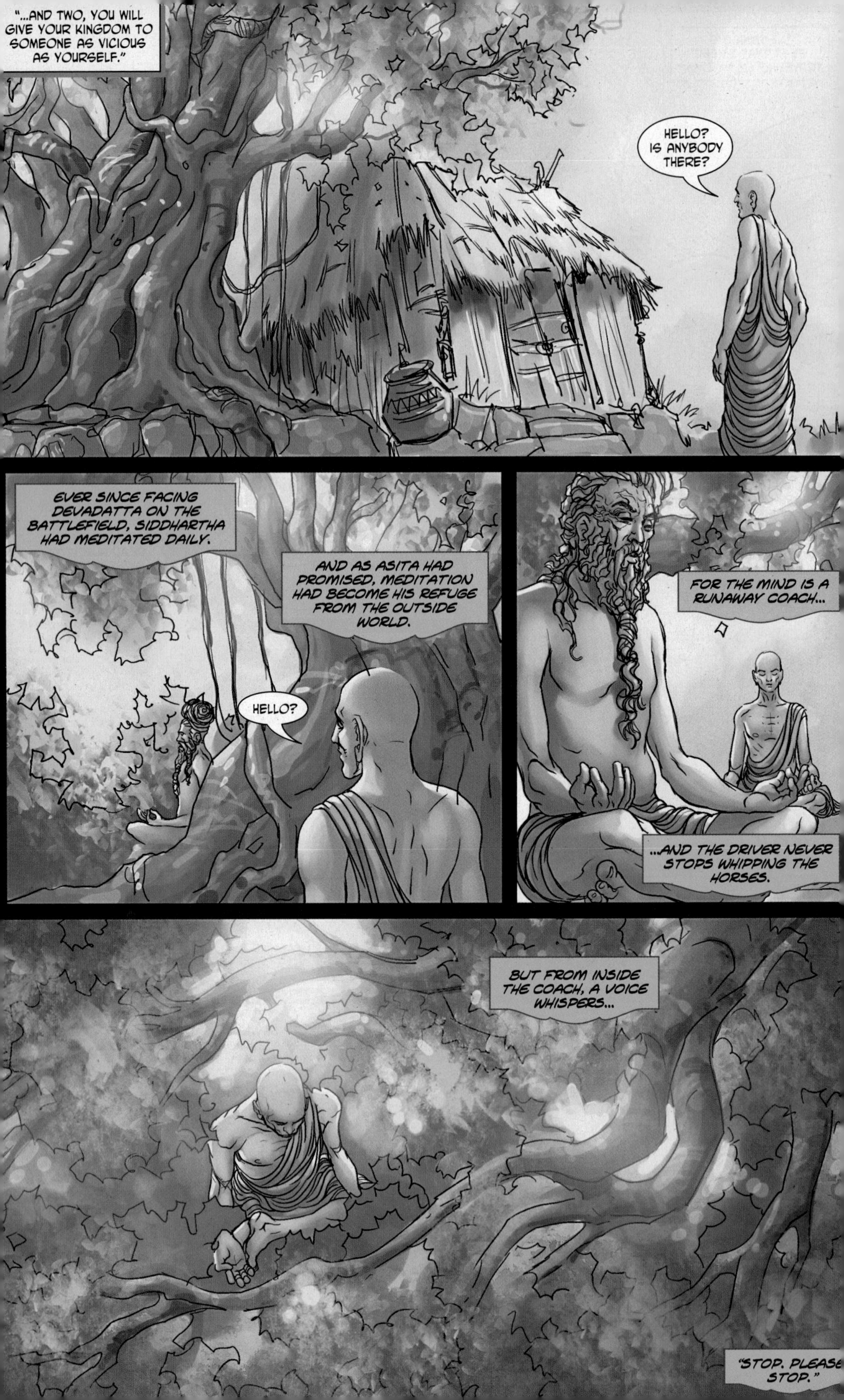
"...AND TWO, YOU WILL GIVE YOUR KINGDOM TO SOMEONE AS VICIOUS AS YOURSELF."
HELLO? IS ANYBODY THERE?
EVER SINCE FACING DEVADATTA ON THE BATTLEFIELD, SIDDHARTHA HAD MEDITATED DAILY.
AND AS ASITA HAD PROMISED, MEDITATION HAD BECOME HIS REFUGE FROM THE OUTSIDE WORLD.
HELLO?
FOR THE MIND IS A RUNAWAY COACH...
...AND THE DRIVER NEVER STOPS WHIPPING THE HORSES.
BUT FROM INSIDE THE COACH, A VOICE WHISPERS...
"STOP. PLEASE STOP."

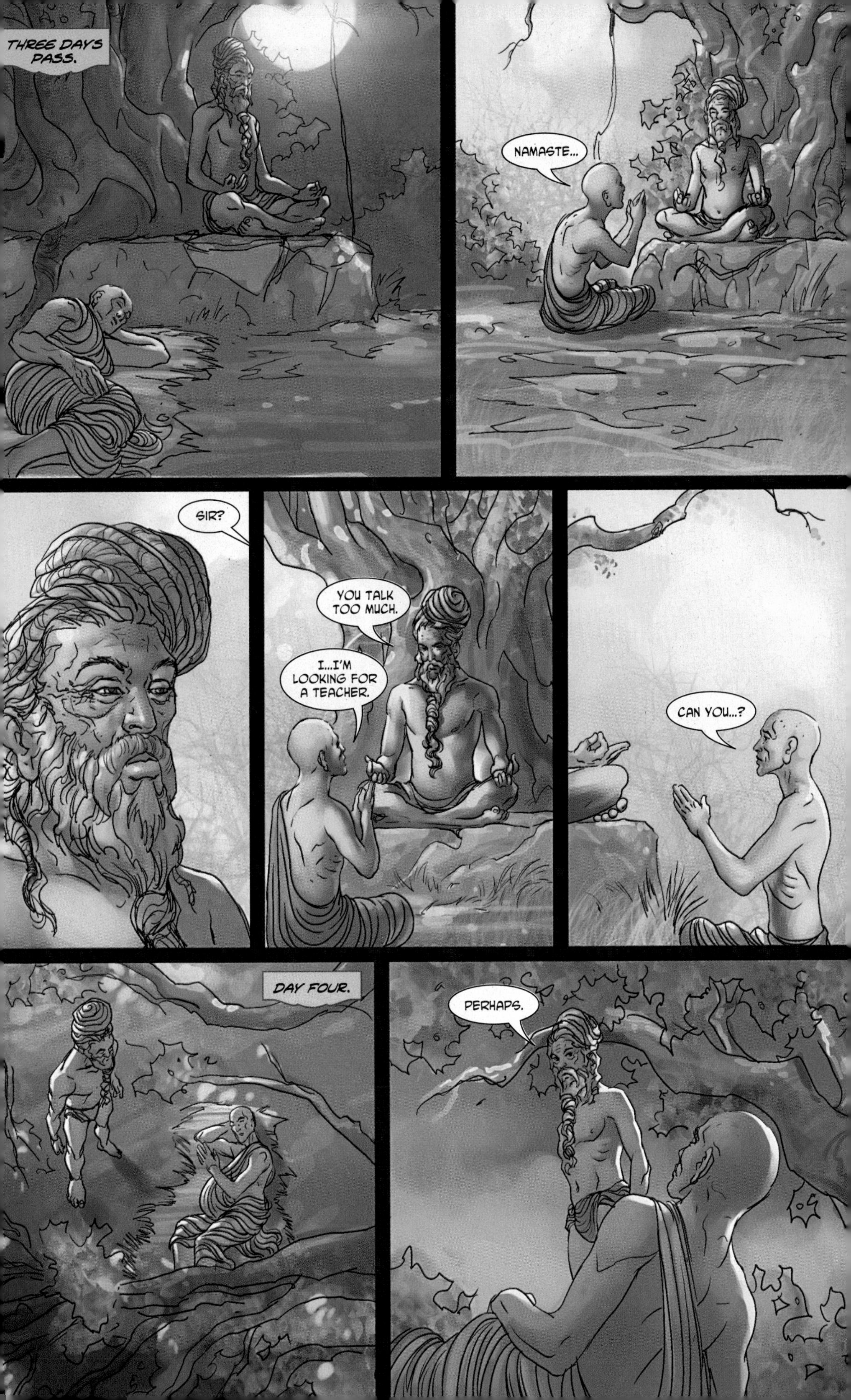
THREE DAYS PASS.
NAMASTE...
SIR?
YOU TALK TOO MUCH.
I...I'M LOOKING FOR A TEACHER.
CAN YOU...?
DAY FOUR.
PERHAPS.

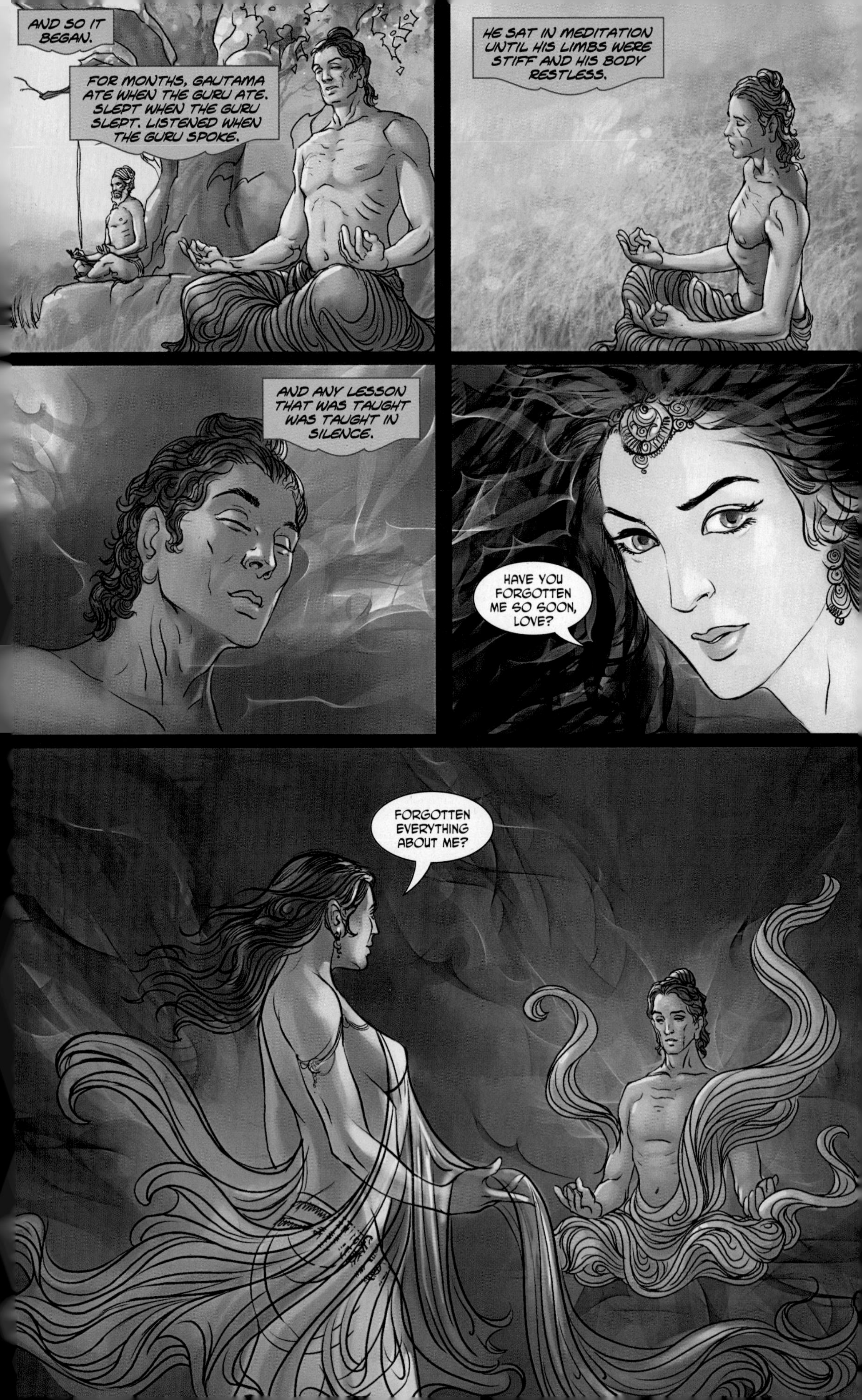
AND SO IT BEGAN.
FOR MONTHS, GAUTAMA ATE WHEN THE GURU ATE. SLEPT WHEN THE GURU SLEPT. LISTENED WHEN THE GURU SPOKE.
HE SAT IN MEDITATION UNTIL HIS LIMBS WERE STIFF AND HIS BODY RESTLESS.
AND ANY LESSON THAT WAS TAUGHT WAS TAUGHT IN SILENCE.
HAVE YOU FORGOTTEN ME SO SOON, LOVE?
FORGOTTEN EVERYTHING ABOUT ME?

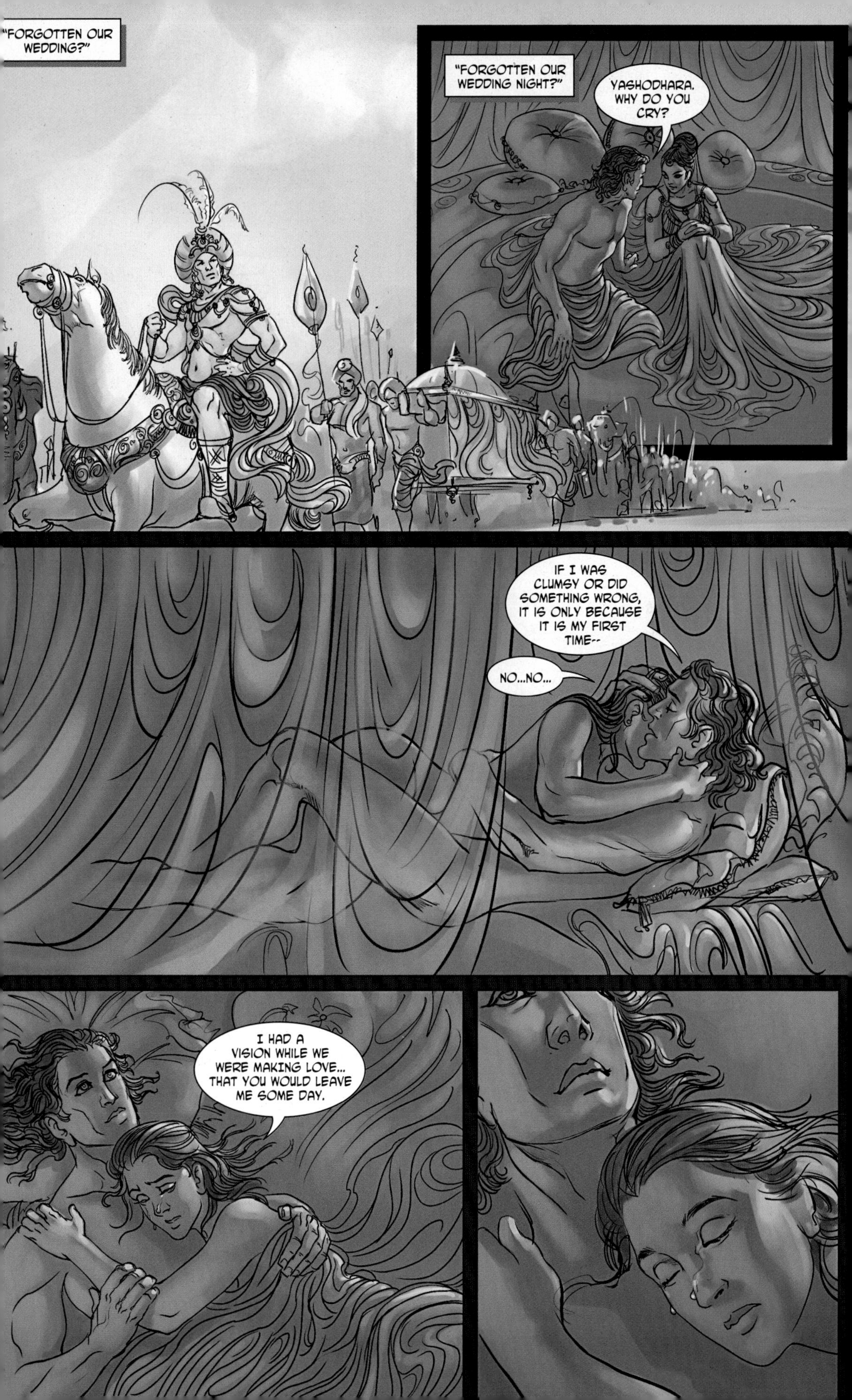
"FORGOTTEN OUR WEDDING?"
"FORGOTTEN OUR WEDDING NIGHT?"
YASHODHARA. WHY DO YOU CRY?
IF I WAS CLUMSY OR DID SOMETHING WRONG, IT IS ONLY BECAUSE IT IS MY FIRST TIME--
NO...NO...
I HAD A VISION WHILE WE WERE MAKING LOVE... THAT YOU WOULD LEAVE ME SOME DAY.

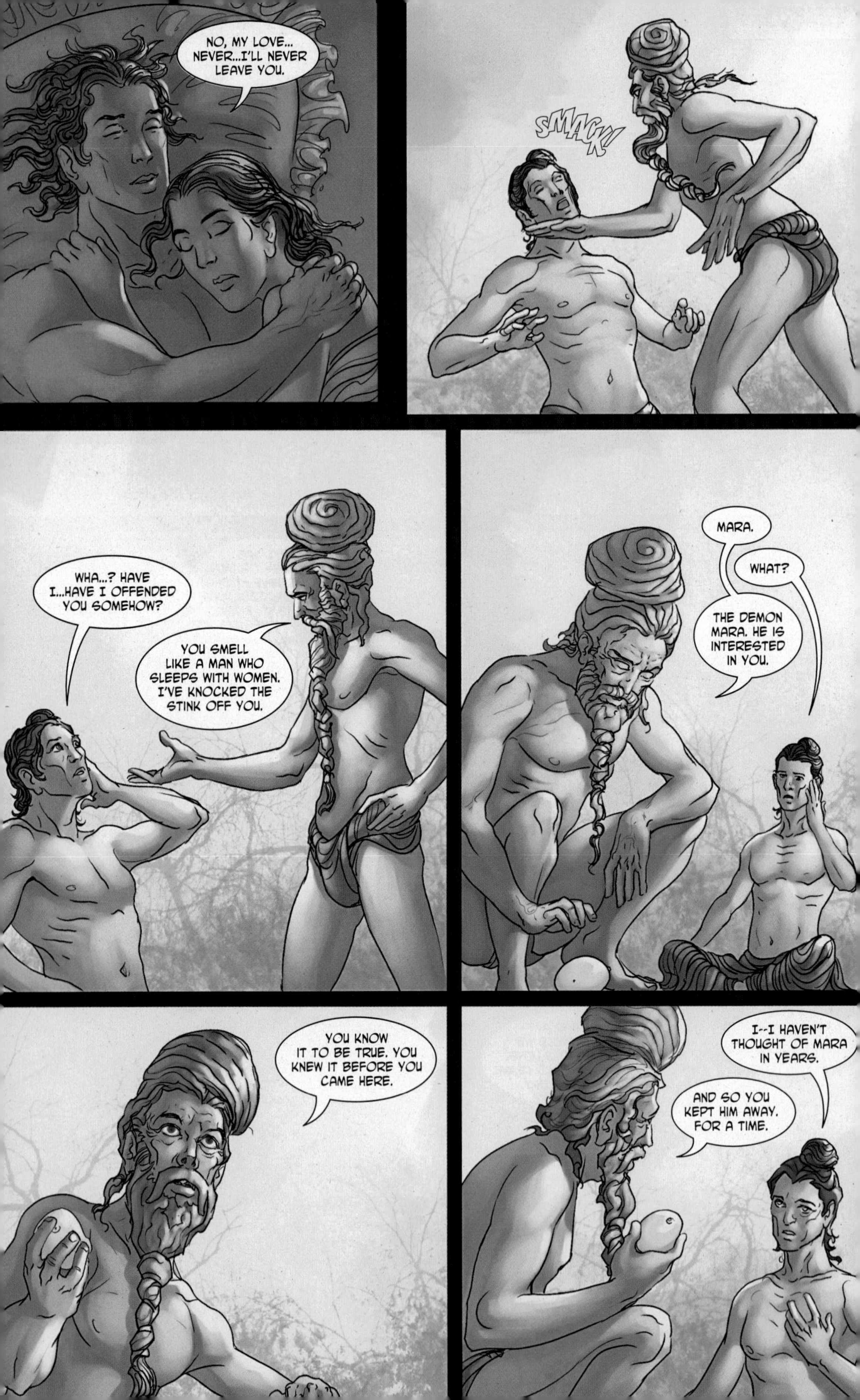
NO, MY LOVE... NEVER...I'LL NEVER LEAVE YOU.
SMACK!
WHA...? HAVE I...HAVE I OFFENDED YOU SOMEHOW?
YOU SMELL LIKE A MAN WHO SLEEPS WITH WOMEN. I'VE KNOCKED THE STINK OFF YOU.
MARA.
WHAT?
THE DEMON MARA. HE IS INTERESTED IN YOU.
YOU KNOW IT TO BE TRUE. YOU KNEW IT BEFORE YOU CAME HERE.
I--I HAVEN'T THOUGHT OF MARA IN YEARS.
AND SO YOU KEPT HIM AWAY. FOR A TIME.

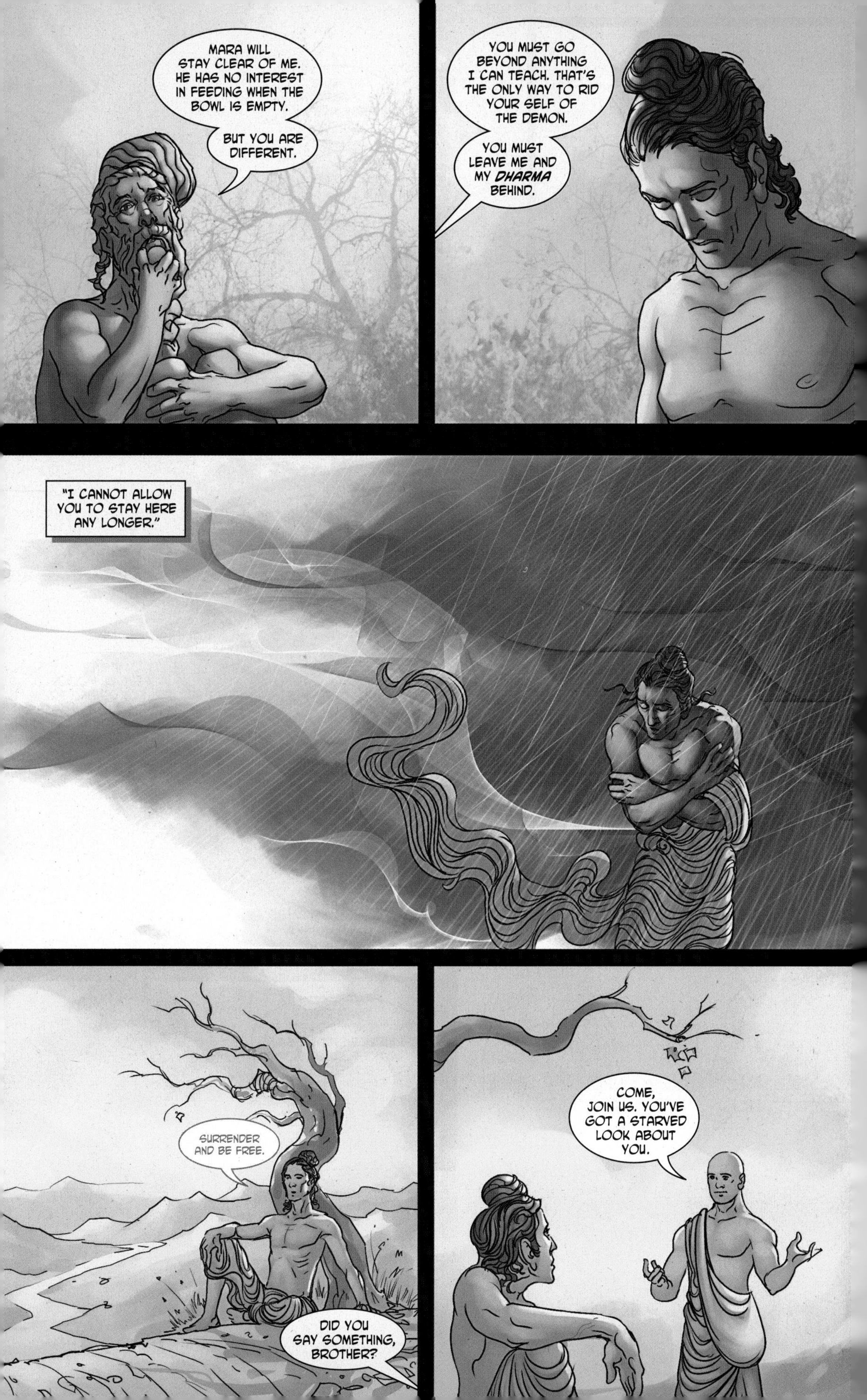
MARA WILL STAY CLEAR OF ME. HE HAS NO INTEREST IN FEEDING WHEN THE BOWL IS EMPTY.
BUT YOU ARE DIFFERENT.
YOU MUST GO BEYOND ANYTHING I CAN TEACH. THAT'S THE ONLY WAY TO RID YOUR SELF OF THE DEMON.
YOU MUST LEAVE ME AND MY *DHARMA* BEHIND.
"I CANNOT ALLOW YOU TO STAY HERE ANY LONGER."
SURRENDER AND BE FREE.
DID YOU SAY SOMETHING, BROTHER?
COME, JOIN US. YOU'VE GOT A STARVED LOOK ABOUT YOU.

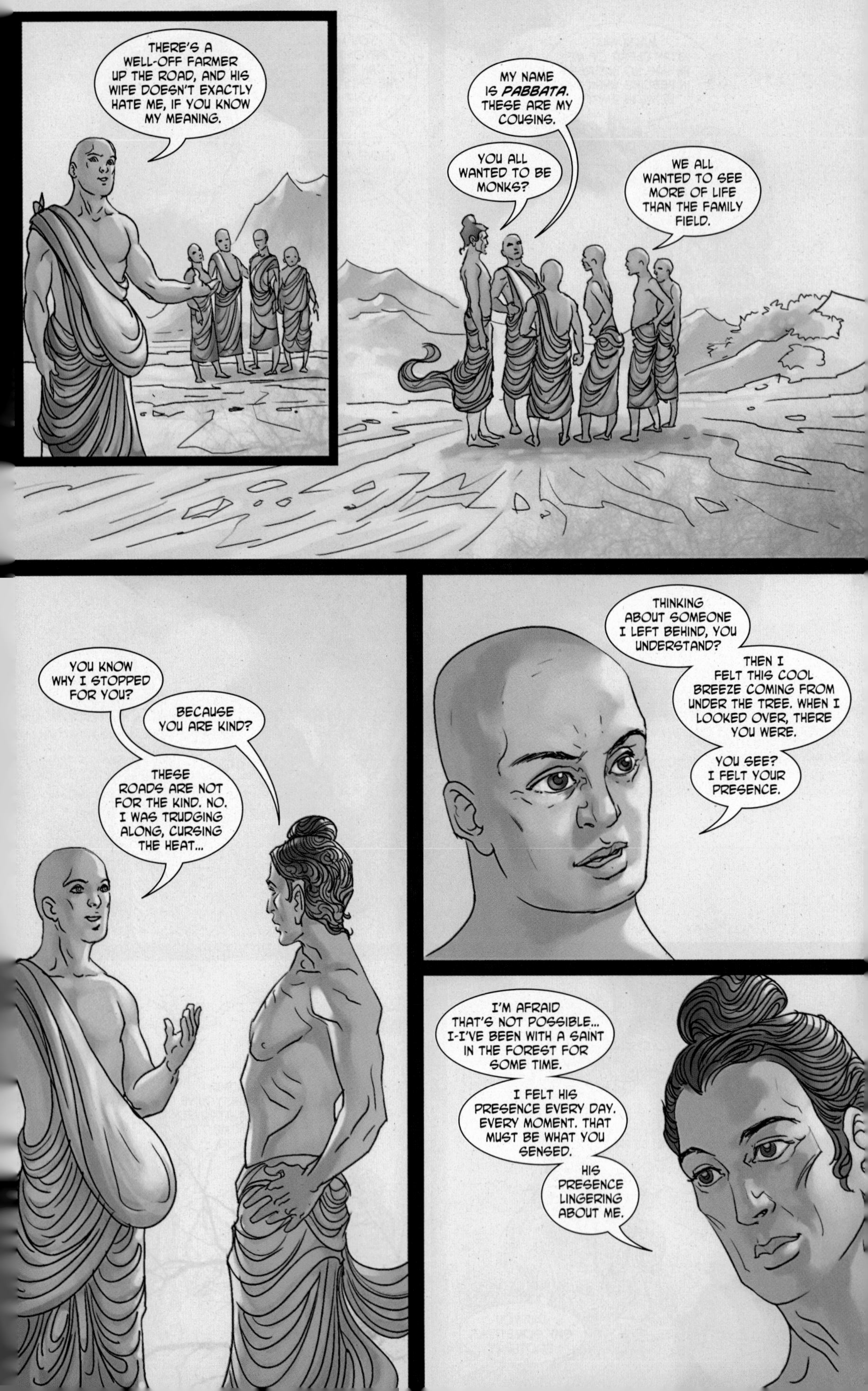
THERE'S A WELL-OFF FARMER UP THE ROAD, AND HIS WIFE DOESN'T EXACTLY HATE ME, IF YOU KNOW MY MEANING.
MY NAME IS *PABBATA*. THESE ARE MY COUSINS.
YOU ALL WANTED TO BE MONKS?
WE ALL WANTED TO SEE MORE OF LIFE THAN THE FAMILY FIELD.
YOU KNOW WHY I STOPPED FOR YOU?
BECAUSE YOU ARE KIND?
THESE ROADS ARE NOT FOR THE KIND. NO. I WAS TRUDGING ALONG, CURSING THE HEAT...
THINKING ABOUT SOMEONE I LEFT BEHIND, YOU UNDERSTAND?
THEN I FELT THIS COOL BREEZE COMING FROM UNDER THE TREE. WHEN I LOOKED OVER, THERE YOU WERE.
YOU SEE? I FELT YOUR PRESENCE.
I'M AFRAID THAT'S NOT POSSIBLE... I-I'VE BEEN WITH A SAINT IN THE FOREST FOR SOME TIME.
I FELT HIS PRESENCE EVERY DAY. EVERY MOMENT. THAT MUST BE WHAT YOU SENSED.
HIS PRESENCE LINGERING ABOUT ME.

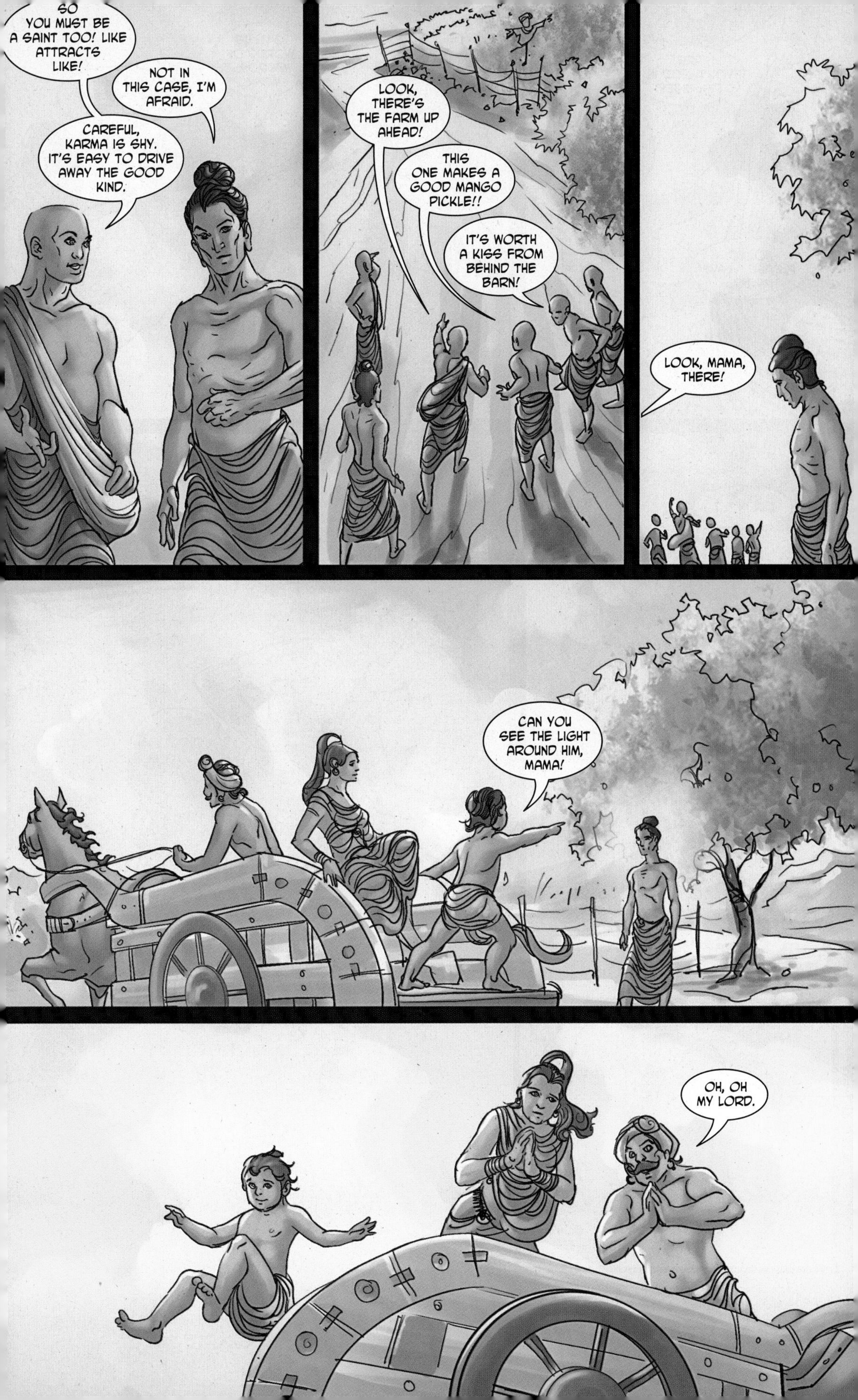
SO YOU MUST BE A SAINT TOO! LIKE ATTRACTS LIKE!
NOT IN THIS CASE, I'M AFRAID.
CAREFUL, KARMA IS SHY. IT'S EASY TO DRIVE AWAY THE GOOD KIND.
LOOK, THERE'S THE FARM UP AHEAD!
THIS ONE MAKES A GOOD MANGO PICKLE!!
IT'S WORTH A KISS FROM BEHIND THE BARN!
LOOK, MAMA, THERE!
CAN YOU SEE THE LIGHT AROUND HIM, MAMA!
OH, OH MY LORD.

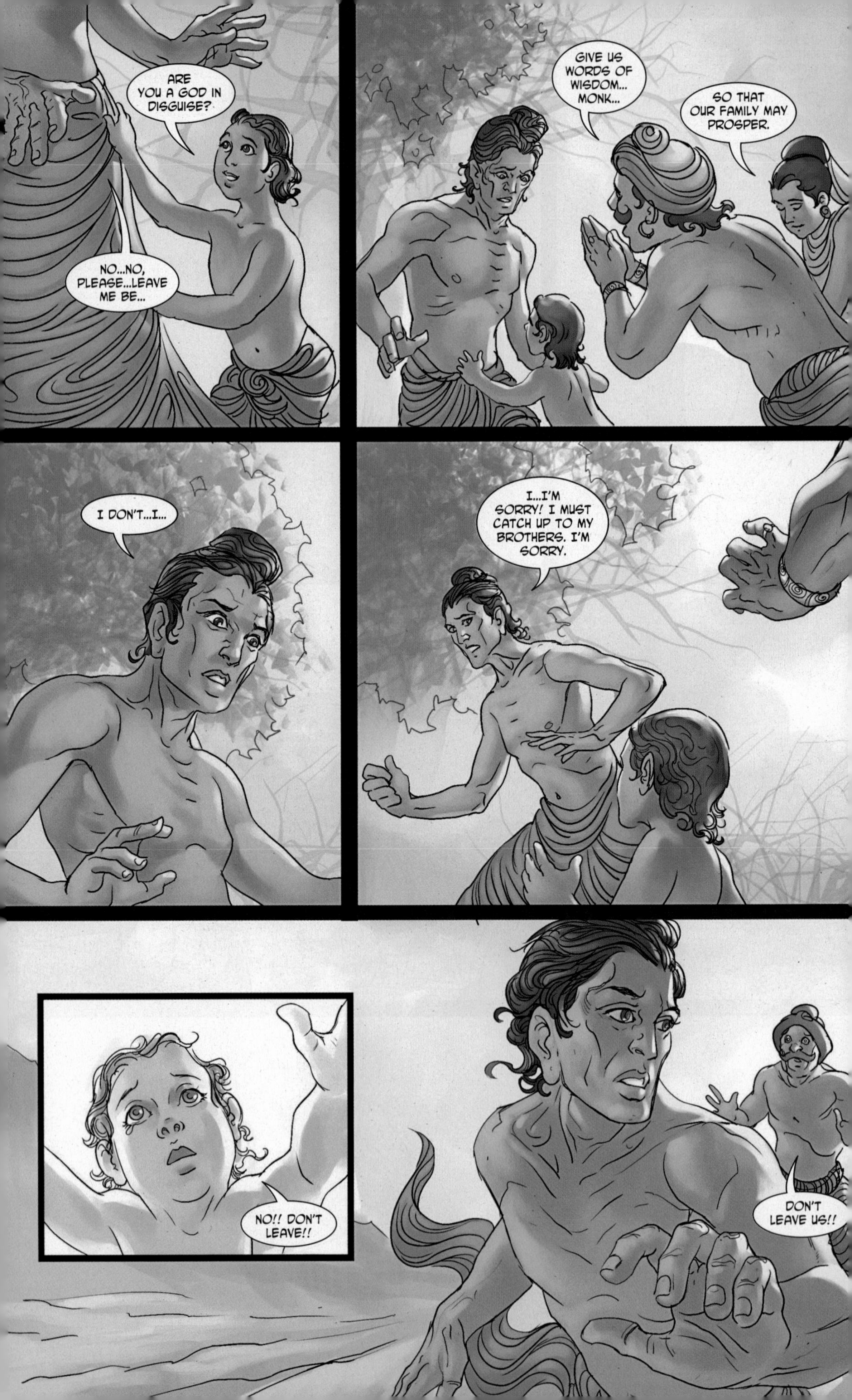
ARE YOU A GOD IN DISGUISE?
NO...NO, PLEASE...LEAVE ME BE...
GIVE US WORDS OF WISDOM... MONK...
SO THAT OUR FAMILY MAY PROSPER.
I DON'T...I...
I...I'M SORRY! I MUST CATCH UP TO MY BROTHERS. I'M SORRY.
NO!! DON'T LEAVE!!
DON'T LEAVE US!!

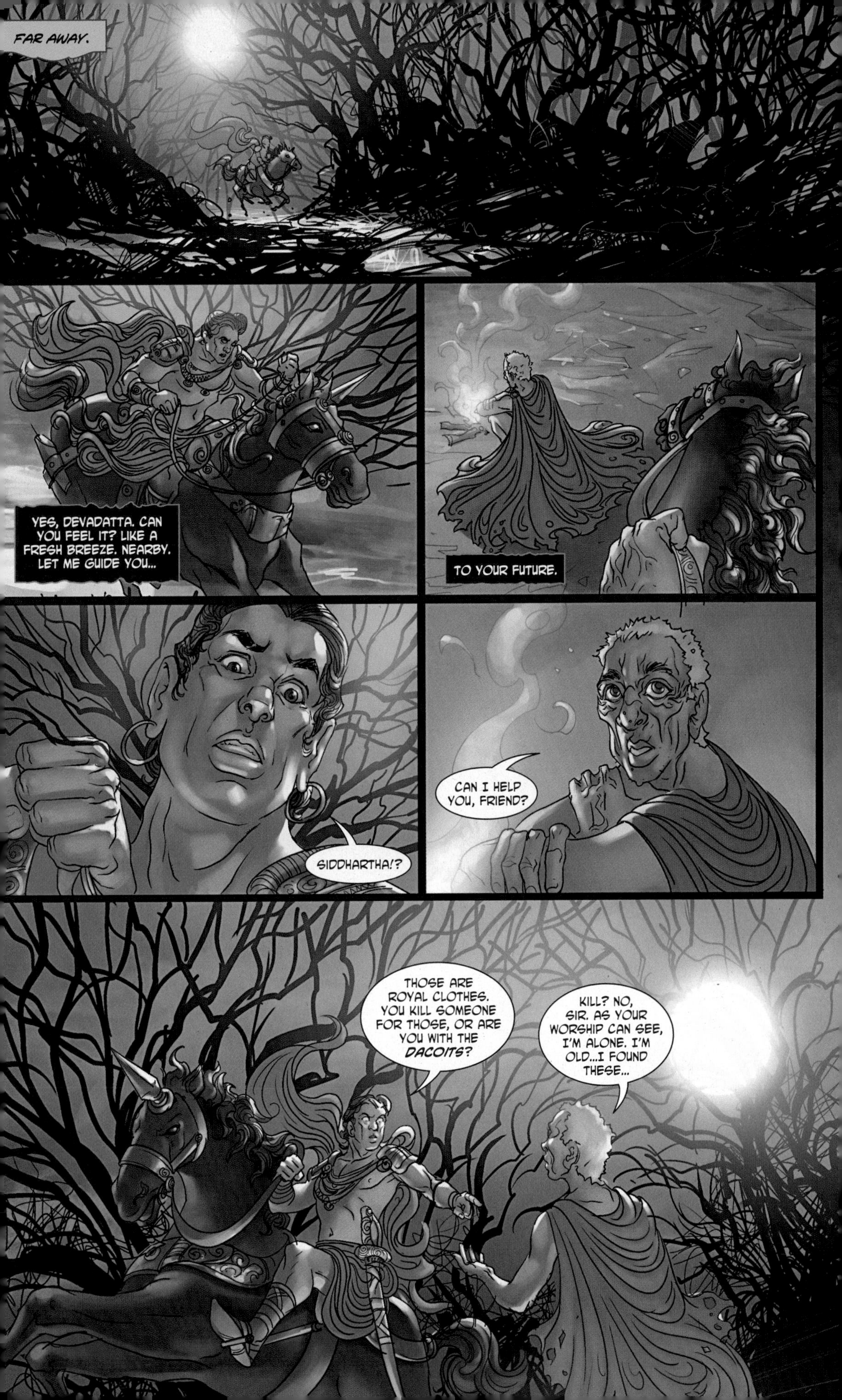
FAR AWAY.
YES, DEVADATTA. CAN YOU FEEL IT? LIKE A FRESH BREEZE. NEARBY. LET ME GUIDE YOU...
TO YOUR FUTURE.
SIDDHARTHA!?
CAN I HELP YOU, FRIEND?
THOSE ARE ROYAL CLOTHES. YOU KILL SOMEONE FOR THOSE, OR ARE YOU WITH THE *DACOITS*?
KILL? NO, SIR. AS YOUR WORSHIP CAN SEE, I'M ALONE. I'M OLD...I FOUND THESE...

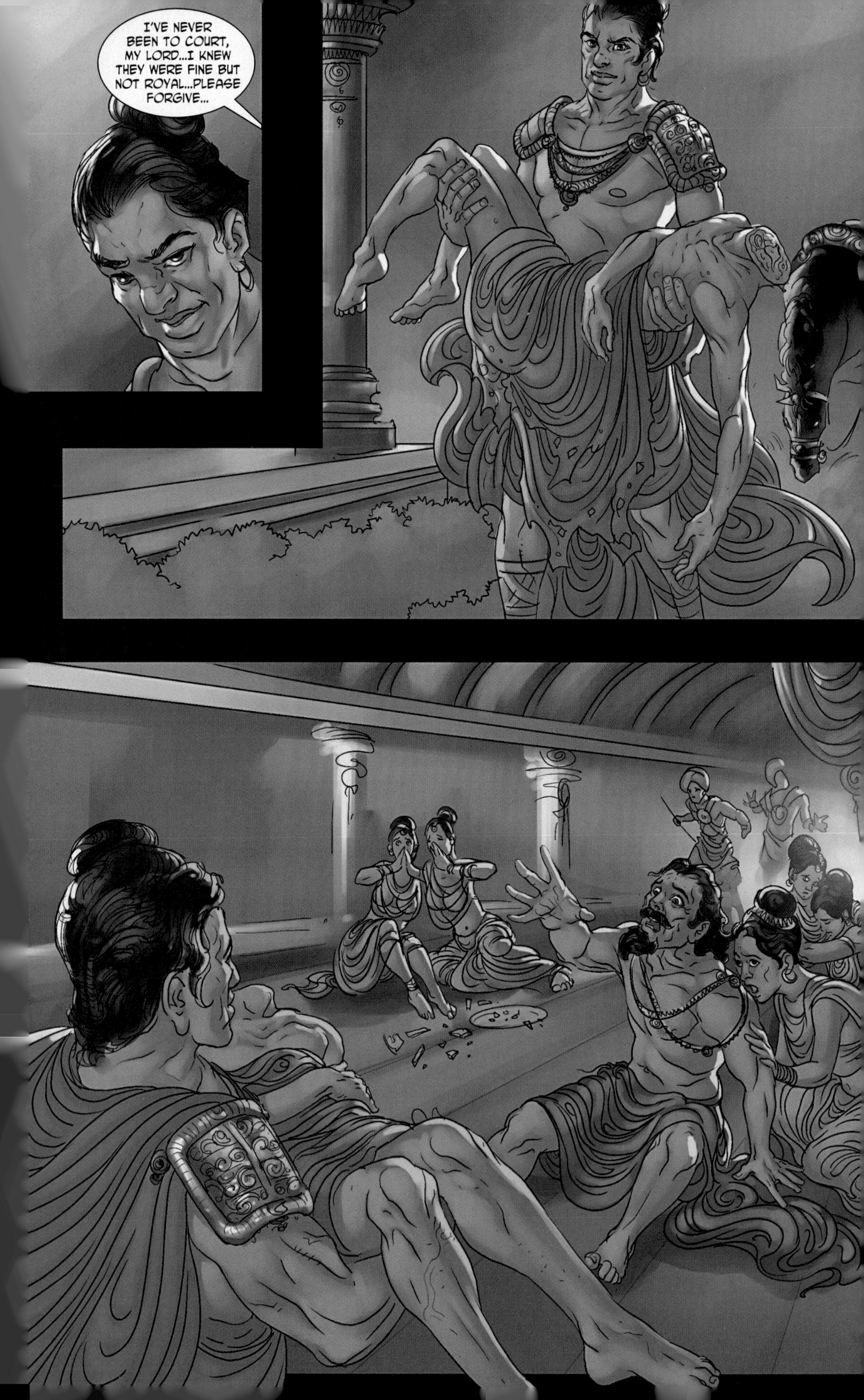
I'VE NEVER BEEN TO COURT, MY LORD...I KNEW THEY WERE FINE BUT NOT ROYAL...PLEASE FORGIVE...

...into the light.

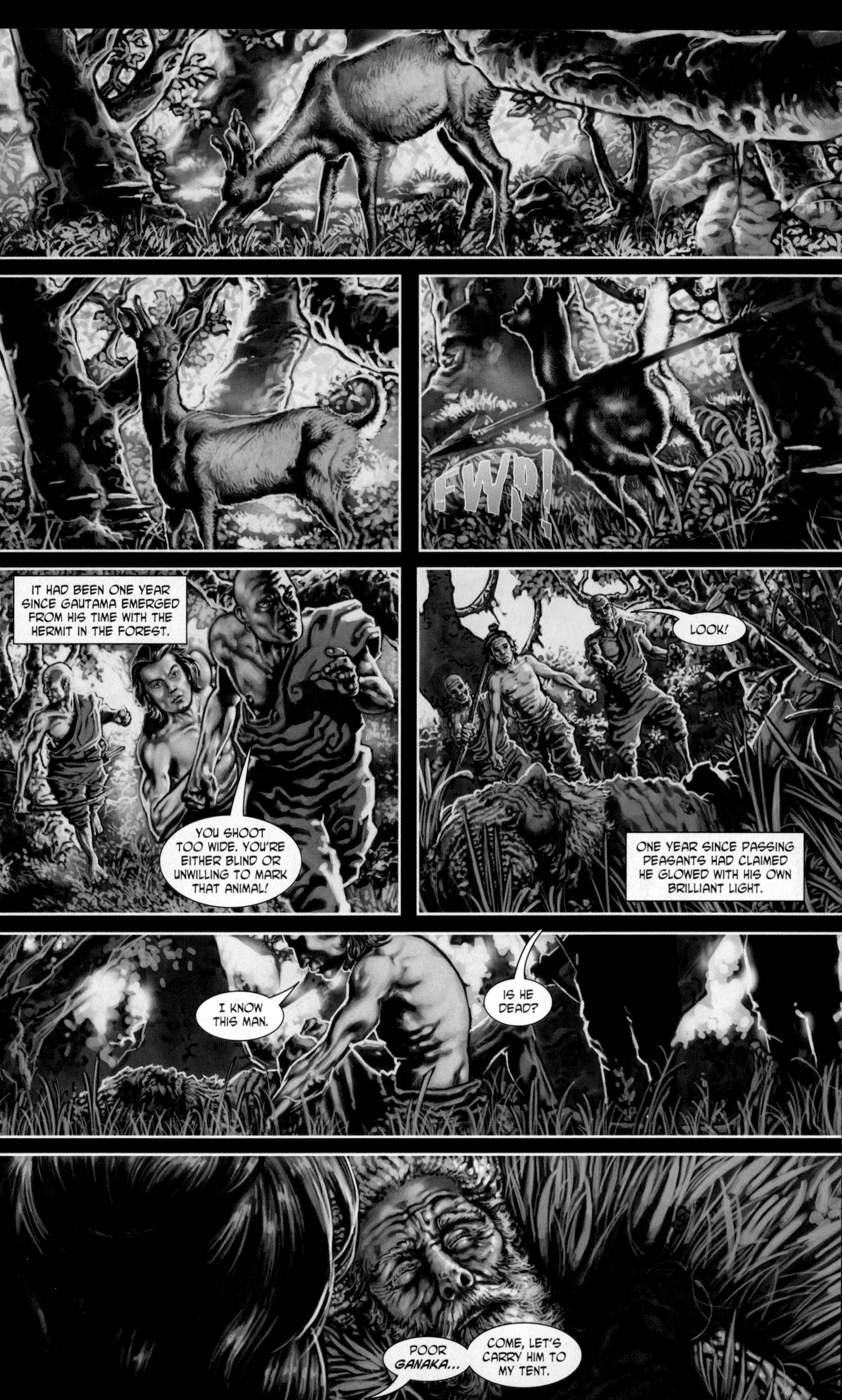
FWP!
IT HAD BEEN ONE YEAR SINCE GAUTAMA EMERGED FROM HIS TIME WITH THE HERMIT IN THE FOREST.
YOU SHOOT TOO WIDE. YOU'RE EITHER BLIND OR UNWILLING TO MARK THAT ANIMAL!
LOOK!
ONE YEAR SINCE PASSING PEASANTS HAD CLAIMED HE GLOWED WITH HIS OWN BRILLIANT LIGHT.
I KNOW THIS MAN.
IS HE DEAD?
POOR GANAKA...
COME, LET'S CARRY HIM TO MY TENT.

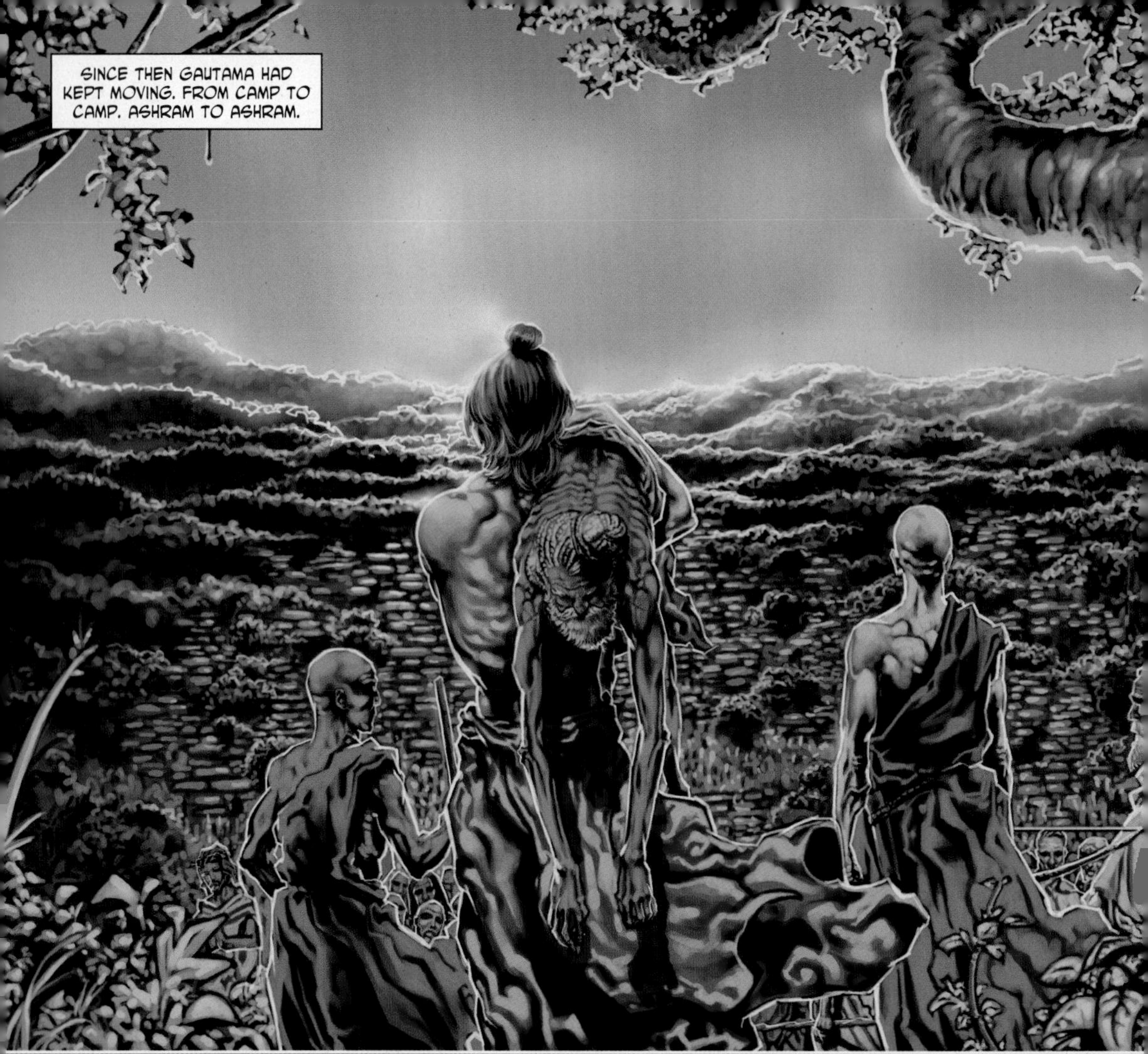
SINCE THEN GAUTAMA HAD KEPT MOVING. FROM CAMP TO CAMP. ASHRAM TO ASHRAM.

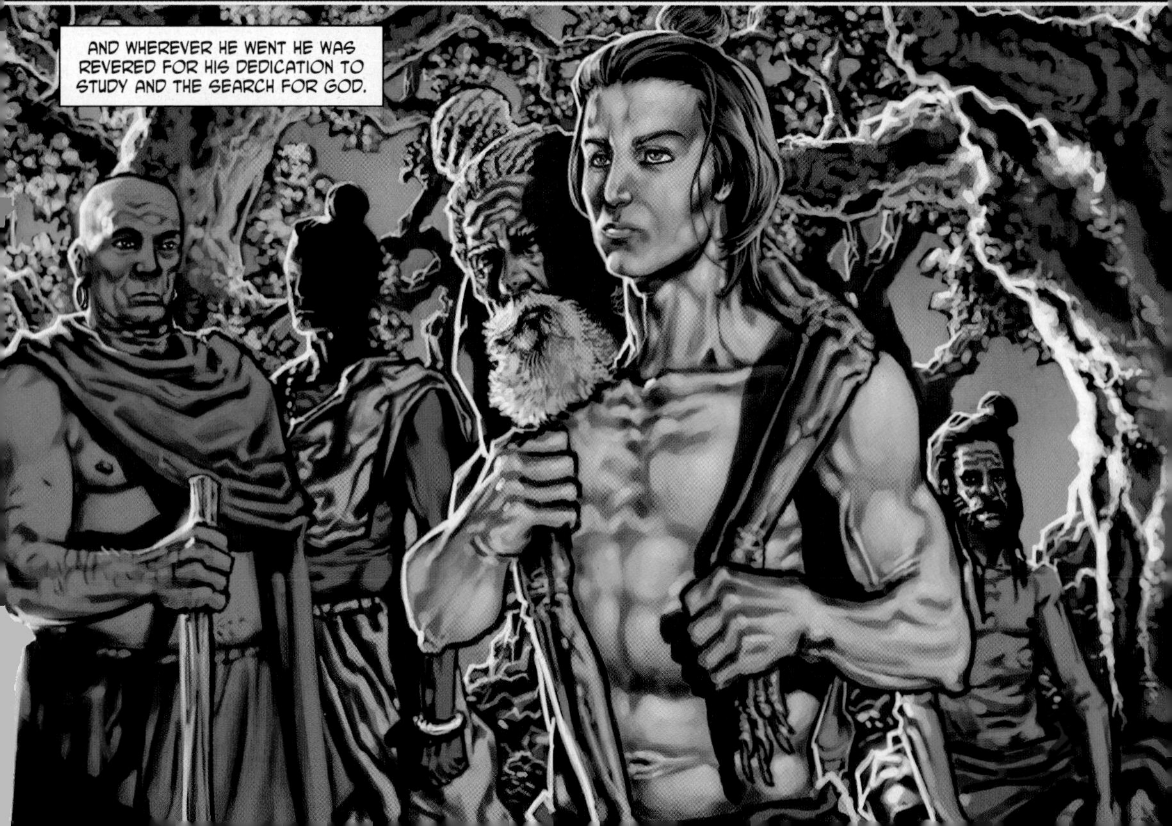
AND WHEREVER HE WENT HE WAS REVERED FOR HIS DEDICATION TO STUDY AND THE SEARCH FOR GOD.

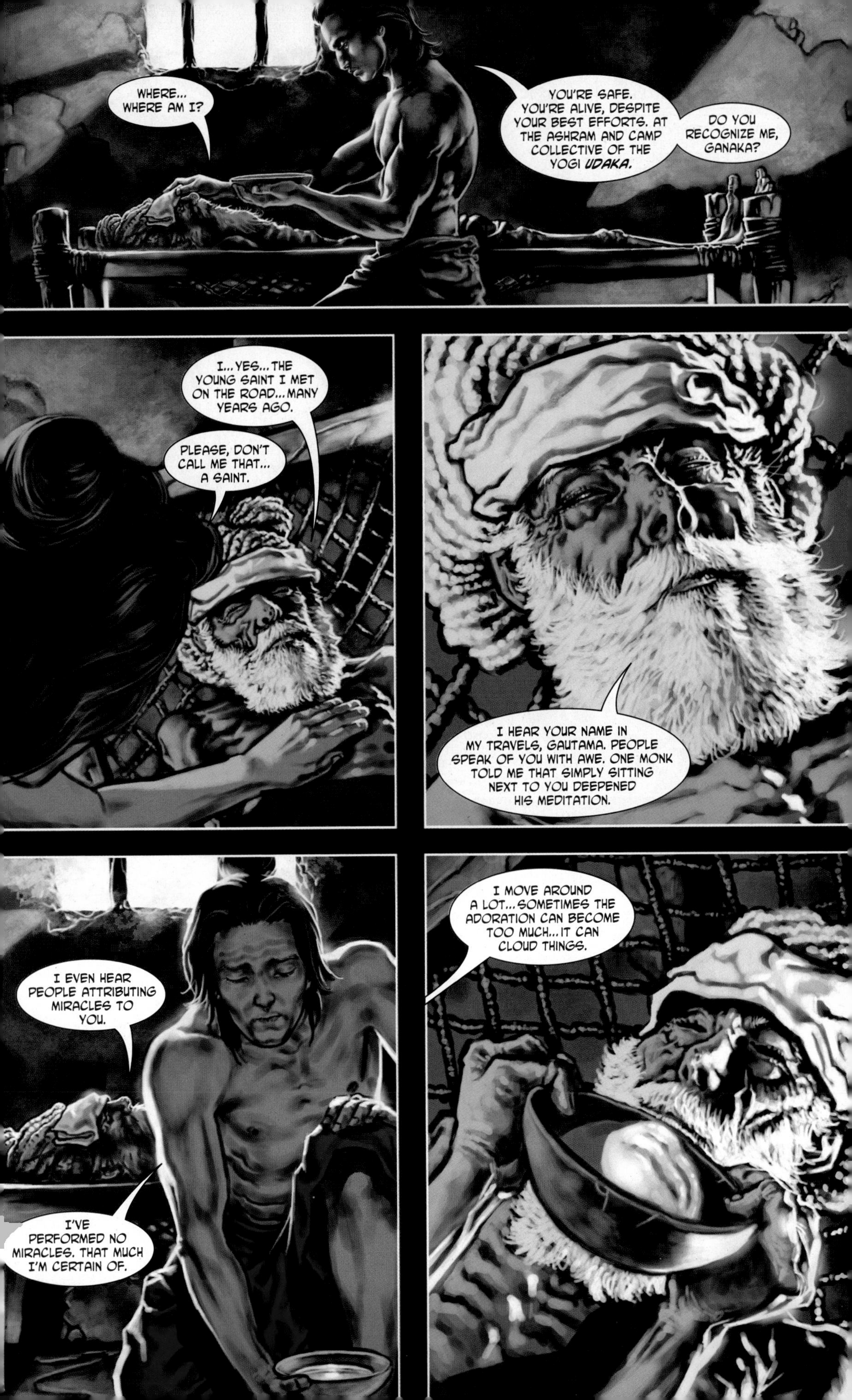
WHERE... WHERE AM I?
YOU'RE SAFE. YOU'RE ALIVE, DESPITE YOUR BEST EFFORTS. AT THE ASHRAM AND CAMP COLLECTIVE OF THE YOGI *UDAKA.*
DO YOU RECOGNIZE ME, GANAKA?
I...YES...THE YOUNG SAINT I MET ON THE ROAD...MANY YEARS AGO.
PLEASE, DON'T CALL ME THAT... A SAINT.
I HEAR YOUR NAME IN MY TRAVELS, GAUTAMA. PEOPLE SPEAK OF YOU WITH AWE. ONE MONK TOLD ME THAT SIMPLY SITTING NEXT TO YOU DEEPENED HIS MEDITATION.
I EVEN HEAR PEOPLE ATTRIBUTING MIRACLES TO YOU.
I'VE PERFORMED NO MIRACLES. THAT MUCH I'M CERTAIN OF.
I MOVE AROUND A LOT...SOMETIMES THE ADORATION CAN BECOME TOO MUCH...IT CAN CLOUD THINGS.

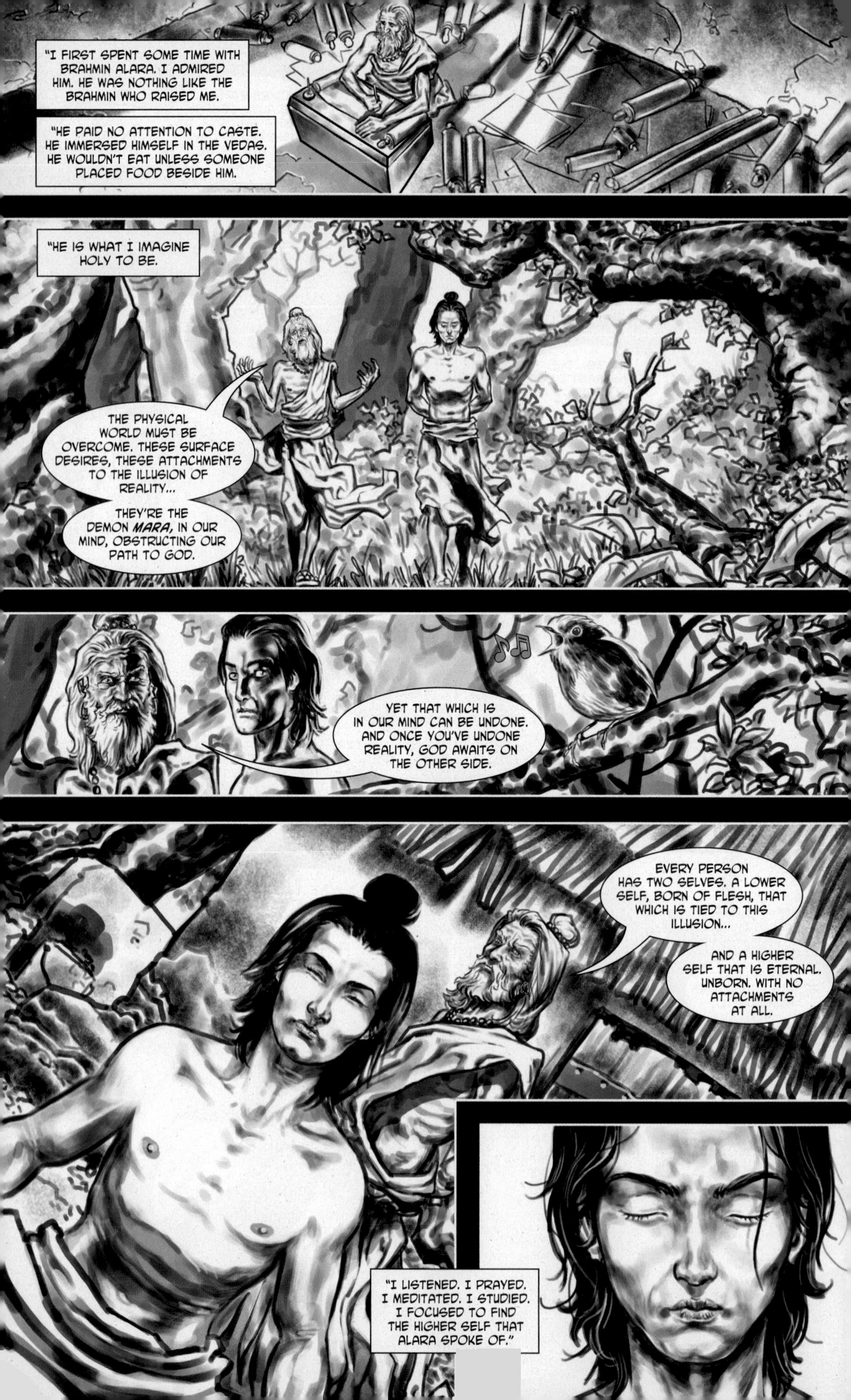
"I FIRST SPENT SOME TIME WITH BRAHMIN ALARA. I ADMIRED HIM. HE WAS NOTHING LIKE THE BRAHMIN WHO RAISED ME.
"HE PAID NO ATTENTION TO CASTE. HE IMMERSED HIMSELF IN THE VEDAS. HE WOULDN'T EAT UNLESS SOMEONE PLACED FOOD BESIDE HIM.
"HE IS WHAT I IMAGINE HOLY TO BE.
THE PHYSICAL WORLD MUST BE OVERCOME. THESE SURFACE DESIRES, THESE ATTACHMENTS TO THE ILLUSION OF REALITY...
THEY'RE THE DEMON *MARA,* IN OUR MIND, OBSTRUCTING OUR PATH TO GOD.
YET THAT WHICH IS IN OUR MIND CAN BE UNDONE. AND ONCE YOU'VE UNDONE REALITY, GOD AWAITS ON THE OTHER SIDE.
EVERY PERSON HAS TWO SELVES. A LOWER SELF, BORN OF FLESH, THAT WHICH IS TIED TO THIS ILLUSION...
AND A HIGHER SELF THAT IS ETERNAL. UNBORN. WITH NO ATTACHMENTS AT ALL.
"I LISTENED. I PRAYED. I MEDITATED. I STUDIED. I FOCUSED TO FIND THE HIGHER SELF THAT ALARA SPOKE OF."

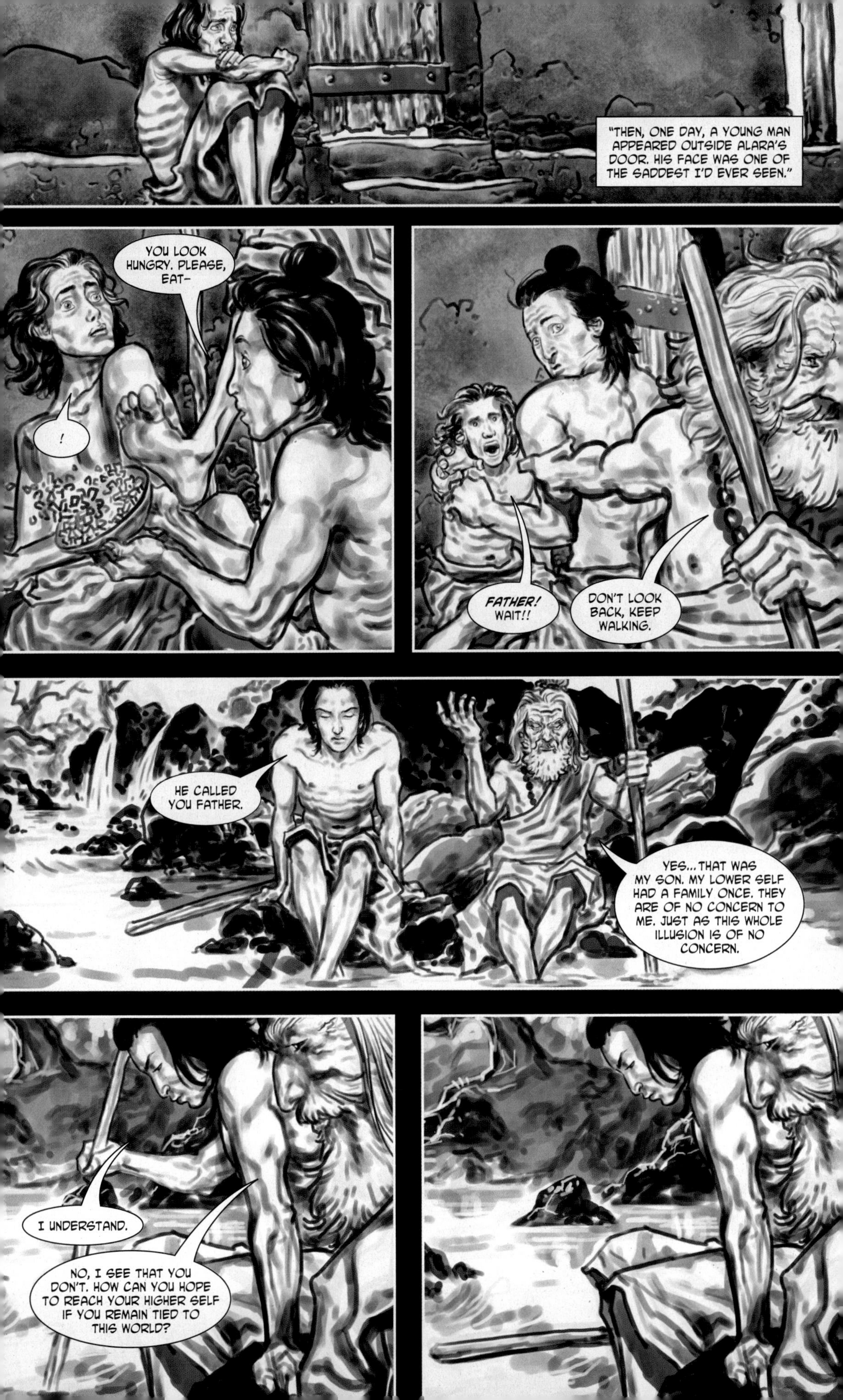
"THEN, ONE DAY, A YOUNG MAN APPEARED OUTSIDE ALARA'S DOOR. HIS FACE WAS ONE OF THE SADDEST I'D EVER SEEN."
YOU LOOK HUNGRY. PLEASE, EAT–
!
FATHER! WAIT!!
DON'T LOOK BACK, KEEP WALKING.
HE CALLED YOU FATHER.
YES... THAT WAS MY SON. MY LOWER SELF HAD A FAMILY ONCE. THEY ARE OF NO CONCERN TO ME. JUST AS THIS WHOLE ILLUSION IS OF NO CONCERN.
I UNDERSTAND.
NO, I SEE THAT YOU DON'T. HOW CAN YOU HOPE TO REACH YOUR HIGHER SELF IF YOU REMAIN TIED TO THIS WORLD?

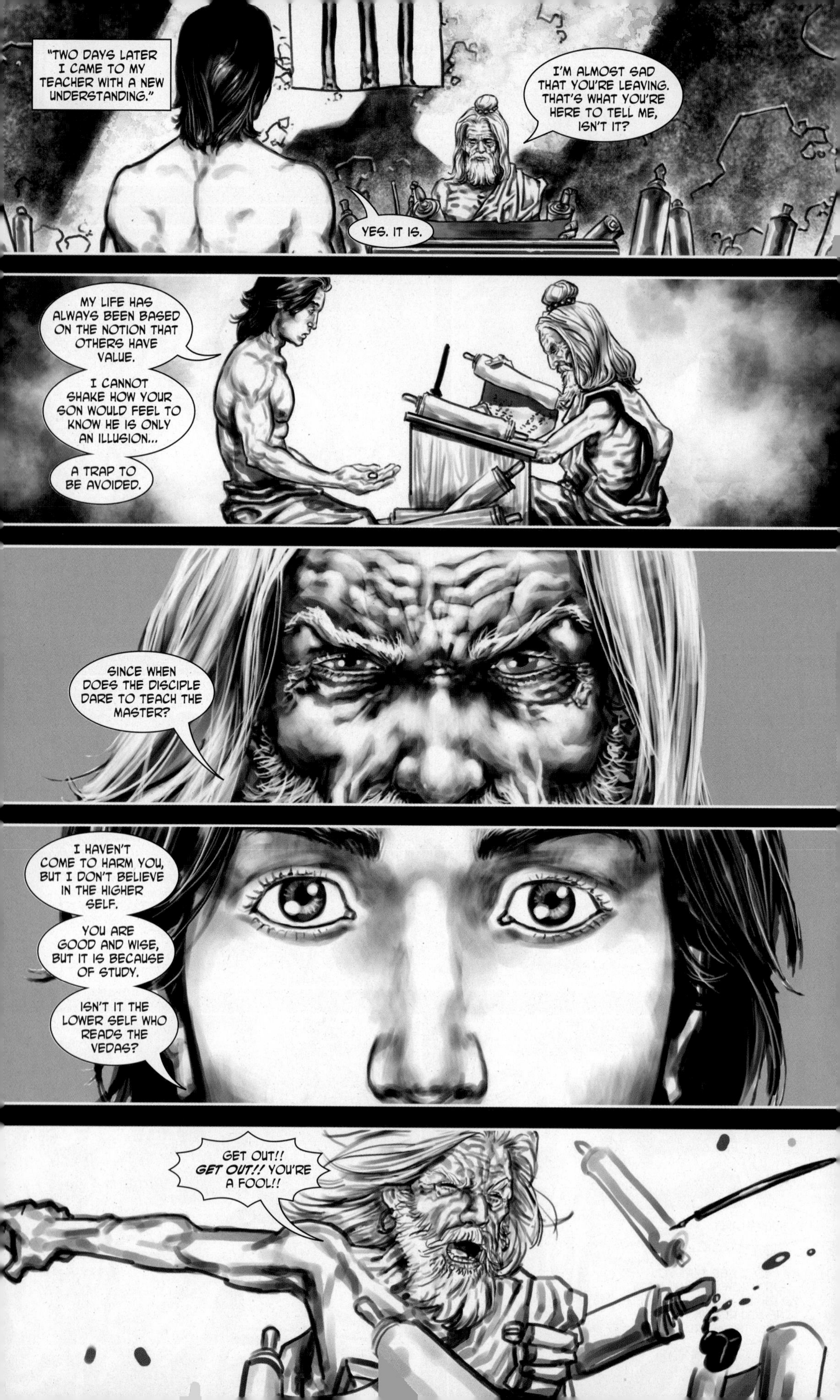

"TWO DAYS LATER I CAME TO MY TEACHER WITH A NEW UNDERSTANDING."
I'M ALMOST SAD THAT YOU'RE LEAVING. THAT'S WHAT YOU'RE HERE TO TELL ME, ISN'T IT?
YES. IT IS.
MY LIFE HAS ALWAYS BEEN BASED ON THE NOTION THAT OTHERS HAVE VALUE.
I CANNOT SHAKE HOW YOUR SON WOULD FEEL TO KNOW HE IS ONLY AN ILLUSION...
A TRAP TO BE AVOIDED.
SINCE WHEN DOES THE DISCIPLE DARE TO TEACH THE MASTER?
I HAVEN'T COME TO HARM YOU, BUT I DON'T BELIEVE IN THE HIGHER SELF.
YOU ARE GOOD AND WISE, BUT IT IS BECAUSE OF STUDY.
ISN'T IT THE LOWER SELF WHO READS THE VEDAS?
GET OUT!! *GET OUT!!* YOU'RE A FOOL!!

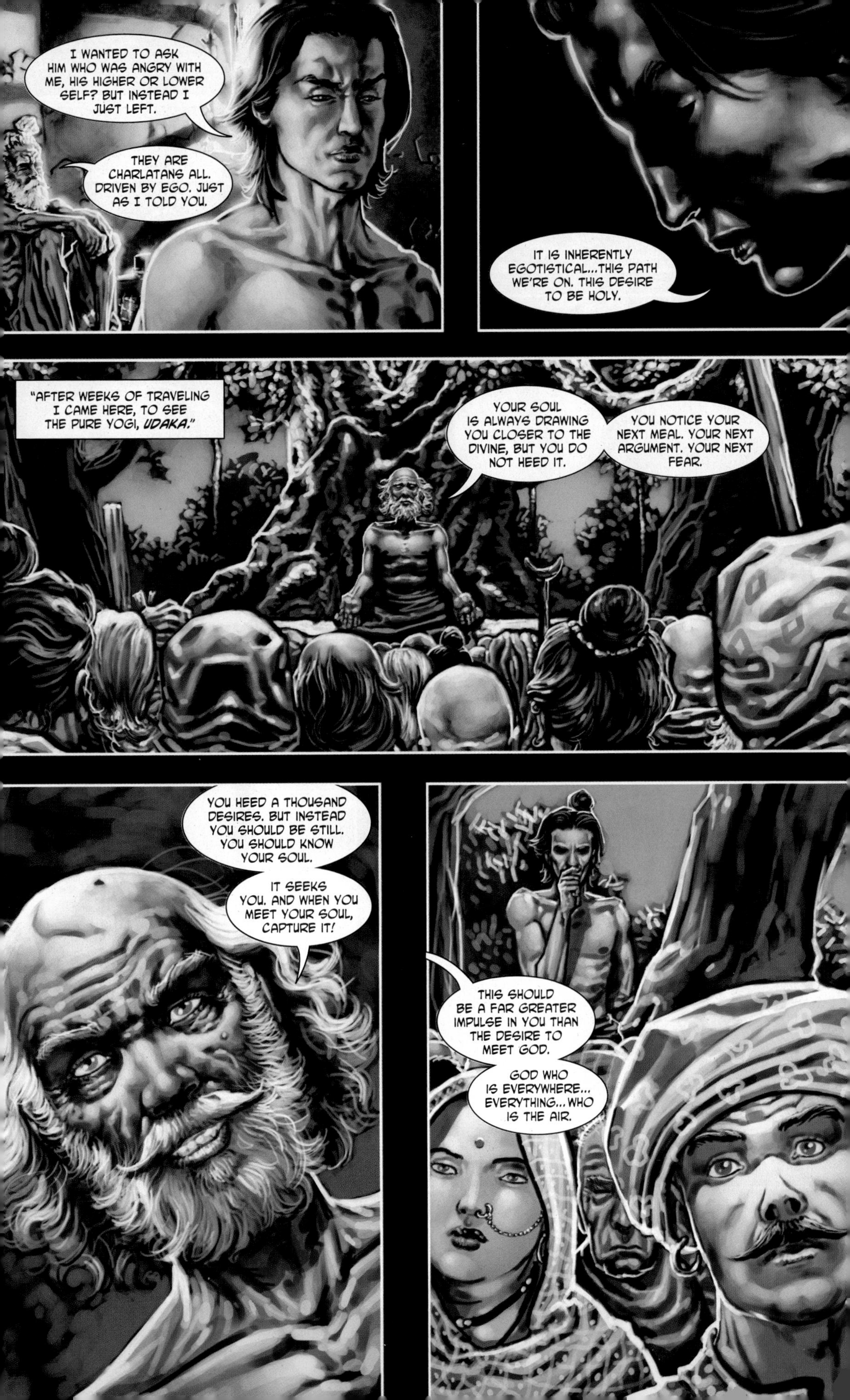
I WANTED TO ASK HIM WHO WAS ANGRY WITH ME, HIS HIGHER OR LOWER SELF? BUT INSTEAD I JUST LEFT.
THEY ARE CHARLATANS ALL. DRIVEN BY EGO. JUST AS I TOLD YOU.
IT IS INHERENTLY EGOTISTICAL...THIS PATH WE'RE ON. THIS DESIRE TO BE HOLY.
"AFTER WEEKS OF TRAVELING I CAME HERE, TO SEE THE PURE YOGI, *UDAKA.*"
YOUR SOUL IS ALWAYS DRAWING YOU CLOSER TO THE DIVINE, BUT YOU DO NOT HEED IT.
YOU NOTICE YOUR NEXT MEAL. YOUR NEXT ARGUMENT. YOUR NEXT FEAR.
YOU HEED A THOUSAND DESIRES. BUT INSTEAD YOU SHOULD BE STILL. YOU SHOULD KNOW YOUR SOUL.
IT SEEKS YOU. AND WHEN YOU MEET YOUR SOUL, CAPTURE IT!
THIS SHOULD BE A FAR GREATER IMPULSE IN YOU THAN THE DESIRE TO MEET GOD.
GOD WHO IS EVERYWHERE... EVERYTHING... WHO IS THE AIR.

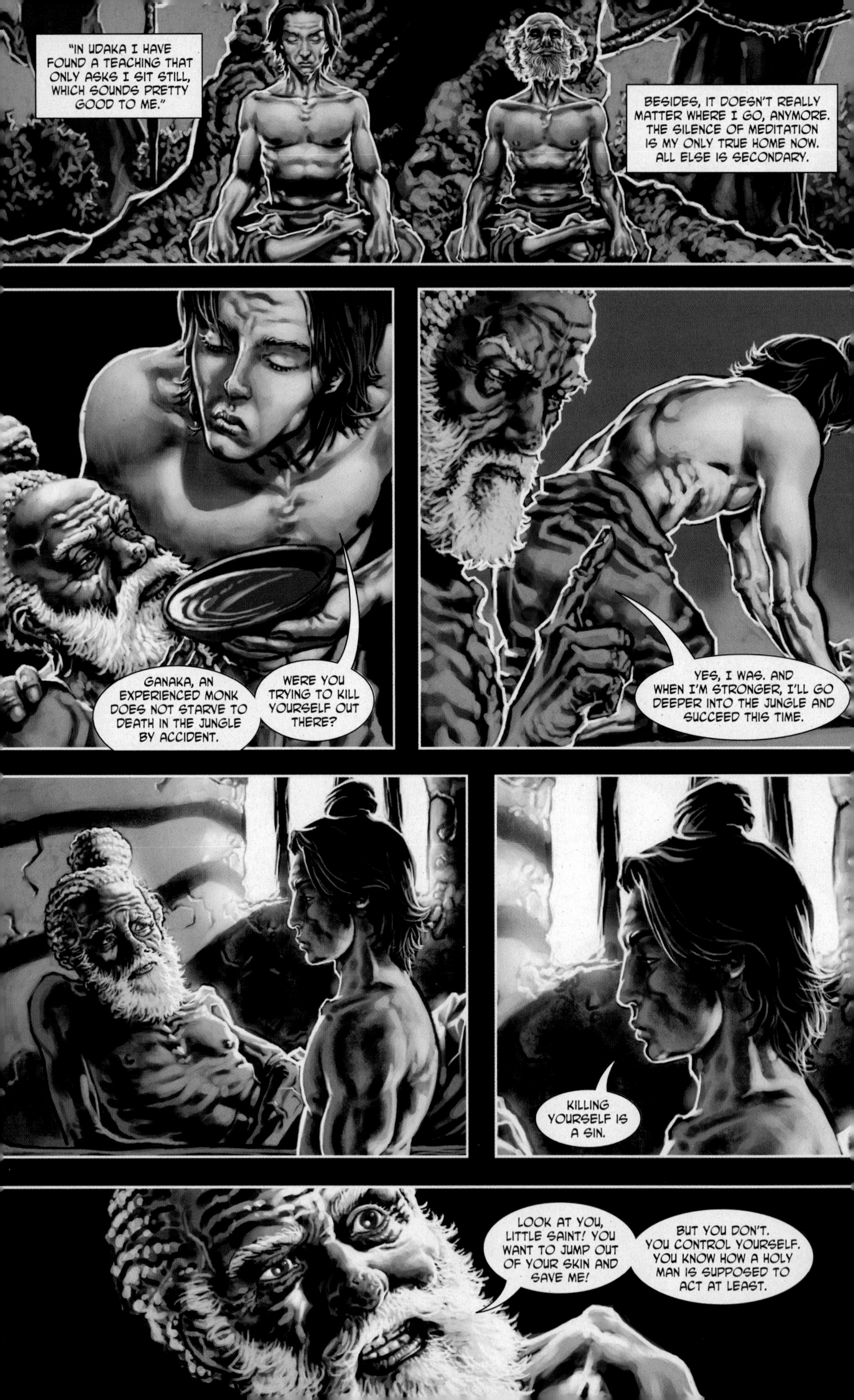
"IN UDAKA I HAVE FOUND A TEACHING THAT ONLY ASKS I SIT STILL, WHICH SOUNDS PRETTY GOOD TO ME."
BESIDES, IT DOESN'T REALLY MATTER WHERE I GO, ANYMORE. THE SILENCE OF MEDITATION IS MY ONLY TRUE HOME NOW. ALL ELSE IS SECONDARY.
GANAKA, AN EXPERIENCED MONK DOES NOT STARVE TO DEATH IN THE JUNGLE BY ACCIDENT.
WERE YOU TRYING TO KILL YOURSELF OUT THERE?
YES, I WAS. AND WHEN I'M STRONGER, I'LL GO DEEPER INTO THE JUNGLE AND SUCCEED THIS TIME.
KILLING YOURSELF IS A SIN.
LOOK AT YOU, LITTLE SAINT! YOU WANT TO JUMP OUT OF YOUR SKIN AND SAVE ME!
BUT YOU DON'T. YOU CONTROL YOURSELF. YOU KNOW HOW A HOLY MAN IS SUPPOSED TO ACT AT LEAST.

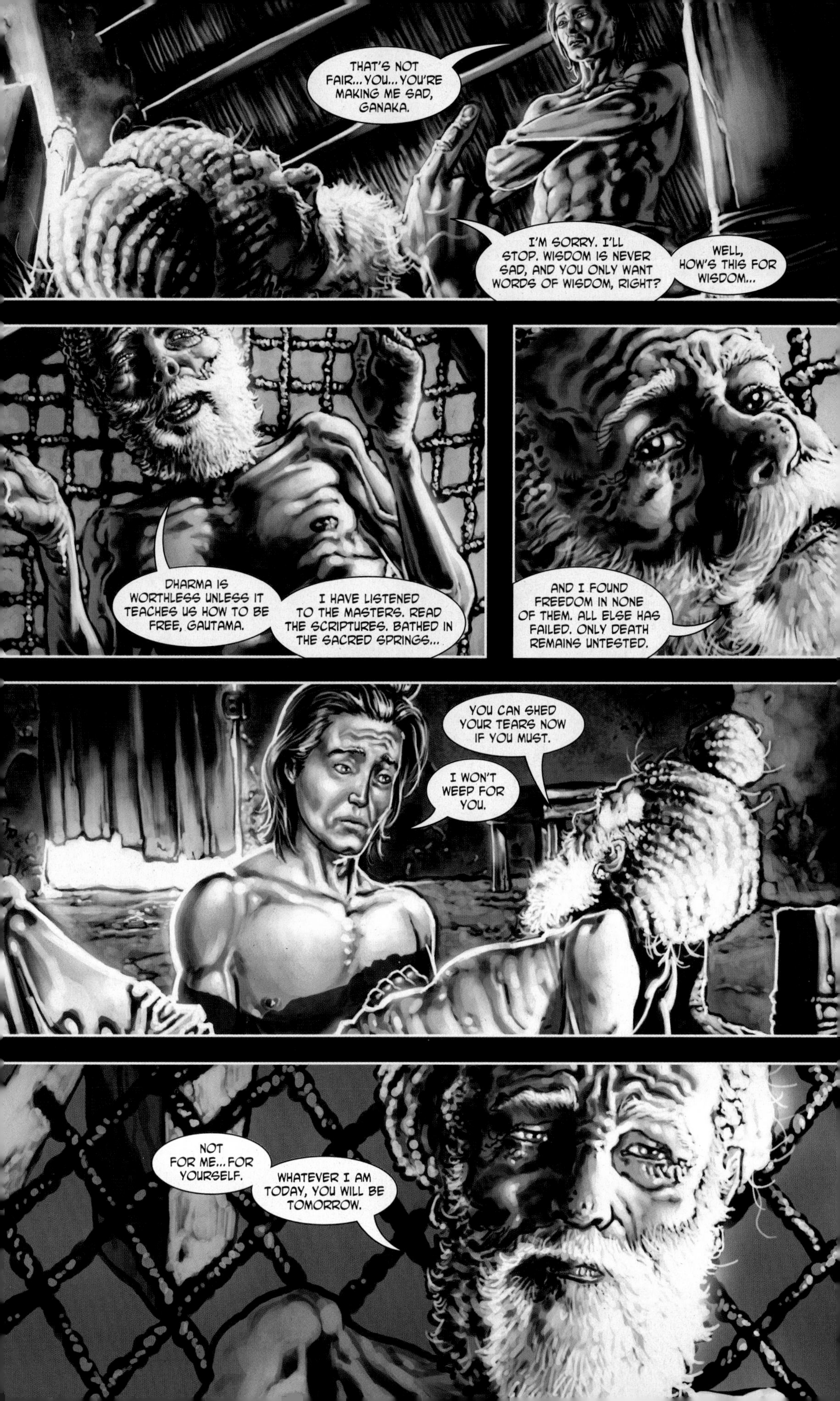

THAT'S NOT FAIR... YOU... YOU'RE MAKING ME SAD, GANAKA.
I'M SORRY. I'LL STOP. WISDOM IS NEVER SAD, AND YOU ONLY WANT WORDS OF WISDOM, RIGHT?
WELL, HOW'S THIS FOR WISDOM...
DHARMA IS WORTHLESS UNLESS IT TEACHES US HOW TO BE FREE, GAUTAMA.
I HAVE LISTENED TO THE MASTERS. READ THE SCRIPTURES. BATHED IN THE SACRED SPRINGS...
AND I FOUND FREEDOM IN NONE OF THEM. ALL ELSE HAS FAILED. ONLY DEATH REMAINS UNTESTED.
YOU CAN SHED YOUR TEARS NOW IF YOU MUST.
I WON'T WEEP FOR YOU.
NOT FOR ME... FOR YOURSELF.
WHATEVER I AM TODAY, YOU WILL BE TOMORROW.

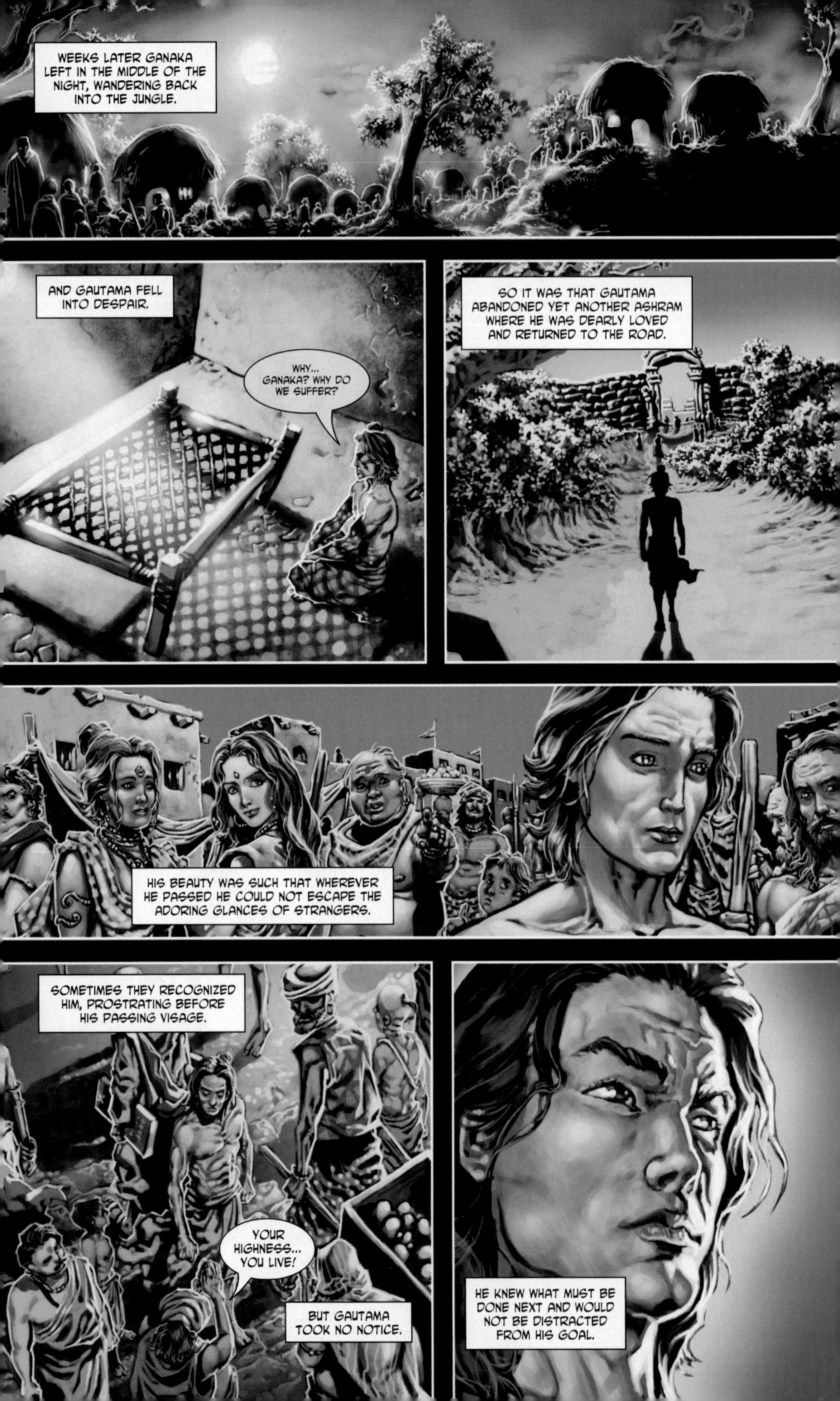
WEEKS LATER GANAKA LEFT IN THE MIDDLE OF THE NIGHT, WANDERING BACK INTO THE JUNGLE.
AND GAUTAMA FELL INTO DESPAIR.
WHY... GANAKA? WHY DO WE SUFFER?
SO IT WAS THAT GAUTAMA ABANDONED YET ANOTHER ASHRAM WHERE HE WAS DEARLY LOVED AND RETURNED TO THE ROAD.
HIS BEAUTY WAS SUCH THAT WHEREVER HE PASSED HE COULD NOT ESCAPE THE ADORING GLANCES OF STRANGERS.
SOMETIMES THEY RECOGNIZED HIM, PROSTRATING BEFORE HIS PASSING VISAGE.
YOUR HIGHNESS... YOU LIVE!
BUT GAUTAMA TOOK NO NOTICE.
HE KNEW WHAT MUST BE DONE NEXT AND WOULD NOT BE DISTRACTED FROM HIS GOAL.

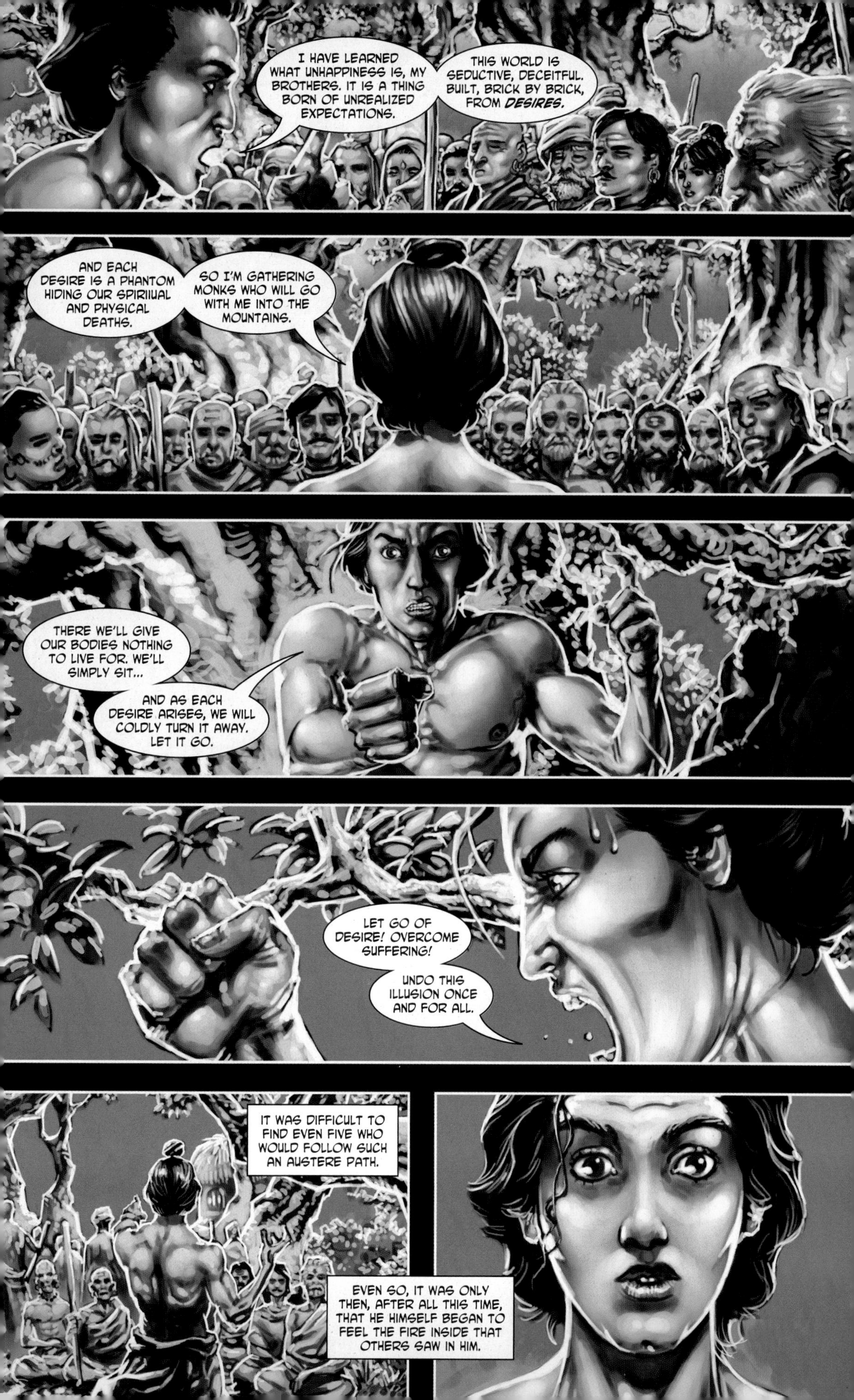
I HAVE LEARNED WHAT UNHAPPINESS IS, MY BROTHERS. IT IS A THING BORN OF UNREALIZED EXPECTATIONS.
THIS WORLD IS SEDUCTIVE, DECEITFUL. BUILT, BRICK BY BRICK, FROM ***DESIRES.***
AND EACH DESIRE IS A PHANTOM HIDING OUR SPIRIIUAL AND PHYSICAL DEATHS.
SO I'M GATHERING MONKS WHO WILL GO WITH ME INTO THE MOUNTAINS.
THERE WE'LL GIVE OUR BODIES NOTHING TO LIVE FOR. WE'LL SIMPLY SIT...
AND AS EACH DESIRE ARISES, WE WILL COLDLY TURN IT AWAY. LET IT GO.
LET GO OF DESIRE! OVERCOME SUFFERING!
UNDO THIS ILLUSION ONCE AND FOR ALL.
IT WAS DIFFICULT TO FIND EVEN FIVE WHO WOULD FOLLOW SUCH AN AUSTERE PATH.
EVEN SO, IT WAS ONLY THEN, AFTER ALL THIS TIME, THAT HE HIMSELF BEGAN TO FEEL THE FIRE INSIDE THAT OTHERS SAW IN HIM.

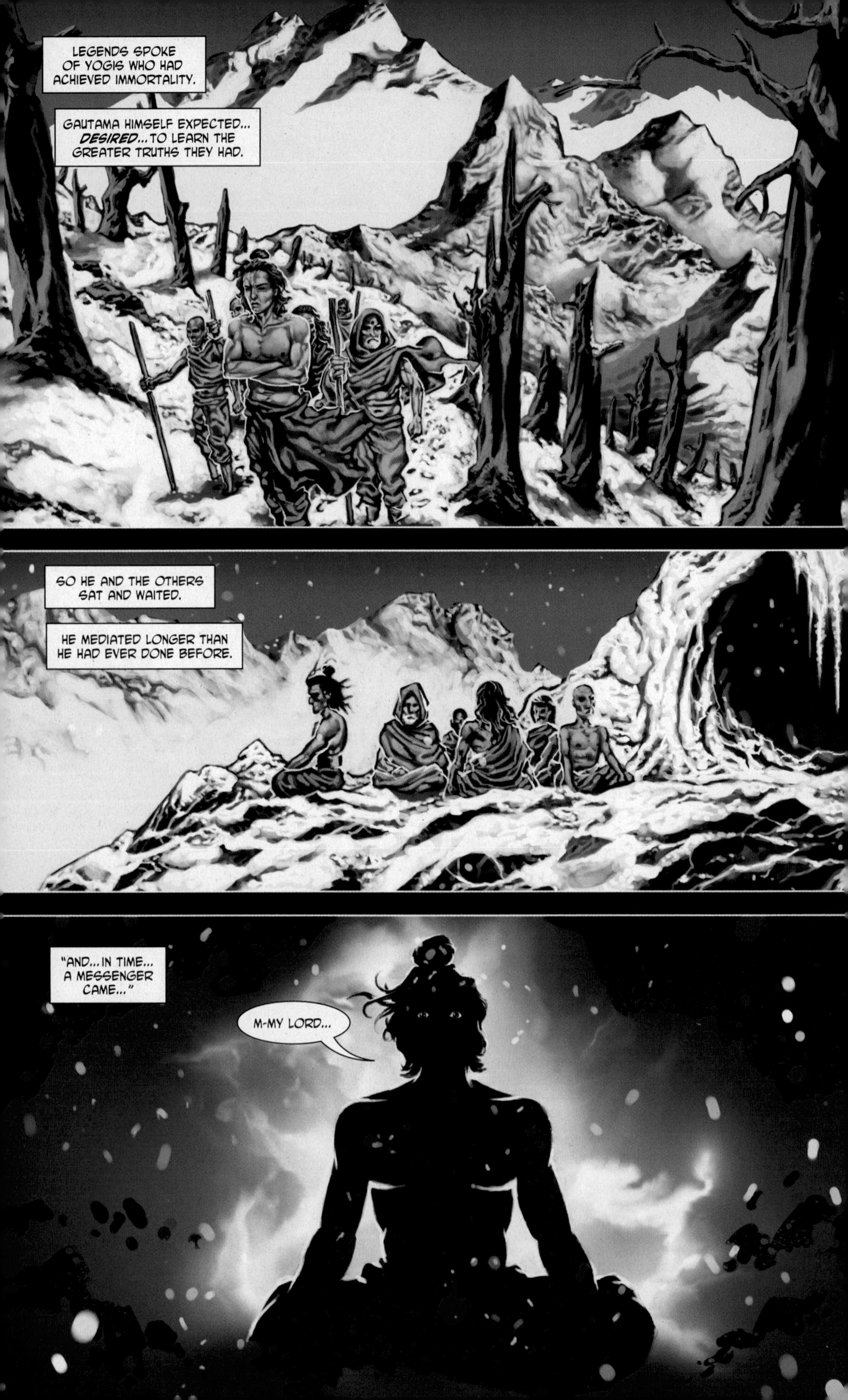
LEGENDS SPOKE OF YOGIS WHO HAD ACHIEVED IMMORTALITY.
GAUTAMA HIMSELF EXPECTED... *DESIRED*...TO LEARN THE GREATER TRUTHS THEY HAD.
SO HE AND THE OTHERS SAT AND WAITED.
HE MEDIATED LONGER THAN HE HAD EVER DONE BEFORE.
"AND... IN TIME... A MESSENGER CAME..."
M-MY LORD...

KRISHNA.

I'VE WAITED SO LONG... STRUGGLED SO HARD... IT SEEMS I'VE BEEN ON THE PATH TO MEET YOU ALL MY LIFE.

JUST TO ASK...

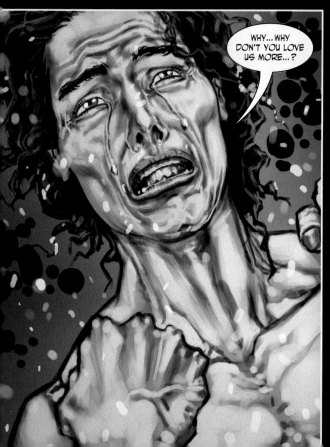

WHY... WHY DON'T YOU LOVE US MORE...?

WHY MUST WE SUFFER SO MUCH?

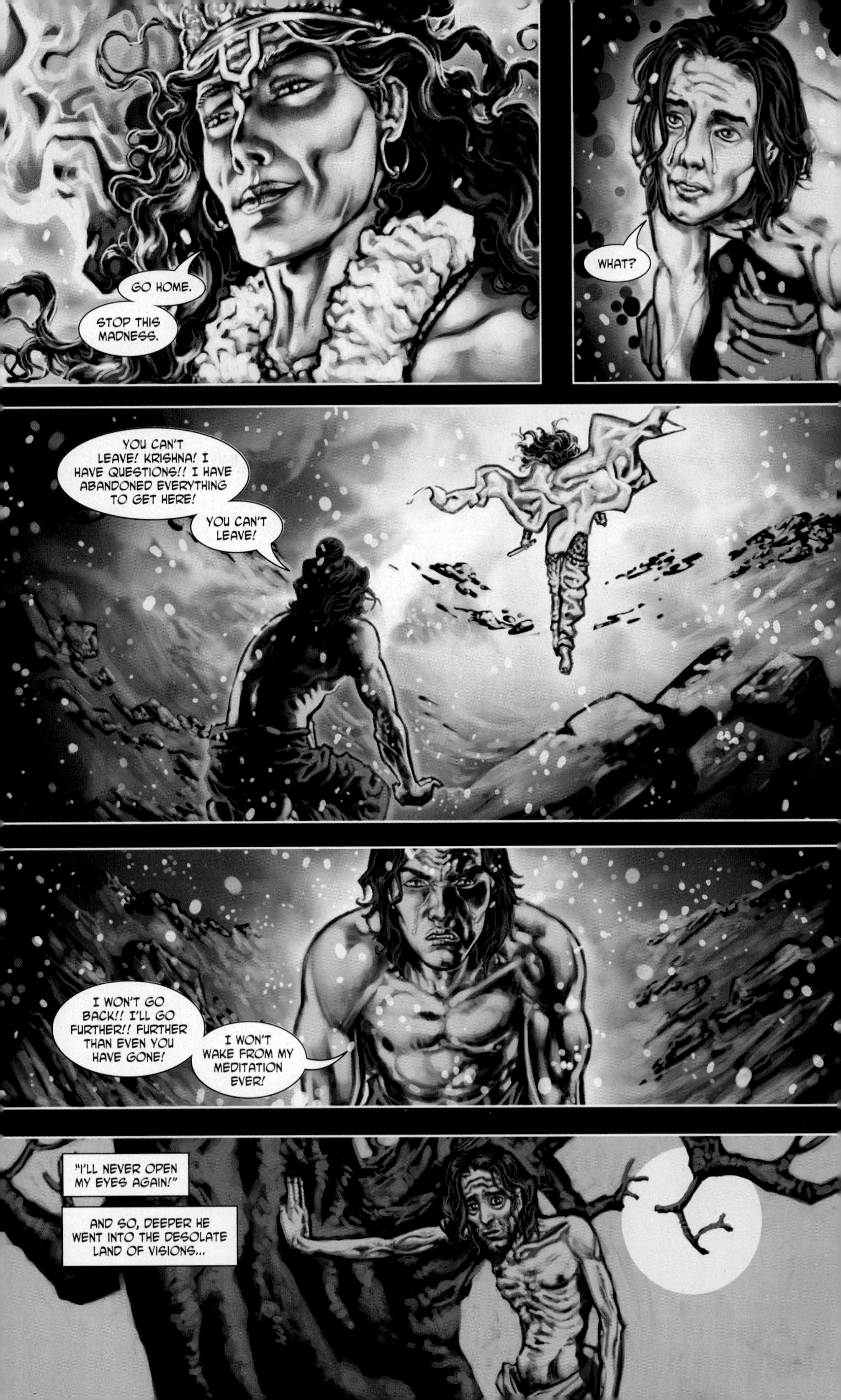
GO HOME.
STOP THIS MADNESS.
WHAT?
YOU CAN'T LEAVE! KRISHNA! I HAVE QUESTIONS!! I HAVE ABANDONED EVERYTHING TO GET HERE!
YOU CAN'T LEAVE!
I WON'T GO BACK!! I'LL GO FURTHER!! FURTHER THAN EVEN YOU HAVE GONE!
I WON'T WAKE FROM MY MEDITATION EVER!
"I'LL NEVER OPEN MY EYES AGAIN!"
AND SO, DEEPER HE WENT INTO THE DESOLATE LAND OF VISIONS...

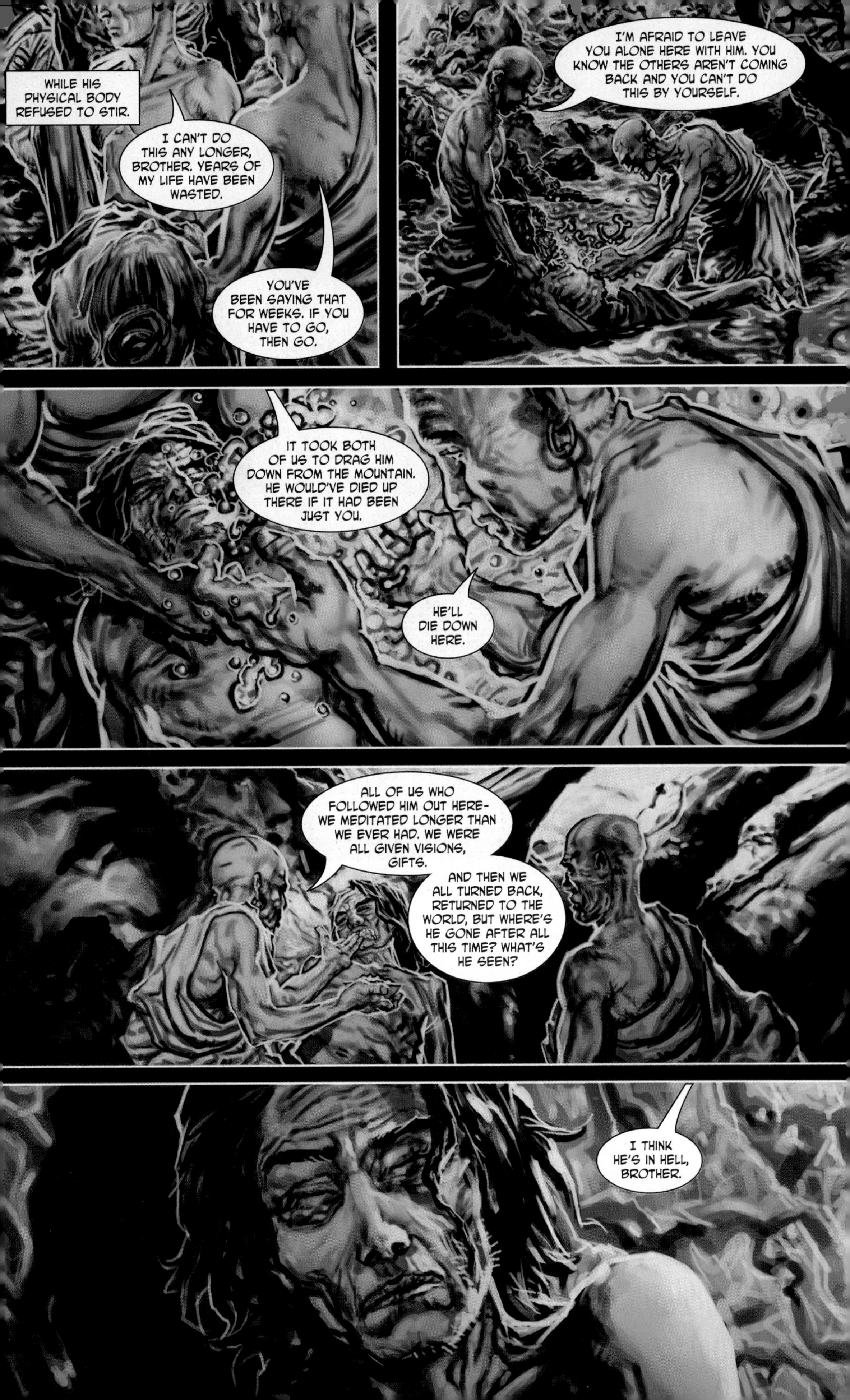

WHILE HIS PHYSICAL BODY REFUSED TO STIR.
I CAN'T DO THIS ANY LONGER, BROTHER. YEARS OF MY LIFE HAVE BEEN WASTED.
YOU'VE BEEN SAYING THAT FOR WEEKS. IF YOU HAVE TO GO, THEN GO.
I'M AFRAID TO LEAVE YOU ALONE HERE WITH HIM. YOU KNOW THE OTHERS AREN'T COMING BACK AND YOU CAN'T DO THIS BY YOURSELF.
IT TOOK BOTH OF US TO DRAG HIM DOWN FROM THE MOUNTAIN. HE WOULD'VE DIED UP THERE IF IT HAD BEEN JUST YOU.
HE'LL DIE DOWN HERE.
ALL OF US WHO FOLLOWED HIM OUT HERE- WE MEDITATED LONGER THAN WE EVER HAD. WE WERE ALL GIVEN VISIONS, GIFTS.
AND THEN WE ALL TURNED BACK, RETURNED TO THE WORLD, BUT WHERE'S HE GONE AFTER ALL THIS TIME? WHAT'S HE SEEN?
I THINK HE'S IN HELL, BROTHER.

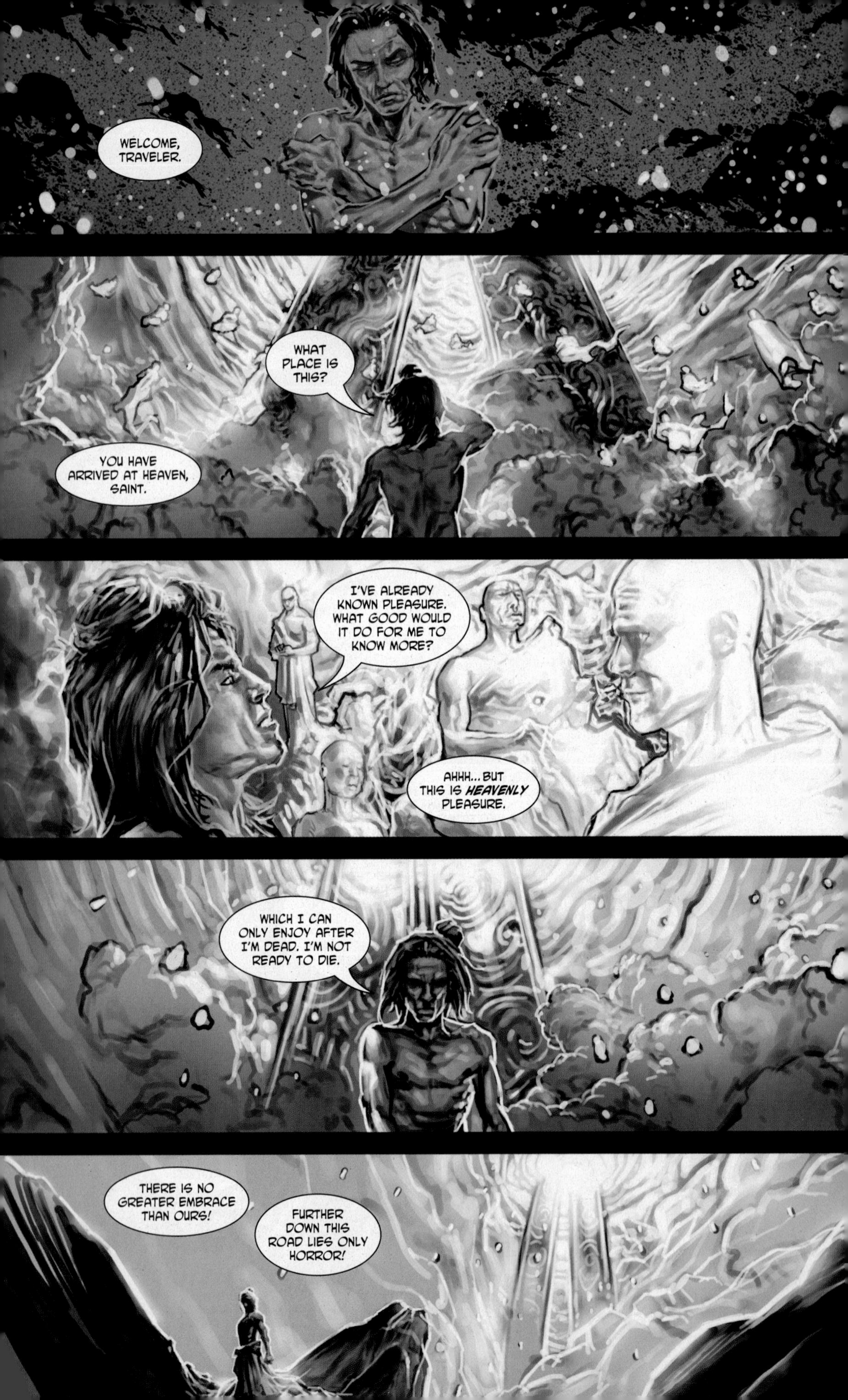
WELCOME, TRAVELER.
WHAT PLACE IS THIS?
YOU HAVE ARRIVED AT HEAVEN, SAINT.
I'VE ALREADY KNOWN PLEASURE. WHAT GOOD WOULD IT DO FOR ME TO KNOW MORE?
AHHH... BUT THIS IS *HEAVENLY* PLEASURE.
WHICH I CAN ONLY ENJOY AFTER I'M DEAD. I'M NOT READY TO DIE.
THERE IS NO GREATER EMBRACE THAN OURS!
FURTHER DOWN THIS ROAD LIES ONLY HORROR!

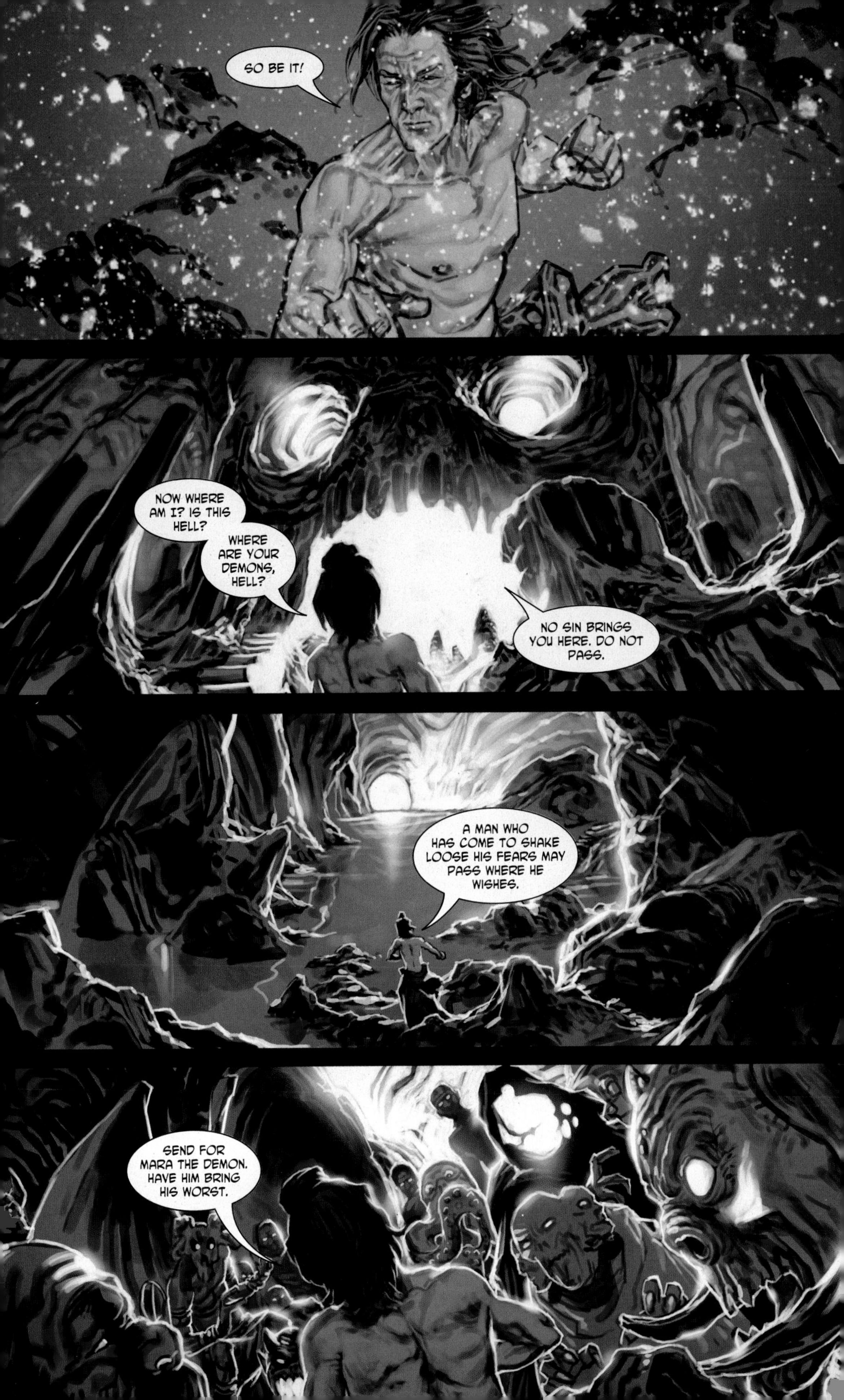
SO BE IT!
NOW WHERE AM I? IS THIS HELL?
WHERE ARE YOUR DEMONS, HELL?
NO SIN BRINGS YOU HERE. DO NOT PASS.
A MAN WHO HAS COME TO SHAKE LOOSE HIS FEARS MAY PASS WHERE HE WISHES.
SEND FOR MARA THE DEMON. HAVE HIM BRING HIS WORST.

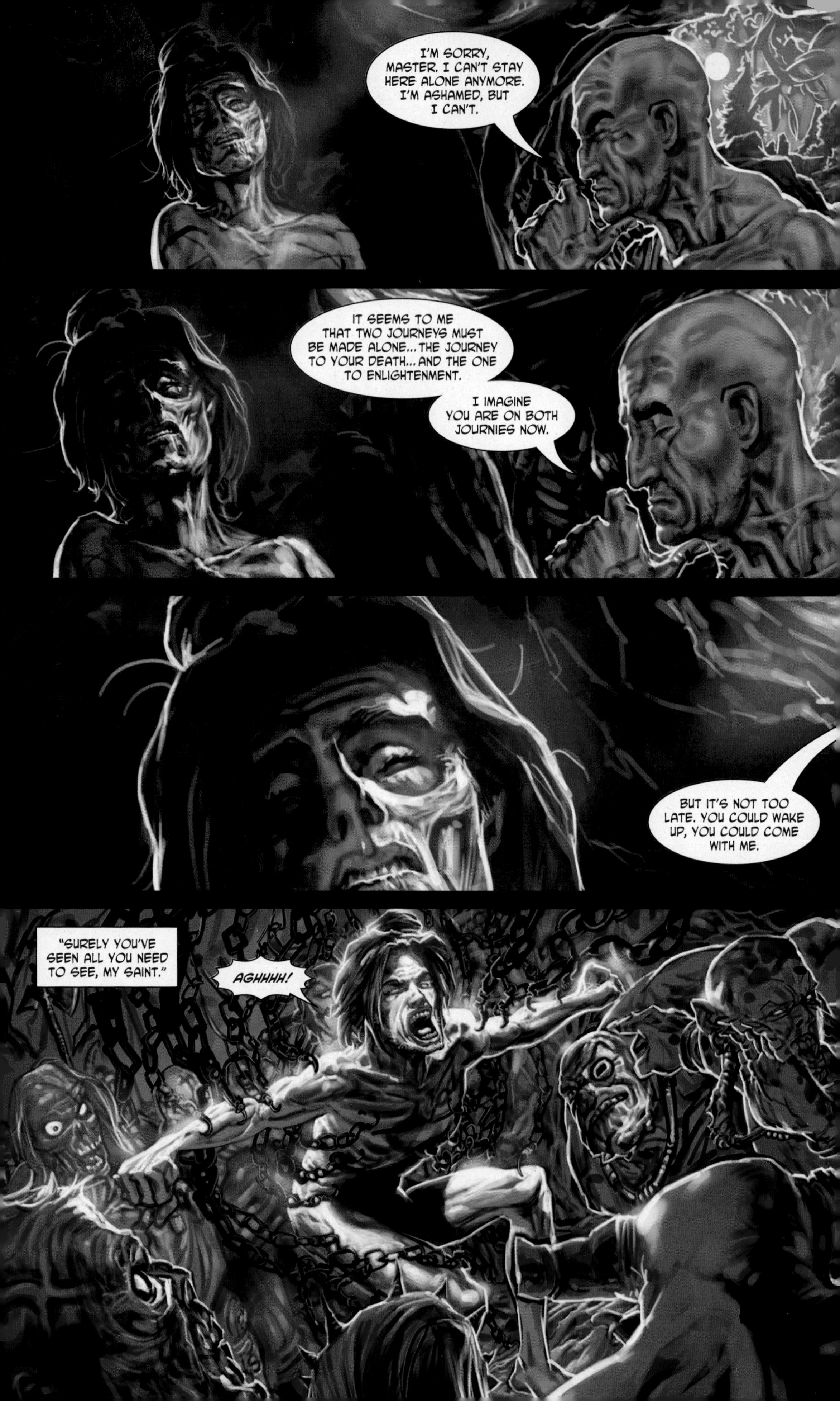
I'M SORRY, MASTER. I CAN'T STAY HERE ALONE ANYMORE. I'M ASHAMED, BUT I CAN'T.
IT SEEMS TO ME THAT TWO JOURNEYS MUST BE MADE ALONE... THE JOURNEY TO YOUR DEATH... AND THE ONE TO ENLIGHTENMENT.
I IMAGINE YOU ARE ON BOTH JOURNIES NOW.
BUT IT'S NOT TOO LATE. YOU COULD WAKE UP, YOU COULD COME WITH ME.
"SURELY YOU'VE SEEN ALL YOU NEED TO SEE, MY SAINT."
AGHHHH!

WHERE IS MARA?! IS HE AFRAID OF ME?!

ALWAYS MANIPULATING THOSE AROUND ME. NEVER FACING ME HIMSELF!

IS HE THE ONE FULL OF FEAR NOW?! *WHERE IS HE!!?*

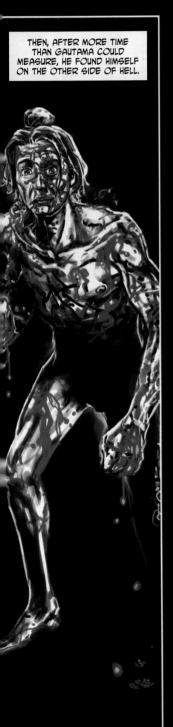

THEN, AFTER MORE TIME THAN GAUTAMA COULD MEASURE, HE FOUND HIMSELF ON THE OTHER SIDE OF HELL.

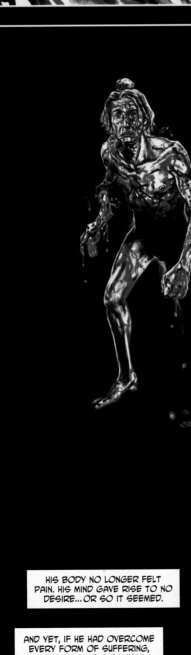

HIS BODY NO LONGER FELT PAIN. HIS MIND GAVE RISE TO NO DESIRE...OR SO IT SEEMED.

AND YET, IF HE HAD OVERCOME EVERY FORM OF SUFFERING, THERE WAS NO SIGN THAT HE HAD REACHED HIS GOAL.

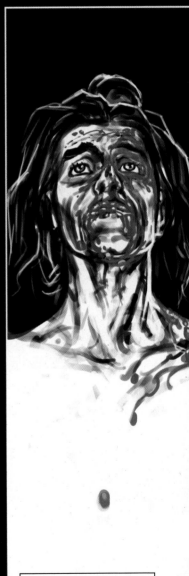

REALIZATION STRUCK...HE STILL DESIRED TO DEFEAT... *DESIRE*...DEATH, SUFFERING.

HE *STILL* DESIRED.

SO GAUTAMA SURRENDERED.

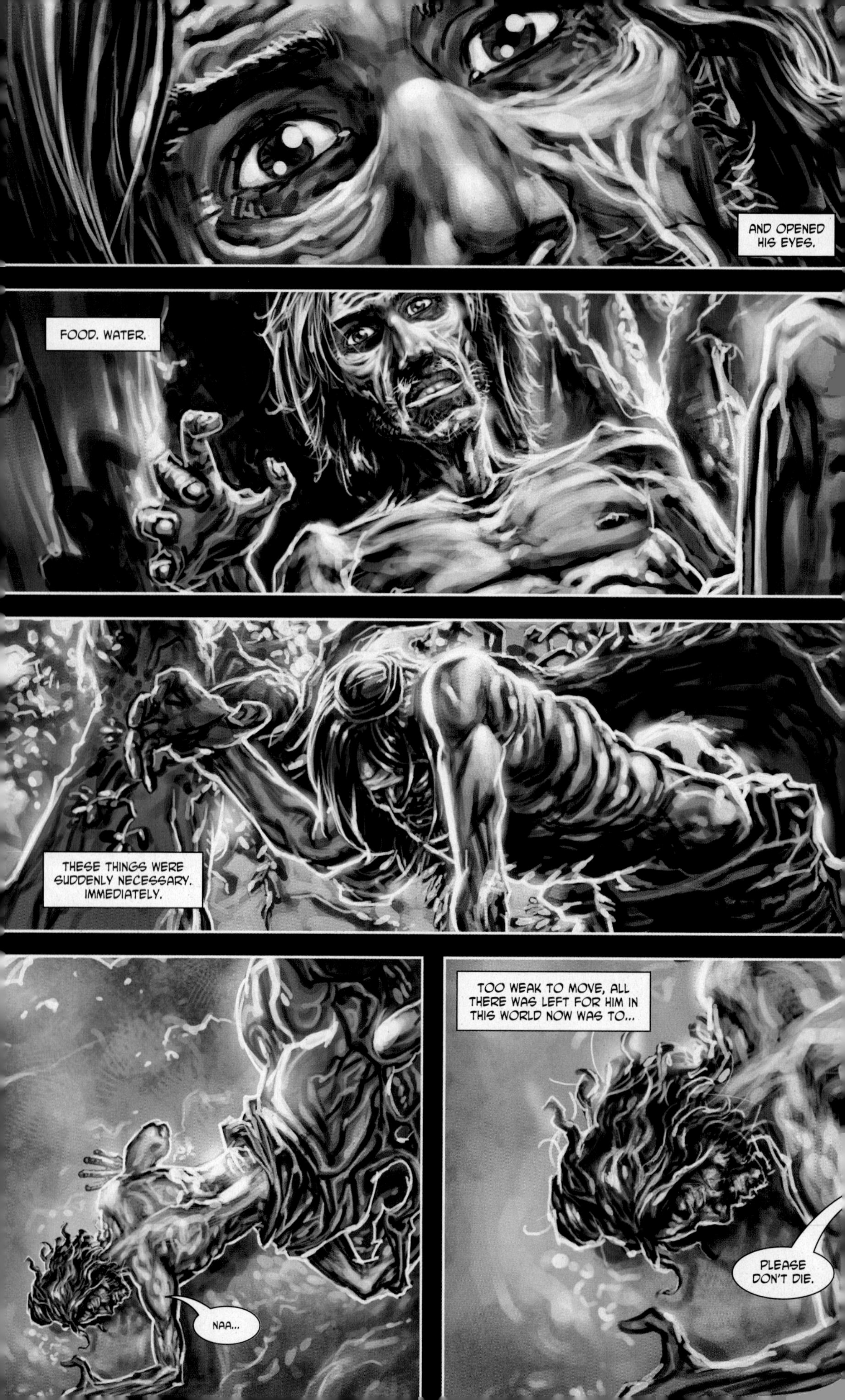
AND OPENED HIS EYES.
FOOD. WATER.
THESE THINGS WERE SUDDENLY NECESSARY. IMMEDIATELY.
NAA...
TOO WEAK TO MOVE, ALL THERE WAS LEFT FOR HIM IN THIS WORLD NOW WAS TO...
PLEASE DON'T DIE.

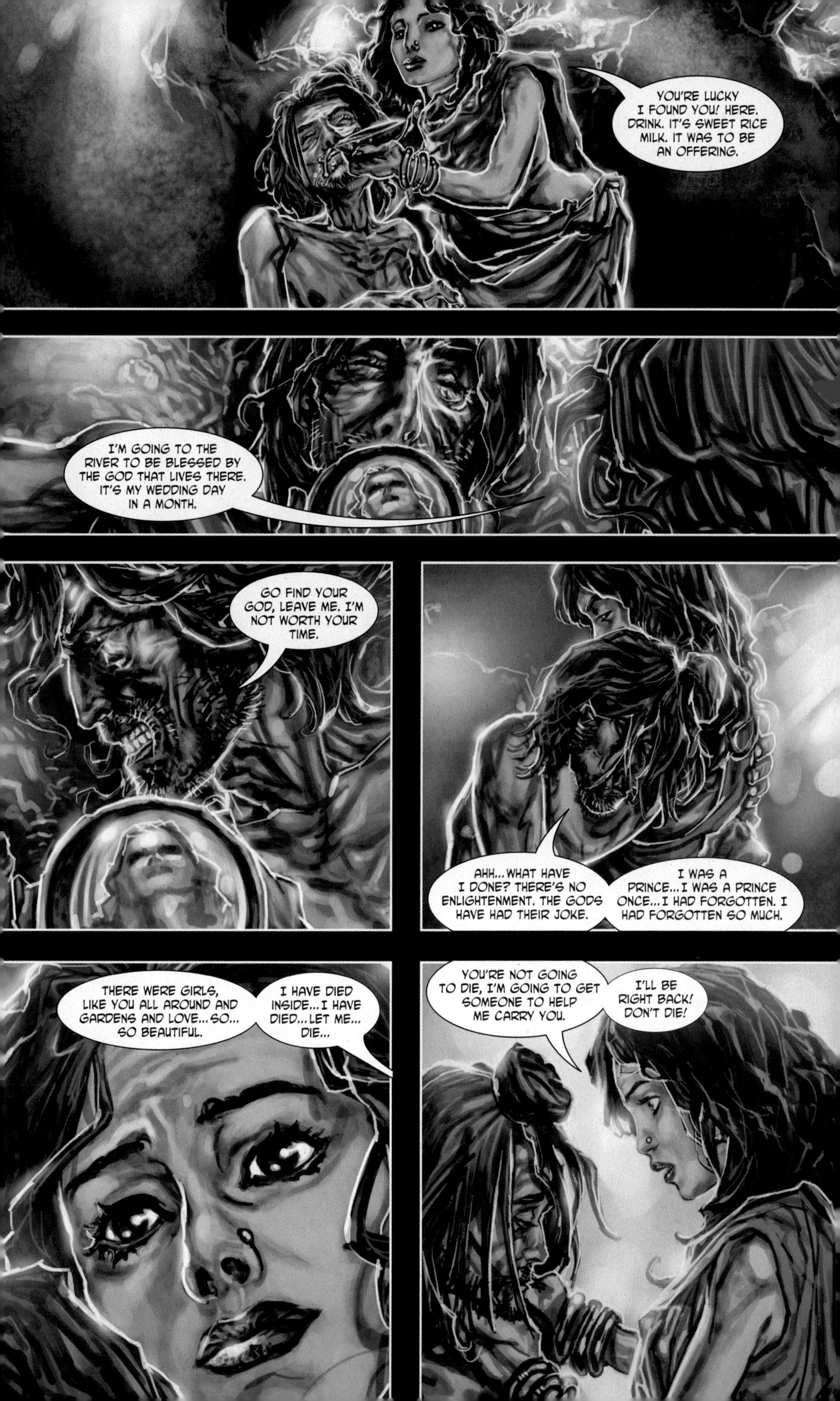
YOU'RE LUCKY I FOUND YOU! HERE. DRINK. IT'S SWEET RICE MILK. IT WAS TO BE AN OFFERING.
I'M GOING TO THE RIVER TO BE BLESSED BY THE GOD THAT LIVES THERE. IT'S MY WEDDING DAY IN A MONTH.
GO FIND YOUR GOD, LEAVE ME. I'M NOT WORTH YOUR TIME.
AHH... WHAT HAVE I DONE? THERE'S NO ENLIGHTENMENT. THE GODS HAVE HAD THEIR JOKE.
I WAS A PRINCE... I WAS A PRINCE ONCE... I HAD FORGOTTEN. I HAD FORGOTTEN SO MUCH.
THERE WERE GIRLS, LIKE YOU ALL AROUND AND GARDENS AND LOVE... SO... SO BEAUTIFUL.
I HAVE DIED INSIDE... I HAVE DIED... LET ME... DIE...
YOU'RE NOT GOING TO DIE, I'M GOING TO GET SOMEONE TO HELP ME CARRY YOU.
I'LL BE RIGHT BACK! DON'T DIE!

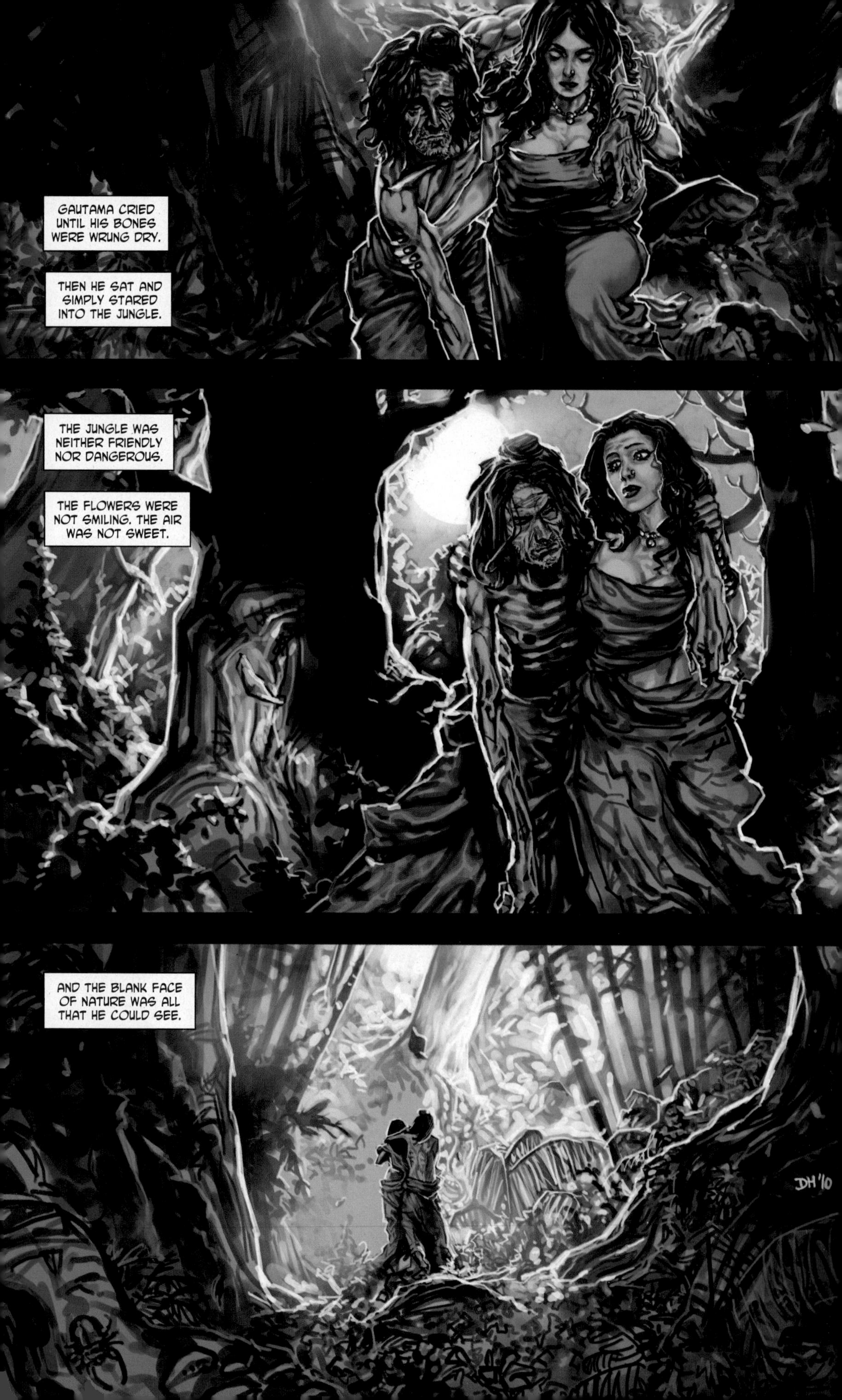
GAUTAMA CRIED UNTIL HIS BONES WERE WRUNG DRY.
THEN HE SAT AND SIMPLY STARED INTO THE JUNGLE.
THE JUNGLE WAS NEITHER FRIENDLY NOR DANGEROUS.
THE FLOWERS WERE NOT SMILING. THE AIR WAS NOT SWEET.
AND THE BLANK FACE OF NATURE WAS ALL THAT HE COULD SEE.
DH '10

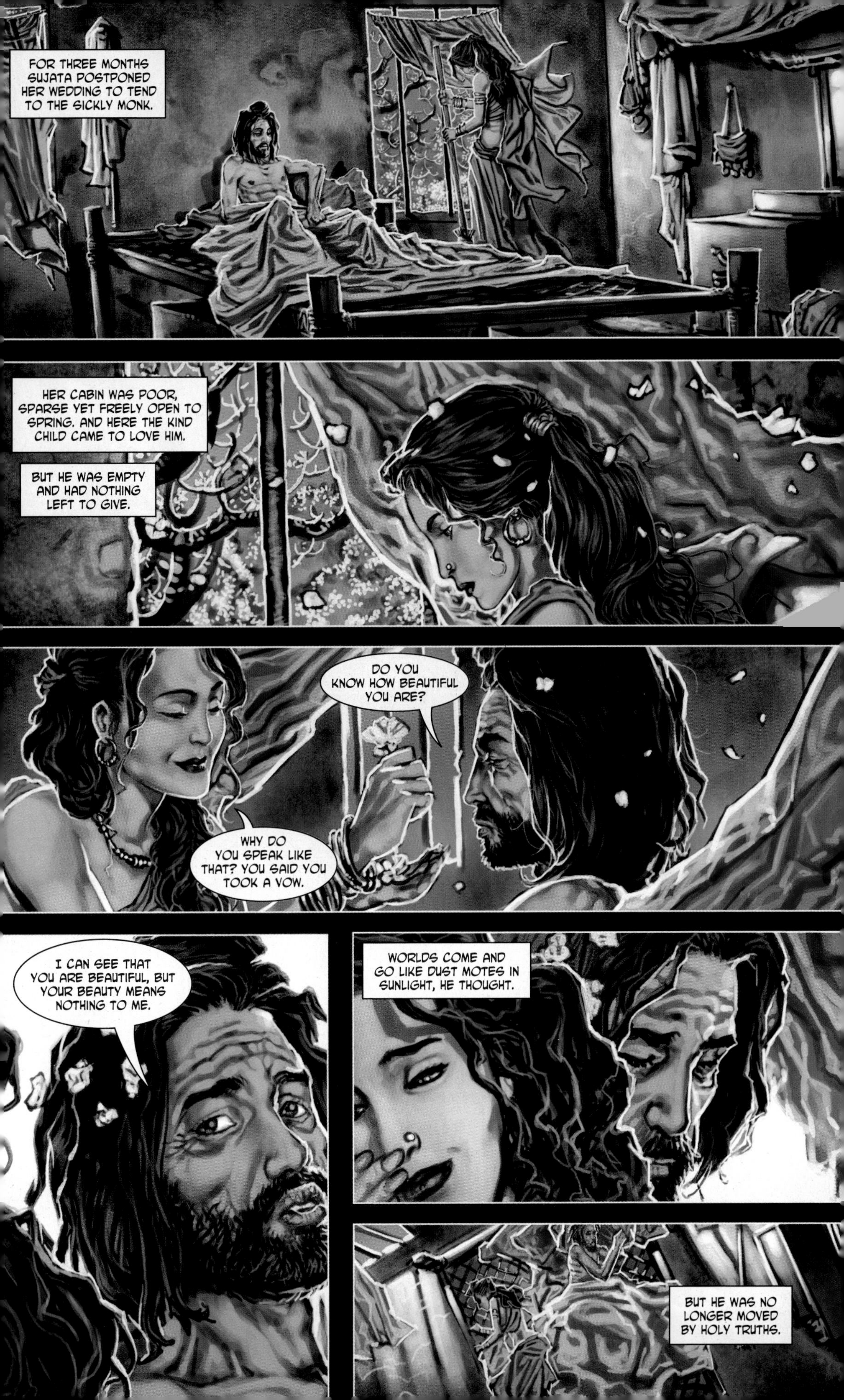
FOR THREE MONTHS SUJATA POSTPONED HER WEDDING TO TEND TO THE SICKLY MONK.
HER CABIN WAS POOR, SPARSE YET FREELY OPEN TO SPRING. AND HERE THE KIND CHILD CAME TO LOVE HIM.
BUT HE WAS EMPTY AND HAD NOTHING LEFT TO GIVE.
DO YOU KNOW HOW BEAUTIFUL YOU ARE?
WHY DO YOU SPEAK LIKE THAT? YOU SAID YOU TOOK A VOW.
I CAN SEE THAT YOU ARE BEAUTIFUL, BUT YOUR BEAUTY MEANS NOTHING TO ME.
WORLDS COME AND GO LIKE DUST MOTES IN SUNLIGHT, HE THOUGHT.
BUT HE WAS NO LONGER MOVED BY HOLY TRUTHS.

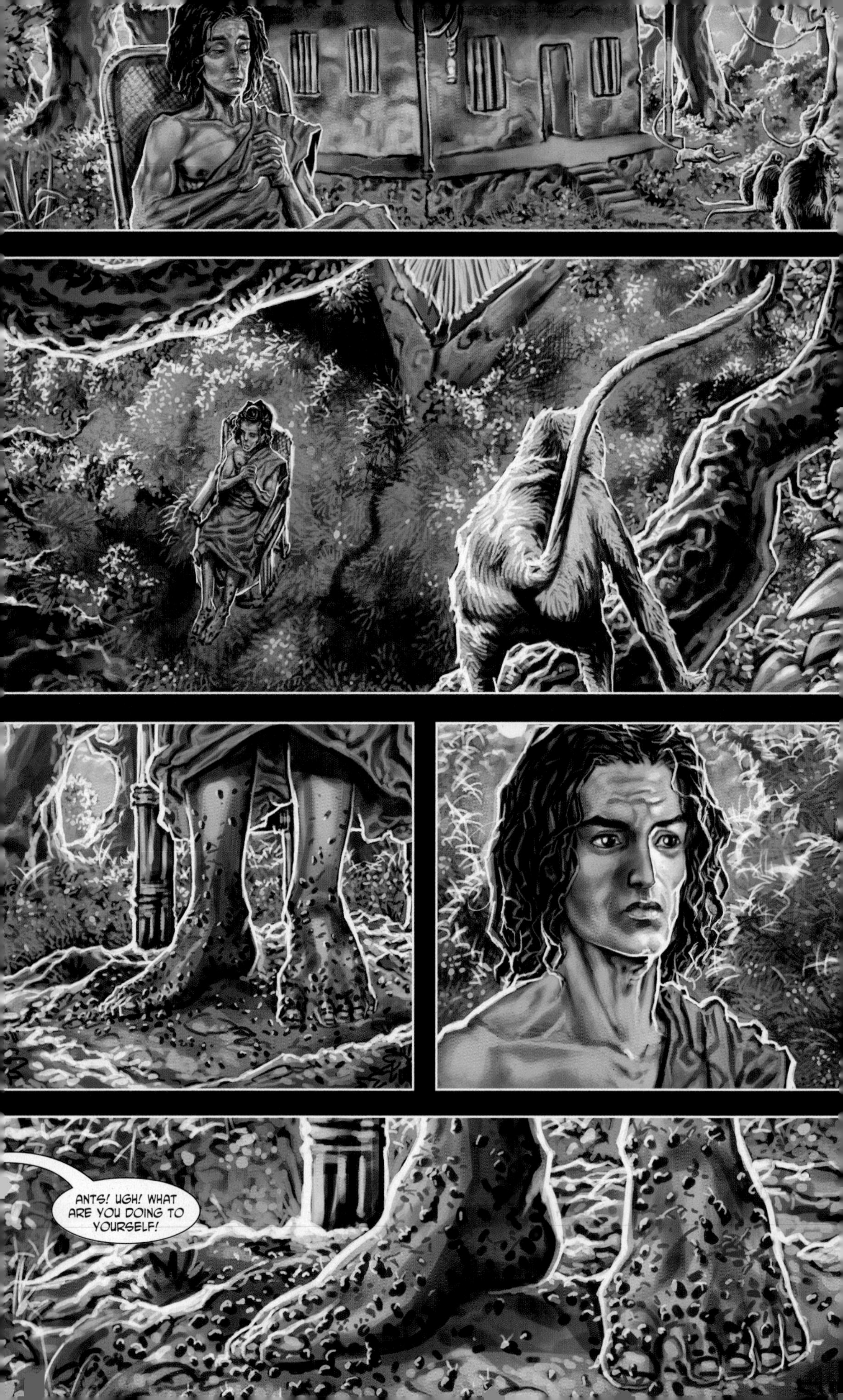
ANTS! UGH! WHAT ARE YOU DOING TO YOURSELF!

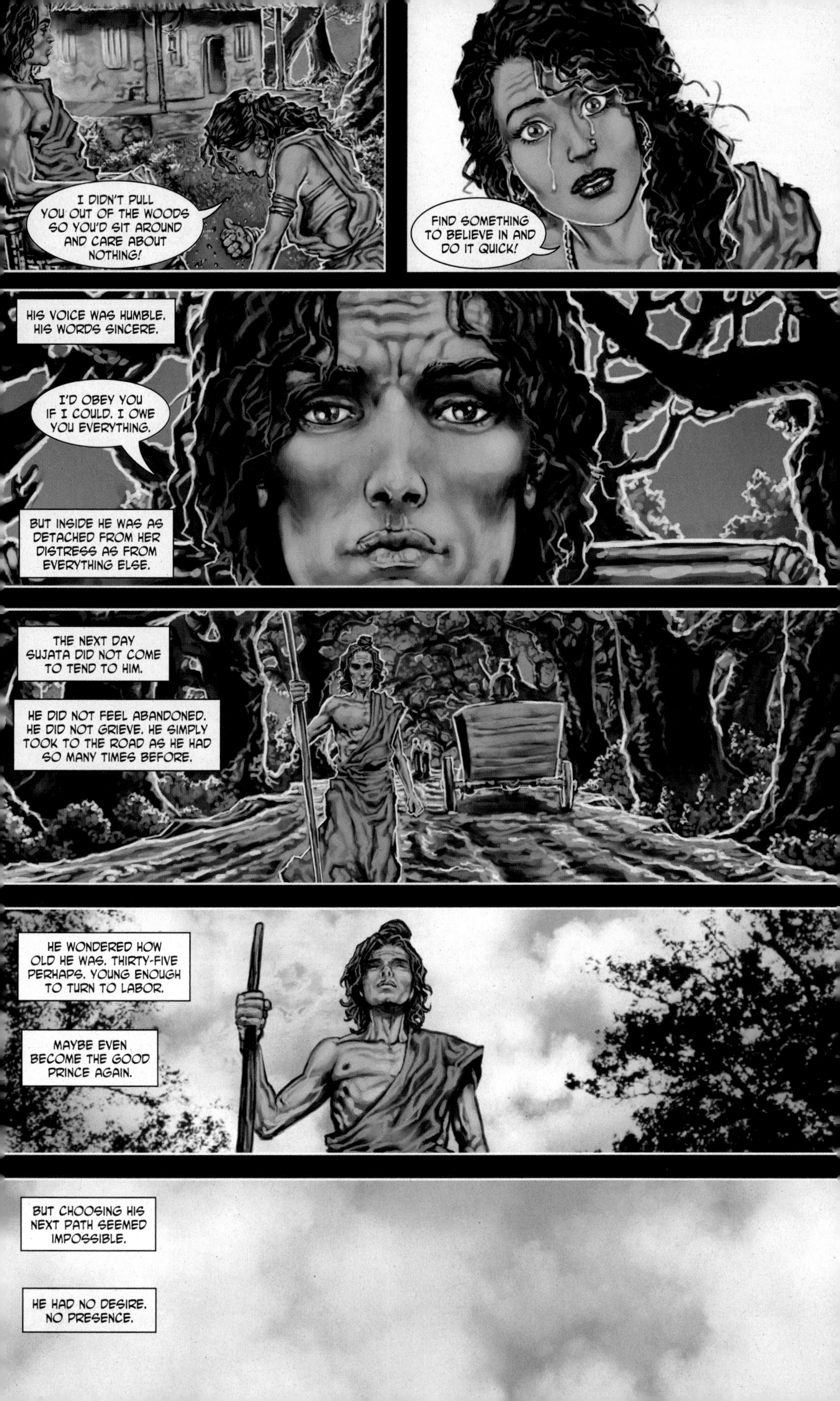
I DIDN'T PULL YOU OUT OF THE WOODS SO YOU'D SIT AROUND AND CARE ABOUT NOTHING!
FIND SOMETHING TO BELIEVE IN AND DO IT QUICK!
HIS VOICE WAS HUMBLE. HIS WORDS SINCERE.
I'D OBEY YOU IF I COULD. I OWE YOU EVERYTHING.
BUT INSIDE HE WAS AS DETACHED FROM HER DISTRESS AS FROM EVERYTHING ELSE.
THE NEXT DAY SUJATA DID NOT COME TO TEND TO HIM.
HE DID NOT FEEL ABANDONED. HE DID NOT GRIEVE. HE SIMPLY TOOK TO THE ROAD AS HE HAD SO MANY TIMES BEFORE.
HE WONDERED HOW OLD HE WAS. THIRTY-FIVE PERHAPS. YOUNG ENOUGH TO TURN TO LABOR.
MAYBE EVEN BECOME THE GOOD PRINCE AGAIN.
BUT CHOOSING HIS NEXT PATH SEEMED IMPOSSIBLE.
HE HAD NO DESIRE. NO PRESENCE.

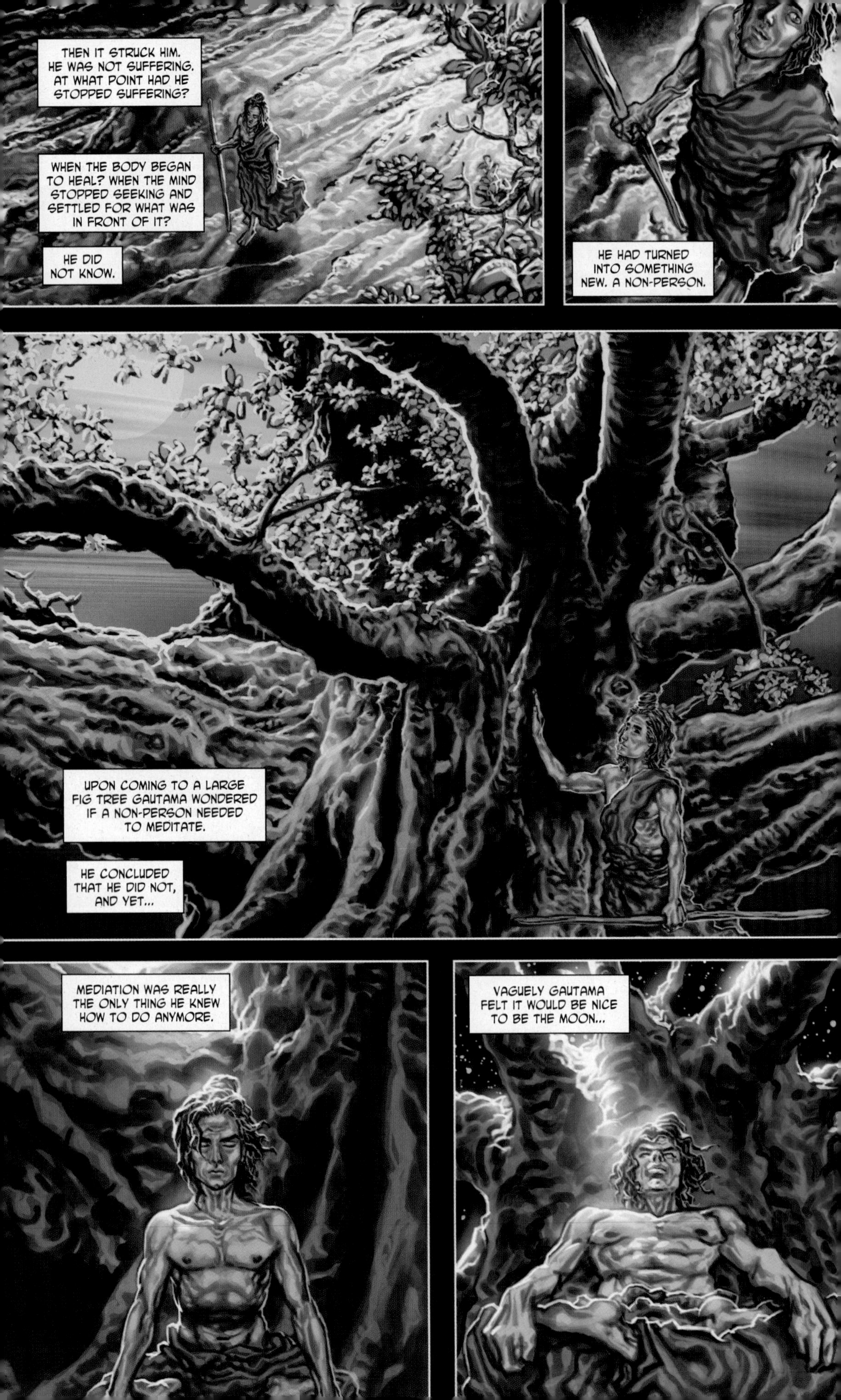
THEN IT STRUCK HIM. HE WAS NOT SUFFERING. AT WHAT POINT HAD HE STOPPED SUFFERING?
WHEN THE BODY BEGAN TO HEAL? WHEN THE MIND STOPPED SEEKING AND SETTLED FOR WHAT WAS IN FRONT OF IT?
HE DID NOT KNOW.
HE HAD TURNED INTO SOMETHING NEW. A NON-PERSON.
UPON COMING TO A LARGE FIG TREE GAUTAMA WONDERED IF A NON-PERSON NEEDED TO MEDITATE.
HE CONCLUDED THAT HE DID NOT, AND YET...
MEDIATION WAS REALLY THE ONLY THING HE KNEW HOW TO DO ANYMORE.
VAGUELY GAUTAMA FELT IT WOULD BE NICE TO BE THE MOON...

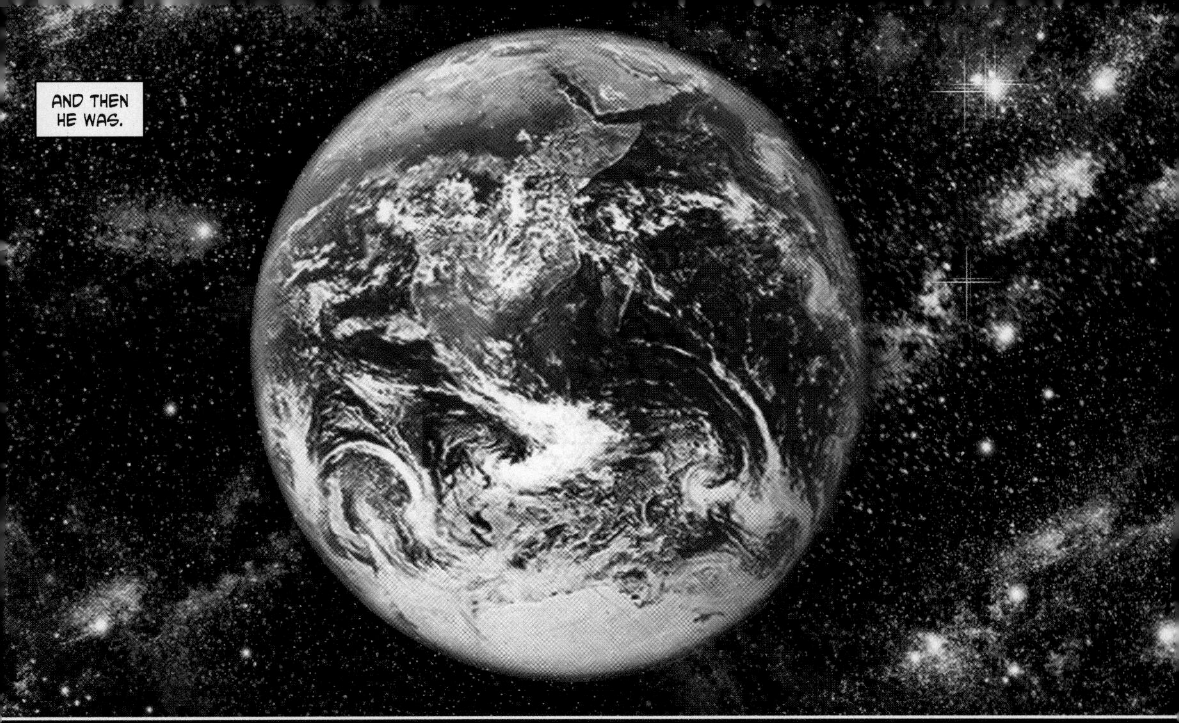
AND THEN HE WAS.

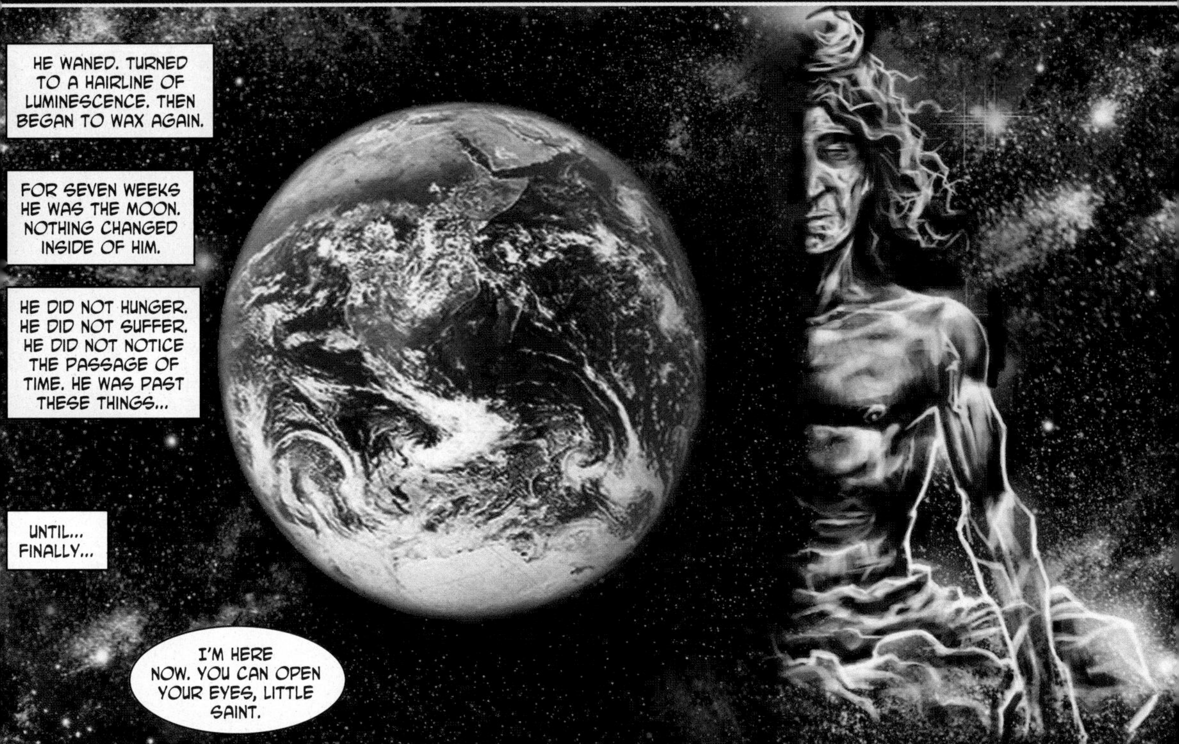
HE WANED. TURNED TO A HAIRLINE OF LUMINESCENCE. THEN BEGAN TO WAX AGAIN.
FOR SEVEN WEEKS HE WAS THE MOON. NOTHING CHANGED INSIDE OF HIM.
HE DID NOT HUNGER. HE DID NOT SUFFER. HE DID NOT NOTICE THE PASSAGE OF TIME. HE WAS PAST THESE THINGS...
UNTIL... FINALLY...
I'M HERE NOW. YOU CAN OPEN YOUR EYES, LITTLE SAINT.

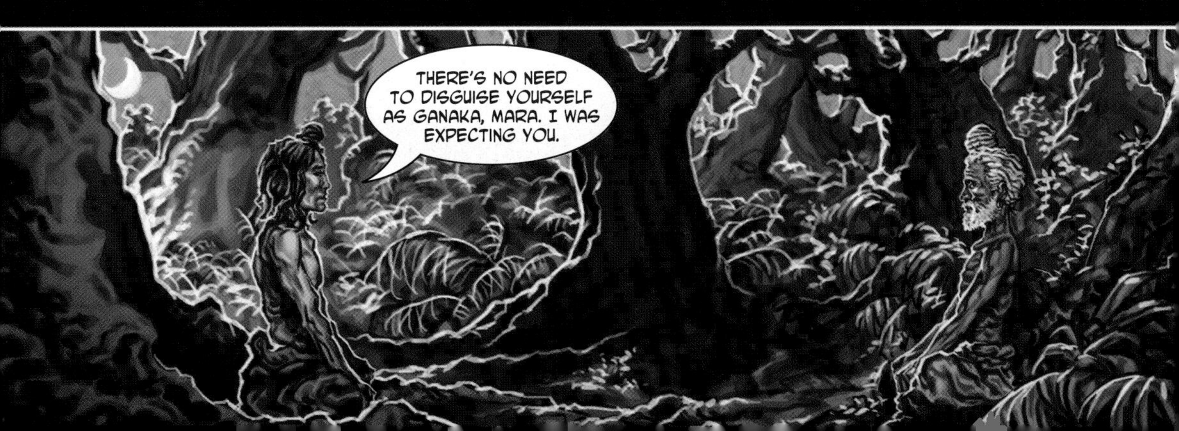
THERE'S NO NEED TO DISGUISE YOURSELF AS GANAKA, MARA. I WAS EXPECTING YOU.

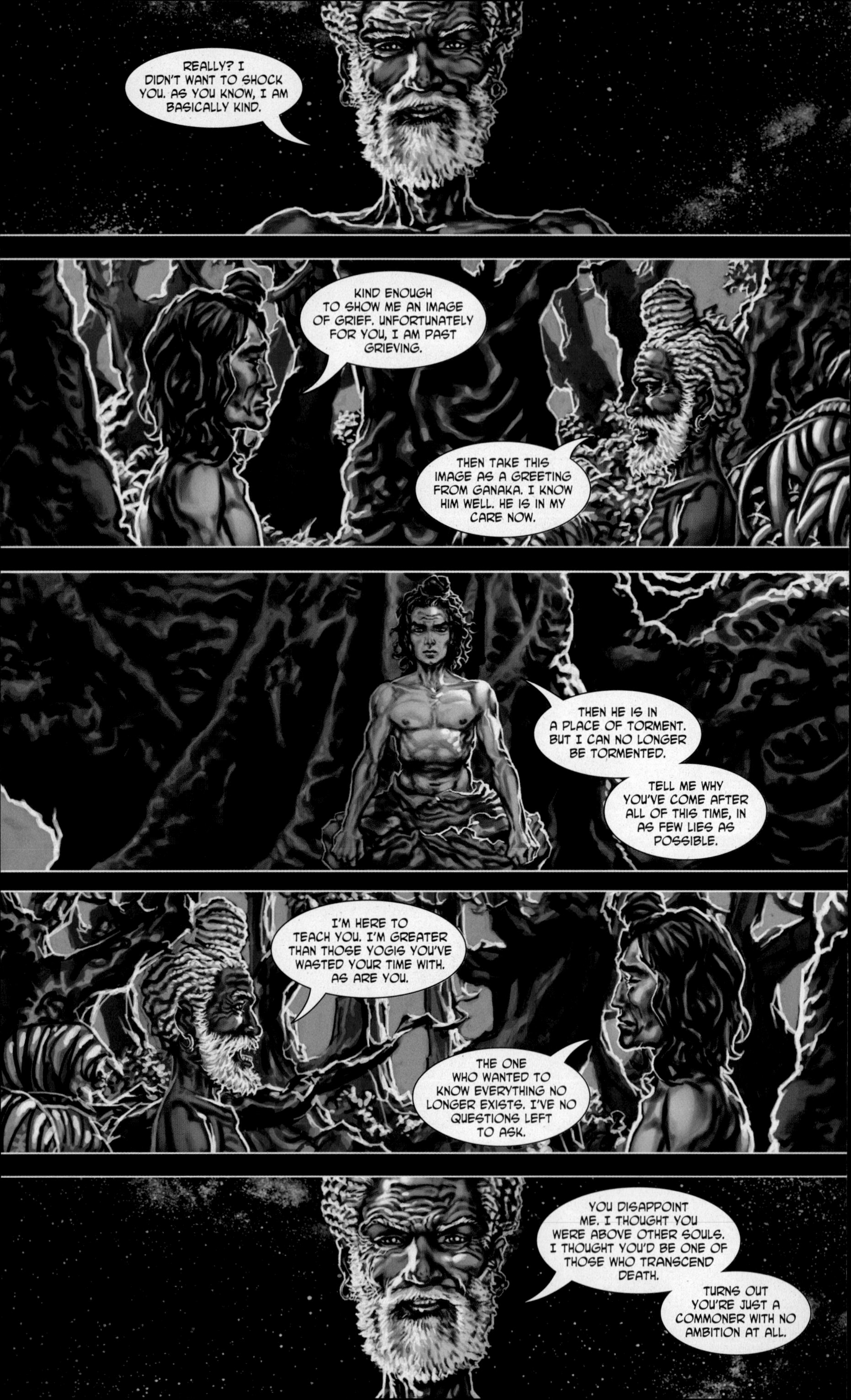
REALLY? I DIDN'T WANT TO SHOCK YOU. AS YOU KNOW, I AM BASICALLY KIND.
KIND ENOUGH TO SHOW ME AN IMAGE OF GRIEF. UNFORTUNATELY FOR YOU, I AM PAST GRIEVING.
THEN TAKE THIS IMAGE AS A GREETING FROM GANAKA. I KNOW HIM WELL. HE IS IN MY CARE NOW.
THEN HE IS IN A PLACE OF TORMENT. BUT I CAN NO LONGER BE TORMENTED.
TELL ME WHY YOU'VE COME AFTER ALL OF THIS TIME, IN AS FEW LIES AS POSSIBLE.
I'M HERE TO TEACH YOU. I'M GREATER THAN THOSE YOGIS YOU'VE WASTED YOUR TIME WITH. AS ARE YOU.
THE ONE WHO WANTED TO KNOW EVERYTHING NO LONGER EXISTS. I'VE NO QUESTIONS LEFT TO ASK.
YOU DISAPPOINT ME. I THOUGHT YOU WERE ABOVE OTHER SOULS. I THOUGHT YOU'D BE ONE OF THOSE WHO TRANSCEND DEATH.
TURNS OUT YOU'RE JUST A COMMONER WITH NO AMBITION AT ALL.

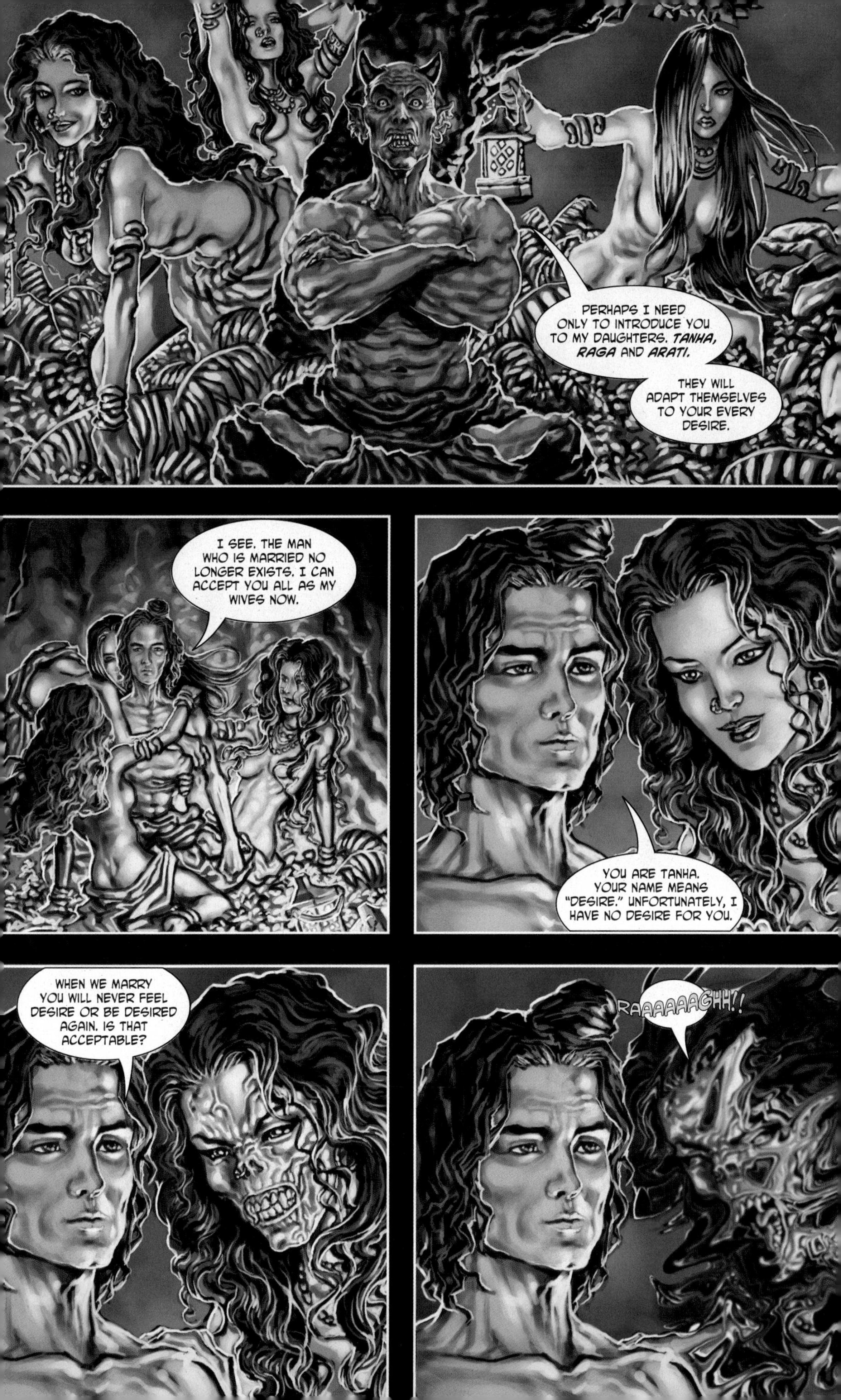
PERHAPS I NEED ONLY TO INTRODUCE YOU TO MY DAUGHTERS. *TANHA, RAGA* AND *ARATI.*
THEY WILL ADAPT THEMSELVES TO YOUR EVERY DESIRE.
I SEE. THE MAN WHO IS MARRIED NO LONGER EXISTS. I CAN ACCEPT YOU ALL AS MY WIVES NOW.
YOU ARE TANHA. YOUR NAME MEANS "DESIRE." UNFORTUNATELY, I HAVE NO DESIRE FOR YOU.
WHEN WE MARRY YOU WILL NEVER FEEL DESIRE OR BE DESIRED AGAIN. IS THAT ACCEPTABLE?
RAAAAAAAGHH!!

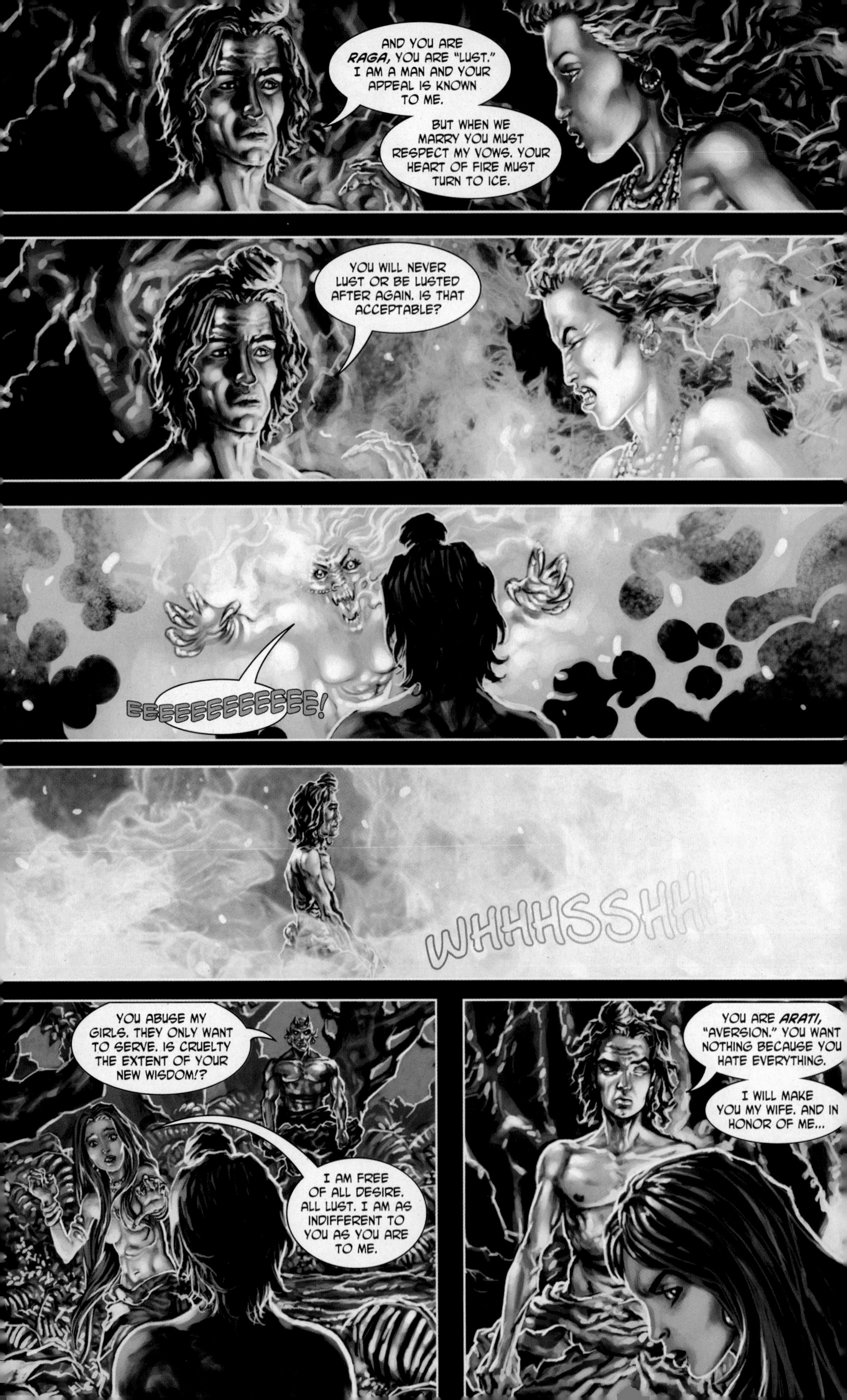
AND YOU ARE RAGA, YOU ARE "LUST." I AM A MAN AND YOUR APPEAL IS KNOWN TO ME.
BUT WHEN WE MARRY YOU MUST RESPECT MY VOWS. YOUR HEART OF FIRE MUST TURN TO ICE.
YOU WILL NEVER LUST OR BE LUSTED AFTER AGAIN. IS THAT ACCEPTABLE?
EEEEEEEEEEEEE!
WHHHSSHH
YOU ABUSE MY GIRLS. THEY ONLY WANT TO SERVE. IS CRUELTY THE EXTENT OF YOUR NEW WISDOM!?
I AM FREE OF ALL DESIRE. ALL LUST. I AM AS INDIFFERENT TO YOU AS YOU ARE TO ME.
YOU ARE ARATI, "AVERSION." YOU WANT NOTHING BECAUSE YOU HATE EVERYTHING.
I WILL MAKE YOU MY WIFE. AND IN HONOR OF ME...

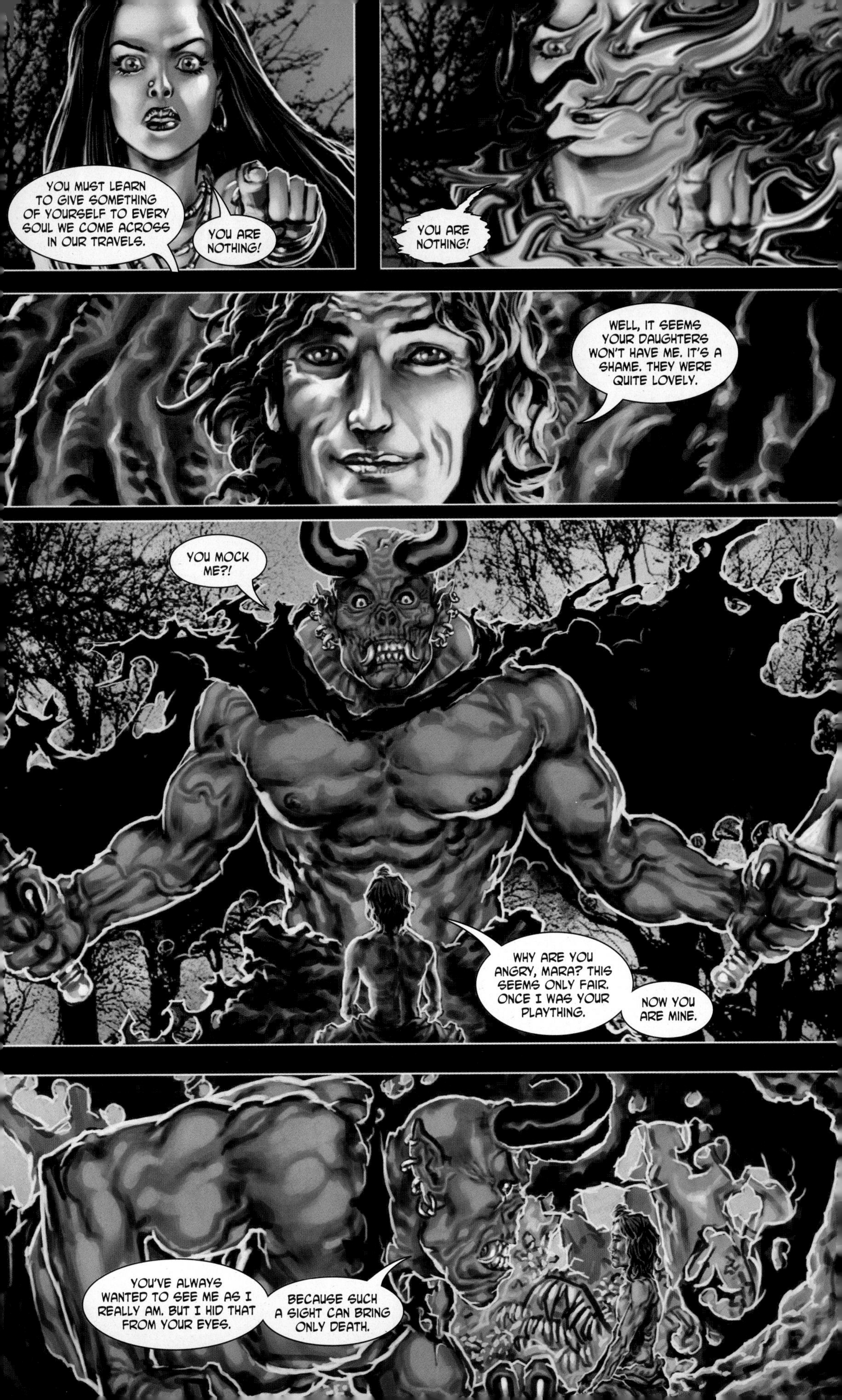

YOU MUST LEARN TO GIVE SOMETHING OF YOURSELF TO EVERY SOUL WE COME ACROSS IN OUR TRAVELS.
YOU ARE NOTHING!
YOU ARE NOTHING!
WELL, IT SEEMS YOUR DAUGHTERS WON'T HAVE ME. IT'S A SHAME. THEY WERE QUITE LOVELY.
YOU MOCK ME?!
WHY ARE YOU ANGRY, MARA? THIS SEEMS ONLY FAIR. ONCE I WAS YOUR PLAYTHING.
NOW YOU ARE MINE.
YOU'VE ALWAYS WANTED TO SEE ME AS I REALLY AM. BUT I HID THAT FROM YOUR EYES.
BECAUSE SUCH A SIGHT CAN BRING ONLY DEATH.

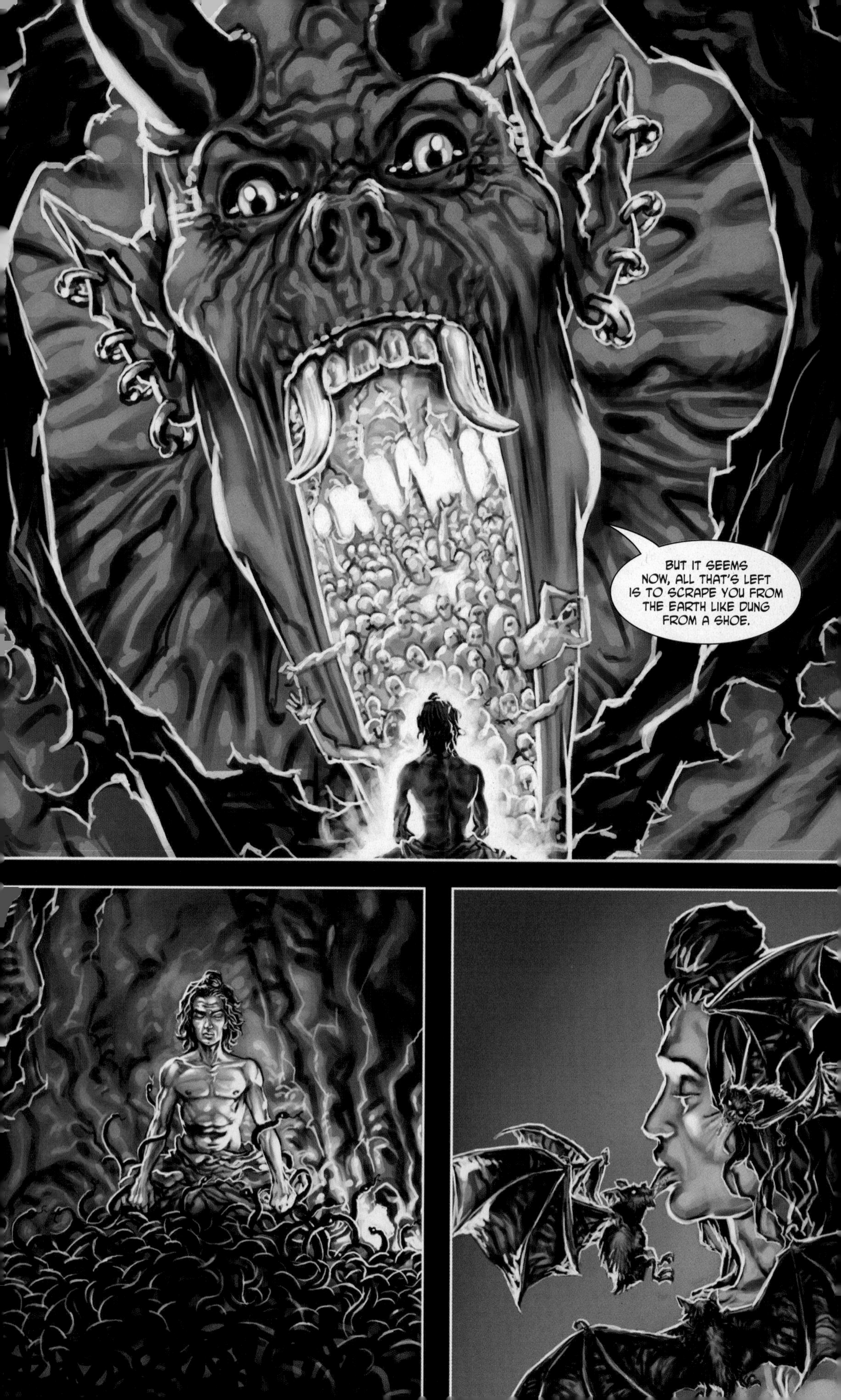
BUT IT SEEMS NOW, ALL THAT'S LEFT IS TO SCRAPE YOU FROM THE EARTH LIKE DUNG FROM A SHOE.

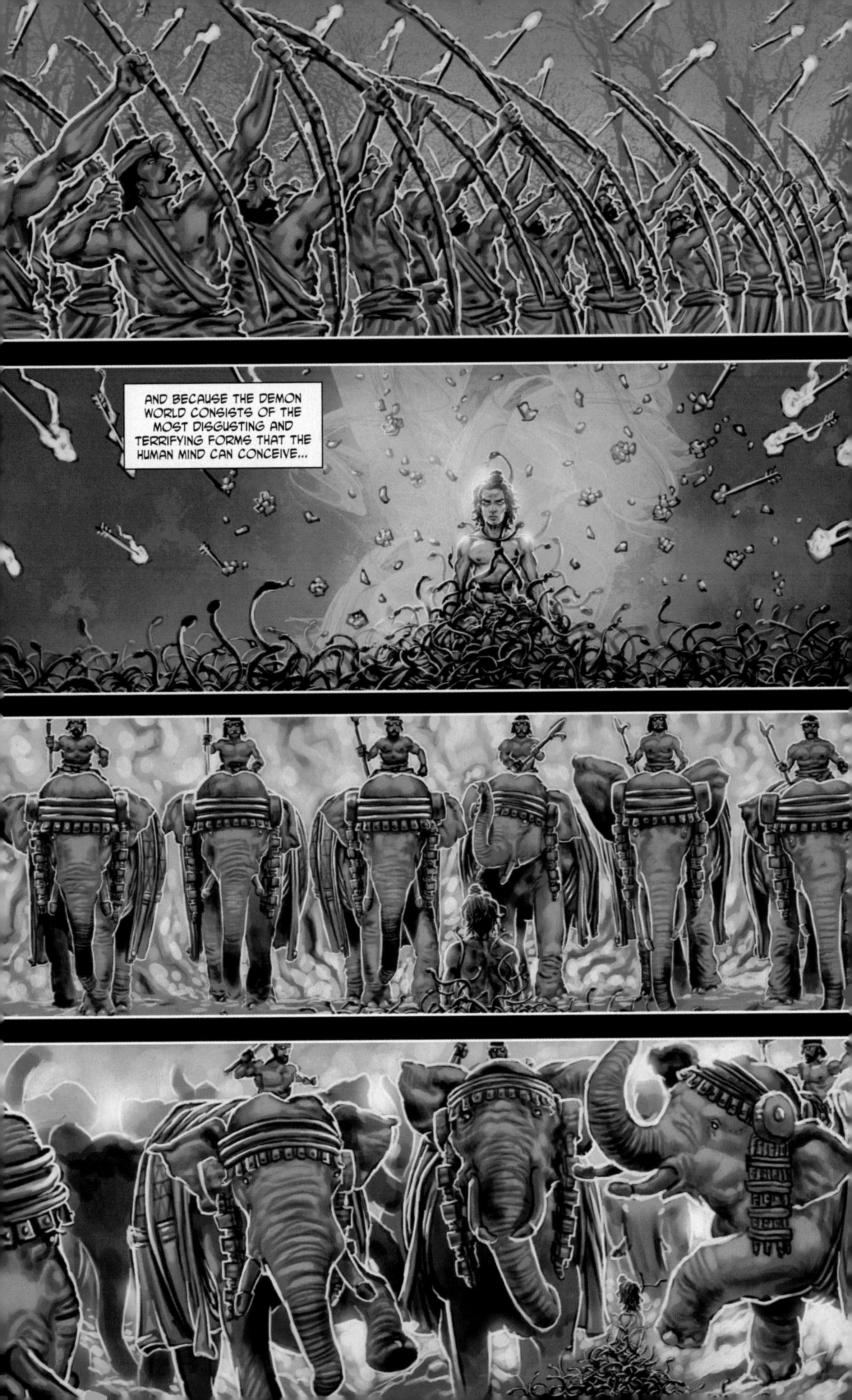
AND BECAUSE THE DEMON WORLD CONSISTS OF THE MOST DISGUSTING AND TERRIFYING FORMS THAT THE HUMAN MIND CAN CONCEIVE...

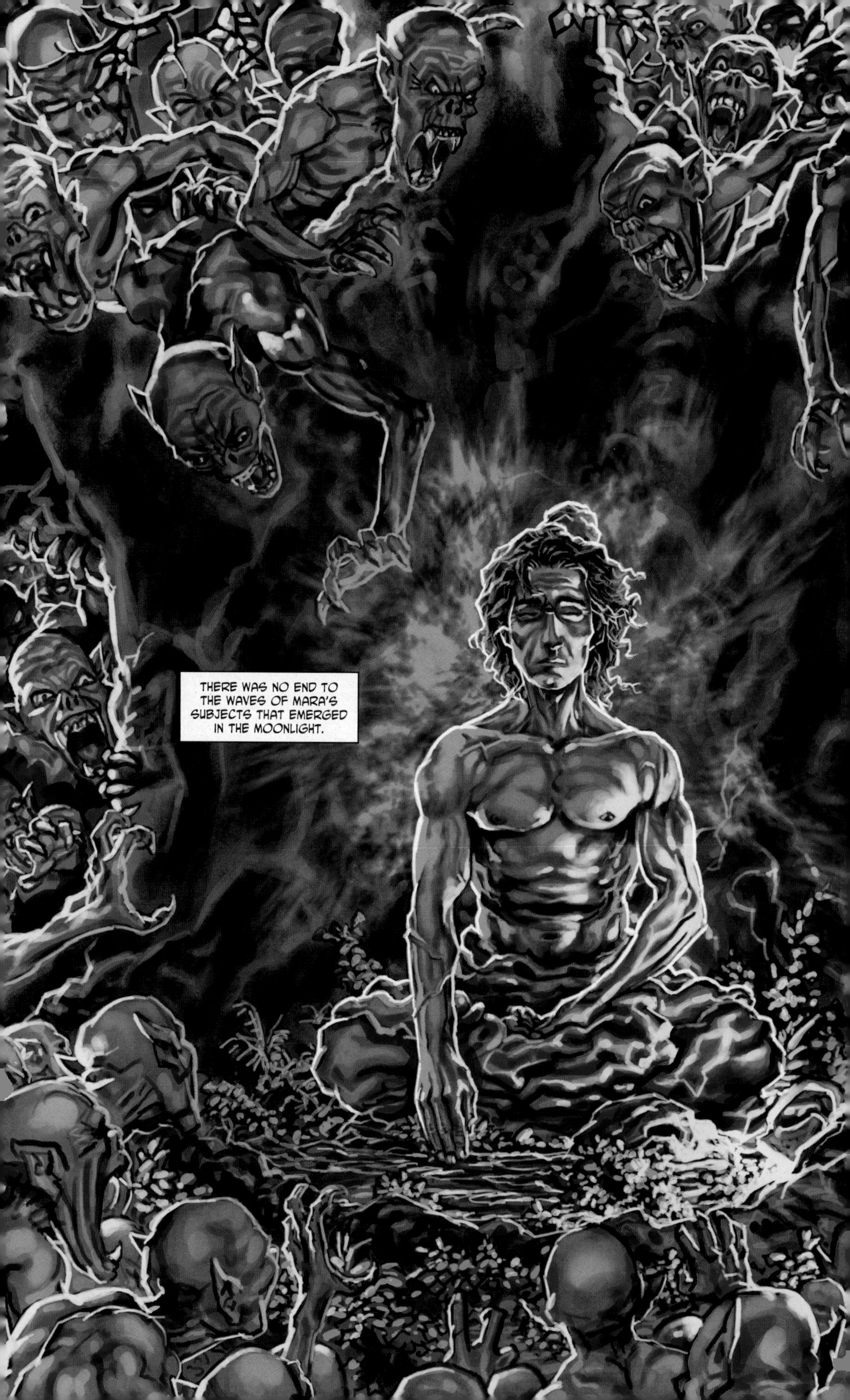
THERE WAS NO END TO THE WAVES OF MARA'S SUBJECTS THAT EMERGED IN THE MOONLIGHT.

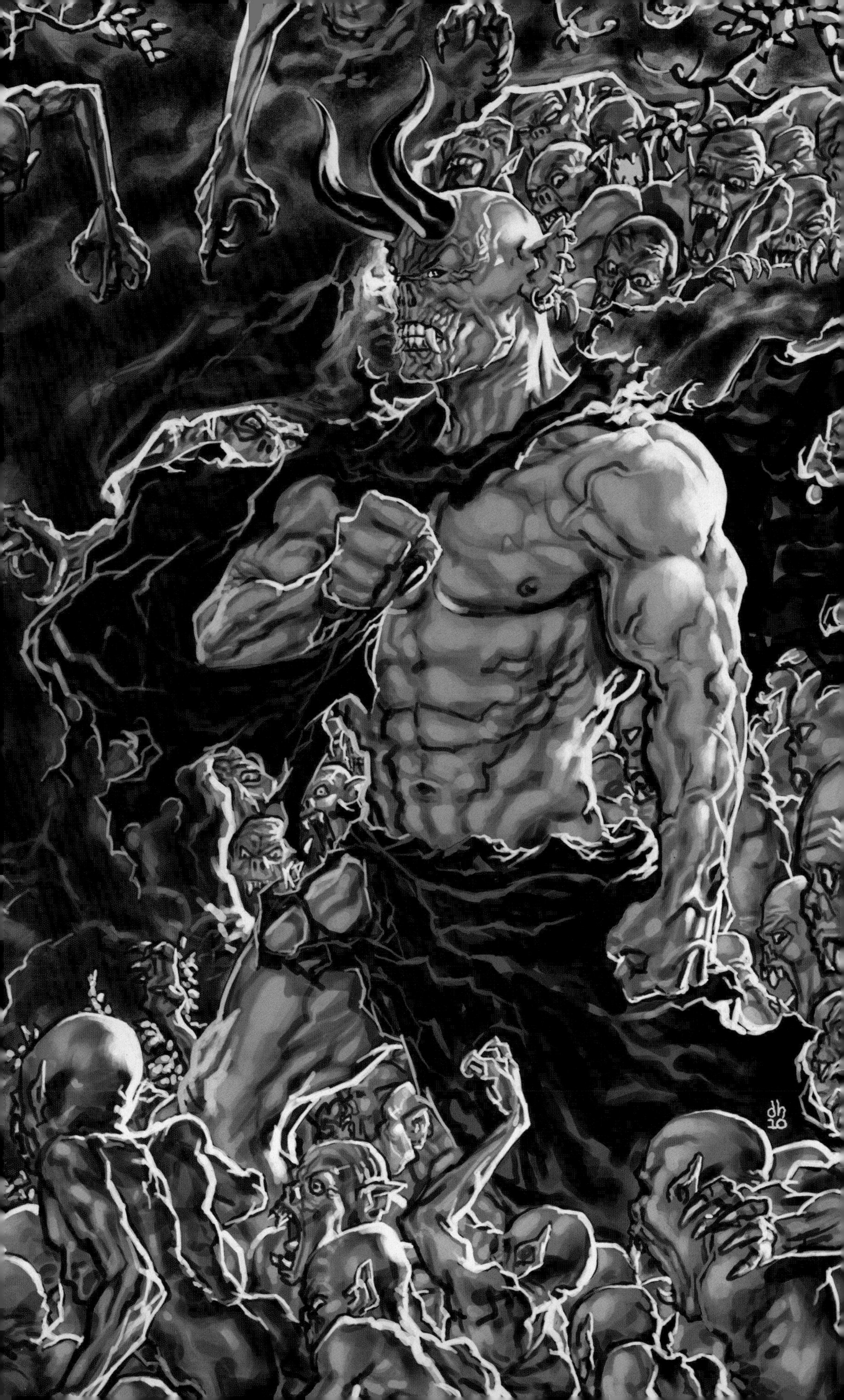

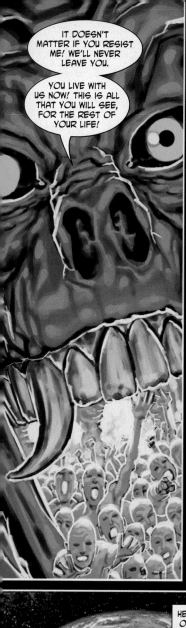

IT DOESN'T MATTER IF YOU RESIST ME! WE'LL NEVER LEAVE YOU.

YOU LIVE WITH US NOW! THIS IS ALL THAT YOU WILL SEE, FOR THE REST OF YOUR LIFE!

I'M NOT RESISTING. YOU ARE ALL WELCOME TO STAY. YOU ARE HERE. I AM NOT.

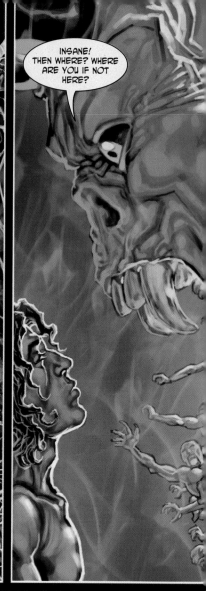

INSANE! THEN WHERE? WHERE ARE YOU IF NOT HERE?

HE FELT THE LAST VEIL OF THE ILLUSION FALL AWAY FROM HIS MIND.

ON THE OTHER SIDE WAS COOL SERENITY. CONCERN FOR NOTHING. THE JOY OF SIMPLY BEING.

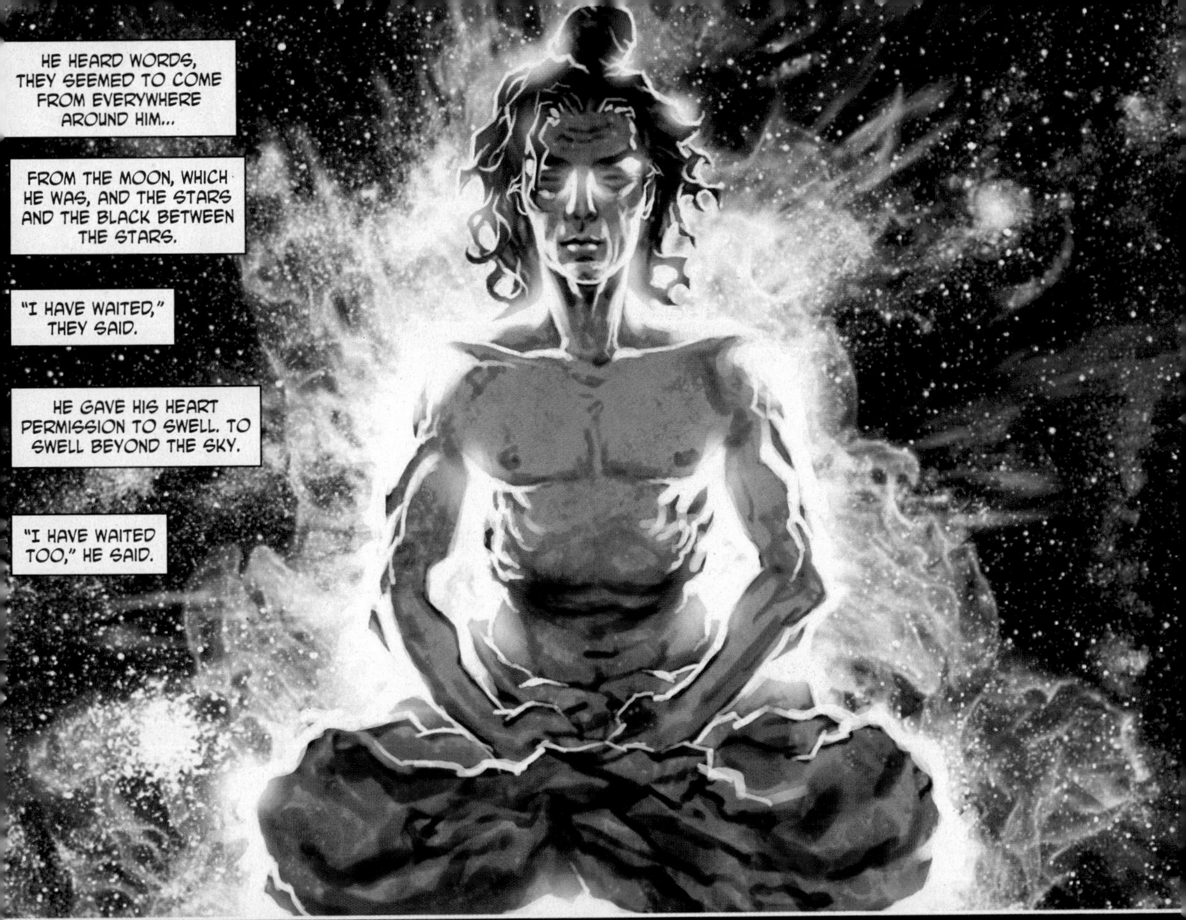
HE HEARD WORDS, THEY SEEMED TO COME FROM EVERYWHERE AROUND HIM...
FROM THE MOON, WHICH HE WAS, AND THE STARS AND THE BLACK BETWEEN THE STARS.
"I HAVE WAITED," THEY SAID.
HE GAVE HIS HEART PERMISSION TO SWELL. TO SWELL BEYOND THE SKY.
"I HAVE WAITED TOO," HE SAID.

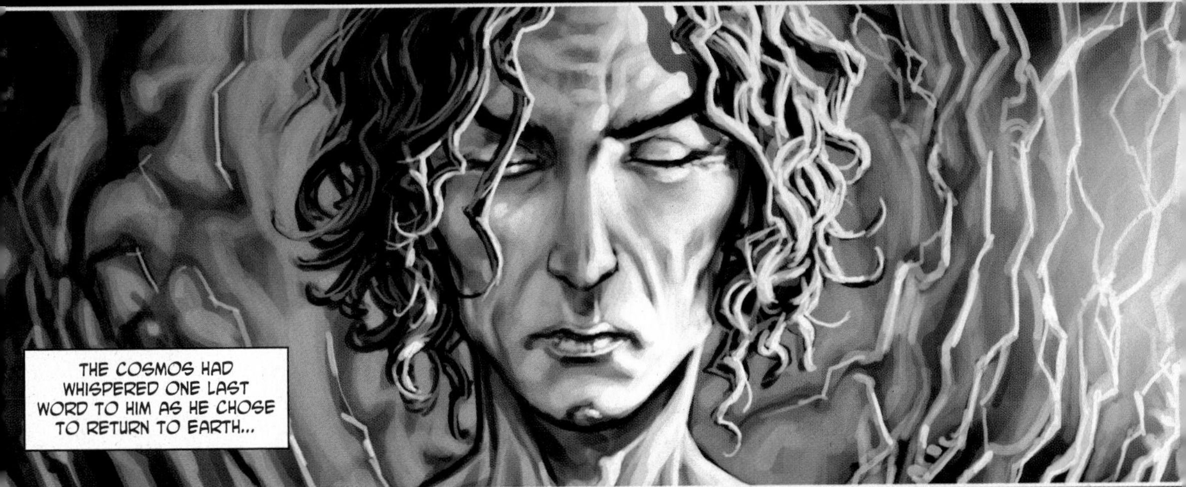
THE COSMOS HAD WHISPERED ONE LAST WORD TO HIM AS HE CHOSE TO RETURN TO EARTH...

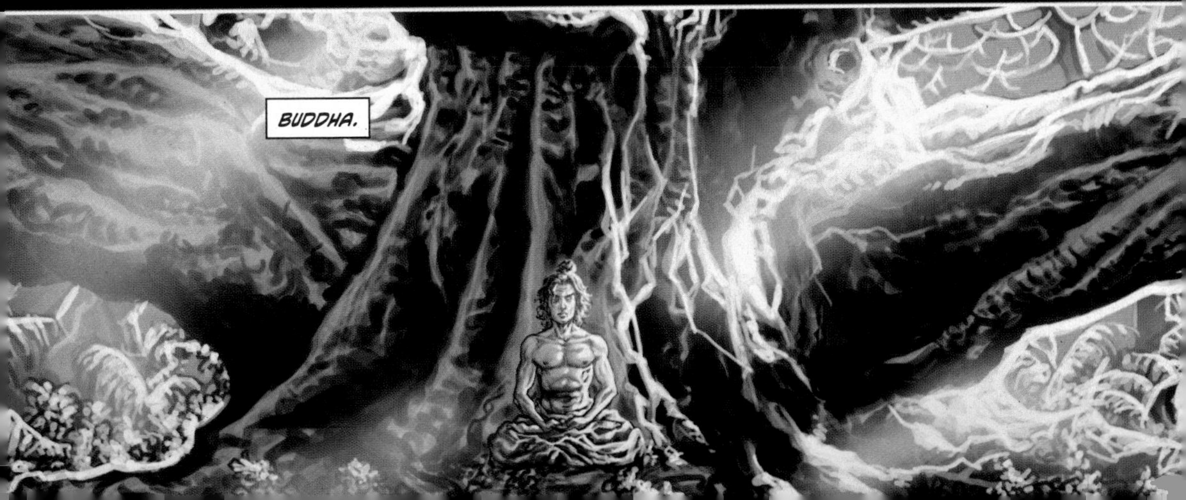
BUDDHA.

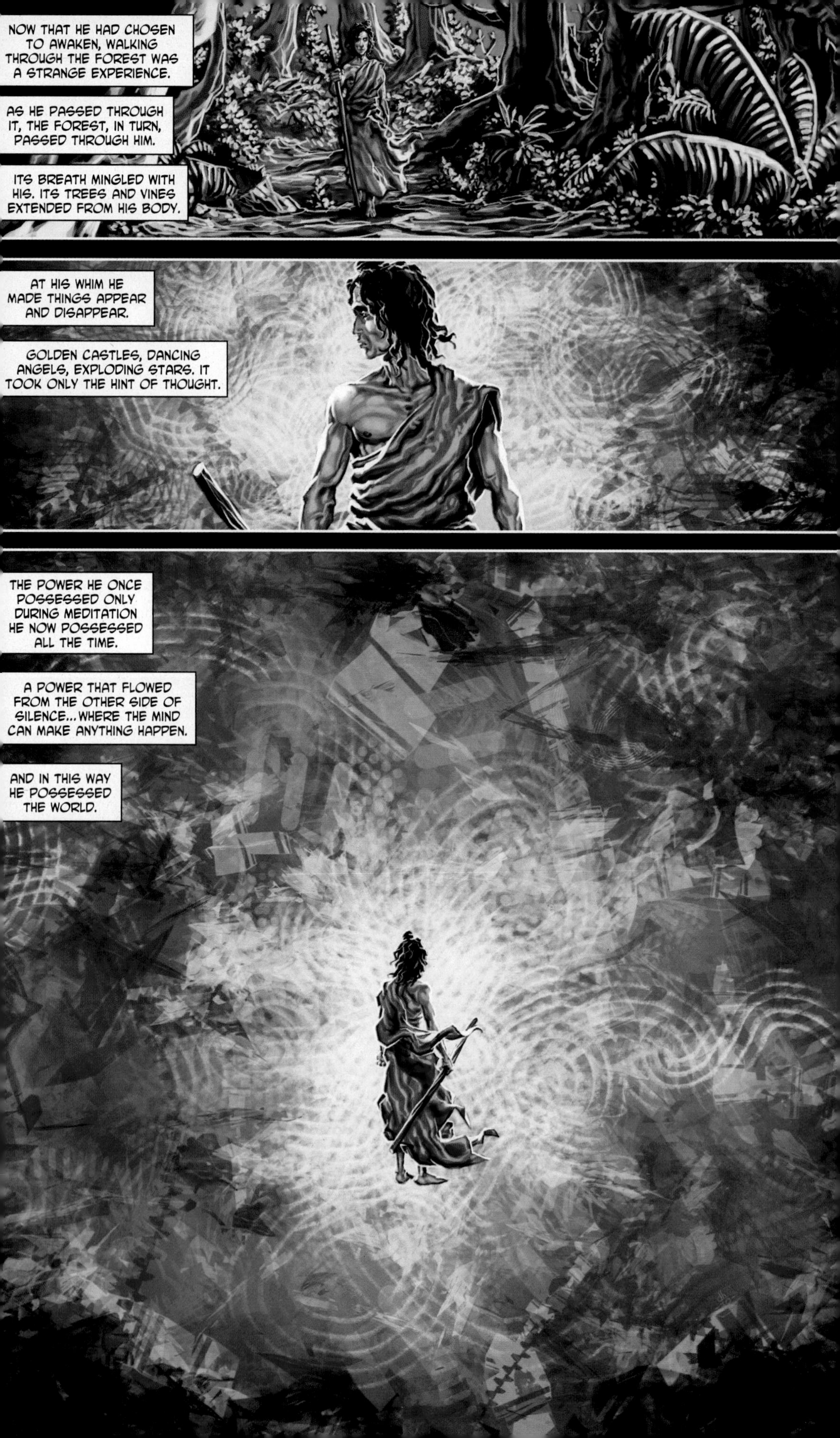
NOW THAT HE HAD CHOSEN TO AWAKEN, WALKING THROUGH THE FOREST WAS A STRANGE EXPERIENCE.
AS HE PASSED THROUGH IT, THE FOREST, IN TURN, PASSED THROUGH HIM.
ITS BREATH MINGLED WITH HIS. ITS TREES AND VINES EXTENDED FROM HIS BODY.
AT HIS WHIM HE MADE THINGS APPEAR AND DISAPPEAR.
GOLDEN CASTLES, DANCING ANGELS, EXPLODING STARS. IT TOOK ONLY THE HINT OF THOUGHT.
THE POWER HE ONCE POSSESSED ONLY DURING MEDITATION HE NOW POSSESSED ALL THE TIME.
A POWER THAT FLOWED FROM THE OTHER SIDE OF SILENCE...WHERE THE MIND CAN MAKE ANYTHING HAPPEN.
AND IN THIS WAY HE POSSESSED THE WORLD.

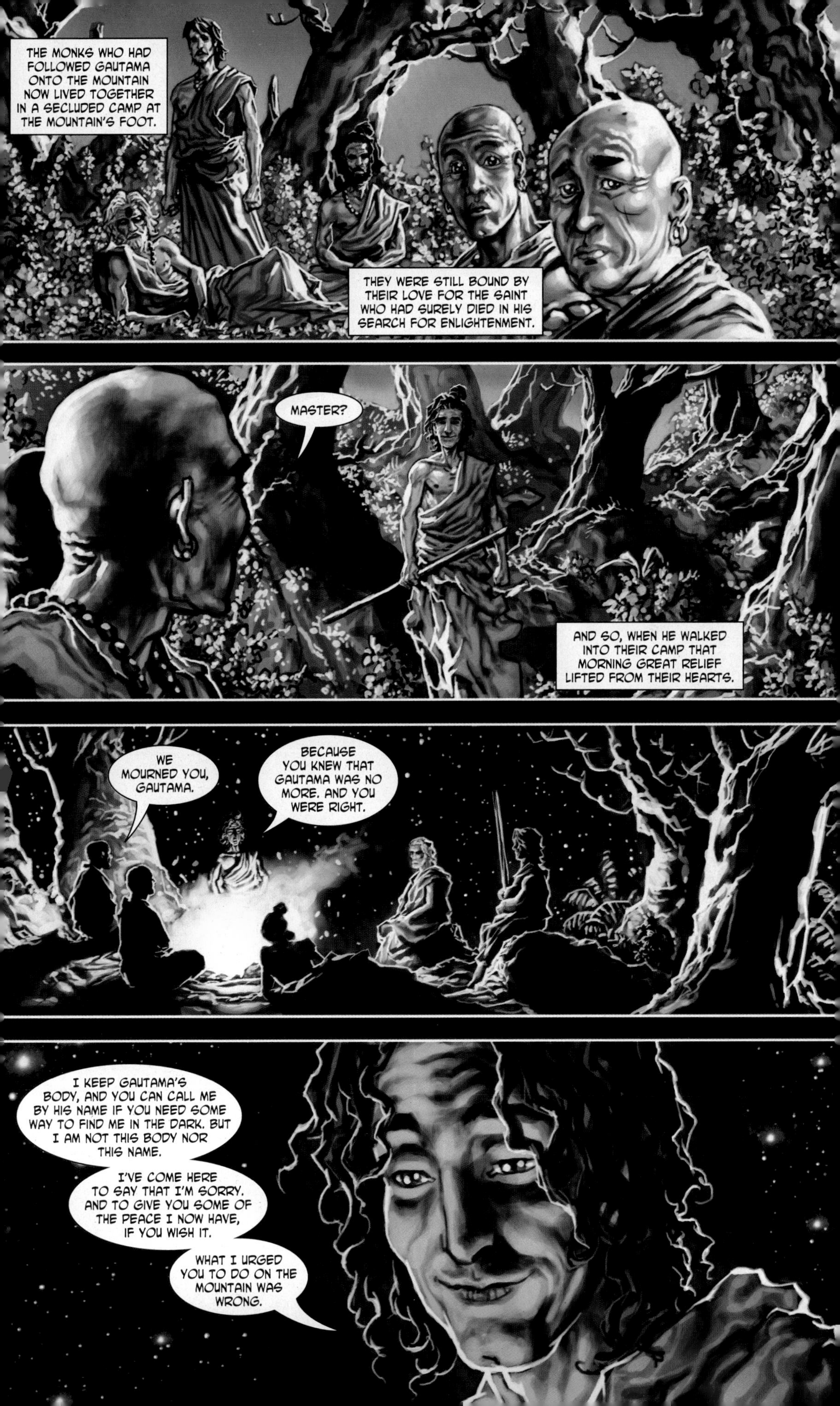
THE MONKS WHO HAD FOLLOWED GAUTAMA ONTO THE MOUNTAIN NOW LIVED TOGETHER IN A SECLUDED CAMP AT THE MOUNTAIN'S FOOT.
THEY WERE STILL BOUND BY THEIR LOVE FOR THE SAINT WHO HAD SURELY DIED IN HIS SEARCH FOR ENLIGHTENMENT.
MASTER?
AND SO, WHEN HE WALKED INTO THEIR CAMP THAT MORNING GREAT RELIEF LIFTED FROM THEIR HEARTS.
WE MOURNED YOU, GAUTAMA.
BECAUSE YOU KNEW THAT GAUTAMA WAS NO MORE. AND YOU WERE RIGHT.
I KEEP GAUTAMA'S BODY, AND YOU CAN CALL ME BY HIS NAME IF YOU NEED SOME WAY TO FIND ME IN THE DARK. BUT I AM NOT THIS BODY NOR THIS NAME.
I'VE COME HERE TO SAY THAT I'M SORRY. AND TO GIVE YOU SOME OF THE PEACE I NOW HAVE, IF YOU WISH IT.
WHAT I URGED YOU TO DO ON THE MOUNTAIN WAS WRONG.

YOU OWE US NOTHING.

I'M NOT SPEAKING OF DEBT. DEBTS END WHEN KARMA ENDS. AND I AM NO LONGER ON THAT WHEEL.

BUT I WAS IN A WAR AGAINST DESIRE. I DESPISED THE WORLD AND MY OWN BODY FOR ITS CRAVINGS, AND I FORCED THIS ONTO YOU.

SURELY THAT'S NOT A MISTAKE. OTHERWISE IT WOULD BE POINTLESS TO TAKE UP THE HOLY LIFE.

HOLINESS IS FOR THE EGO. TO BE HOLY IS TO WANT TO BE DIFFERENT. TO WANT TO BE SAFE. TO WANT TO HAVE HOPE. THESE THINGS ARE TRAPS.

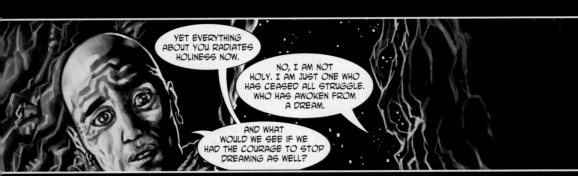

YET EVERYTHING ABOUT YOU RADIATES HOLINESS NOW.

NO, I AM NOT HOLY. I AM JUST ONE WHO HAS CEASED ALL STRUGGLE. WHO HAS AWOKEN FROM A DREAM.

AND WHAT WOULD WE SEE IF WE HAD THE COURAGE TO STOP DREAMING AS WELL?

DEATH.

YOURS, MINE... EVERYONE'S.

WHEN DEATH AND LOSS NO LONGER HAVE MEANING. WHEN YOU ARE NOT AFRAID OF LETTING GO. THEN YOU'LL BE FREE.

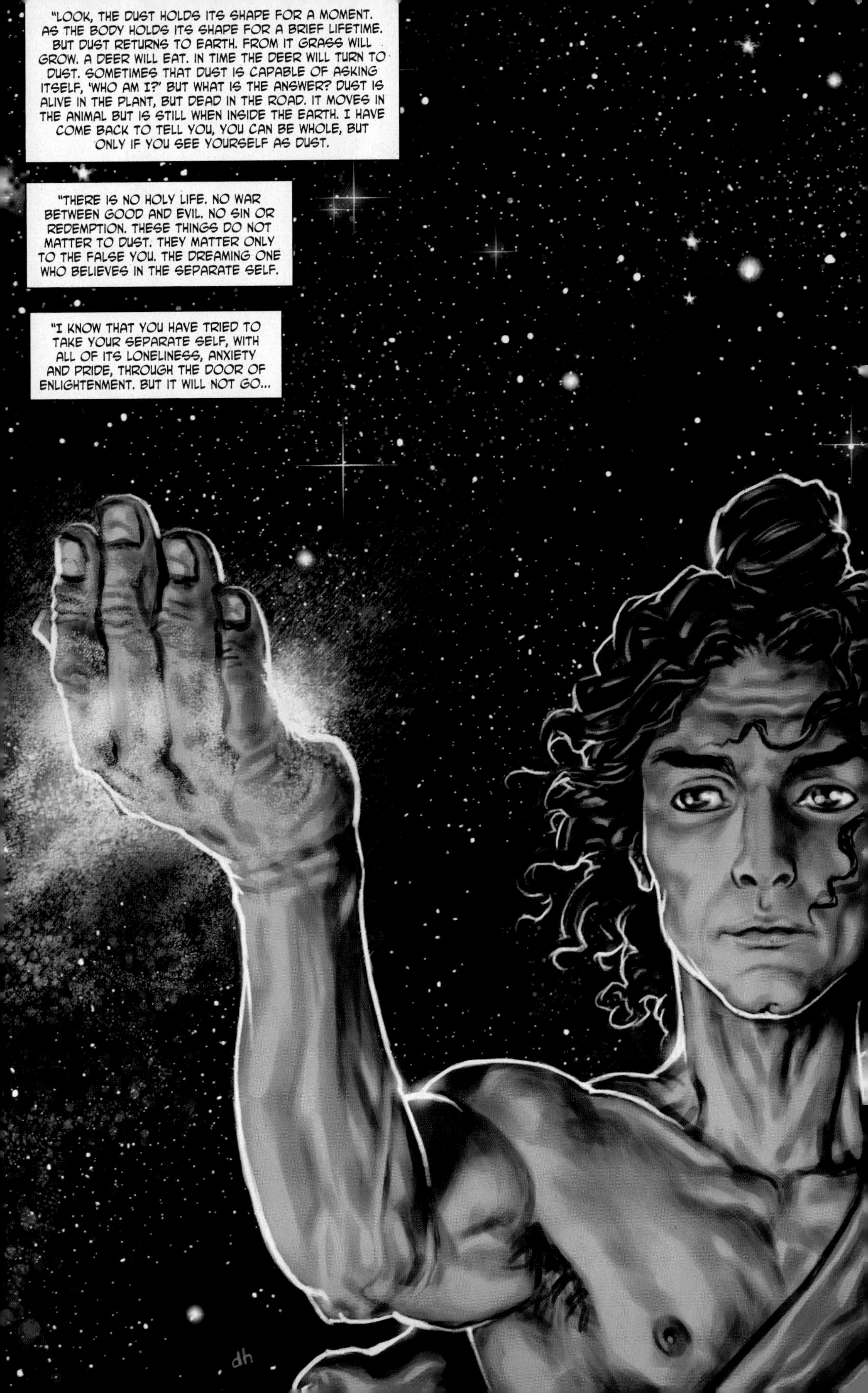
"LOOK, THE DUST HOLDS ITS SHAPE FOR A MOMENT. AS THE BODY HOLDS ITS SHAPE FOR A BRIEF LIFETIME. BUT DUST RETURNS TO EARTH. FROM IT GRASS WILL GROW. A DEER WILL EAT. IN TIME THE DEER WILL TURN TO DUST. SOMETIMES THAT DUST IS CAPABLE OF ASKING ITSELF, 'WHO AM I?' BUT WHAT IS THE ANSWER? DUST IS ALIVE IN THE PLANT, BUT DEAD IN THE ROAD. IT MOVES IN THE ANIMAL BUT IS STILL WHEN INSIDE THE EARTH. I HAVE COME BACK TO TELL YOU, YOU CAN BE WHOLE, BUT ONLY IF YOU SEE YOURSELF AS DUST.
"THERE IS NO HOLY LIFE. NO WAR BETWEEN GOOD AND EVIL. NO SIN OR REDEMPTION. THESE THINGS DO NOT MATTER TO DUST. THEY MATTER ONLY TO THE FALSE YOU. THE DREAMING ONE WHO BELIEVES IN THE SEPARATE SELF.
"I KNOW THAT YOU HAVE TRIED TO TAKE YOUR SEPARATE SELF, WITH ALL OF ITS LONELINESS, ANXIETY AND PRIDE, THROUGH THE DOOR OF ENLIGHTENMENT. BUT IT WILL NOT GO...
dh

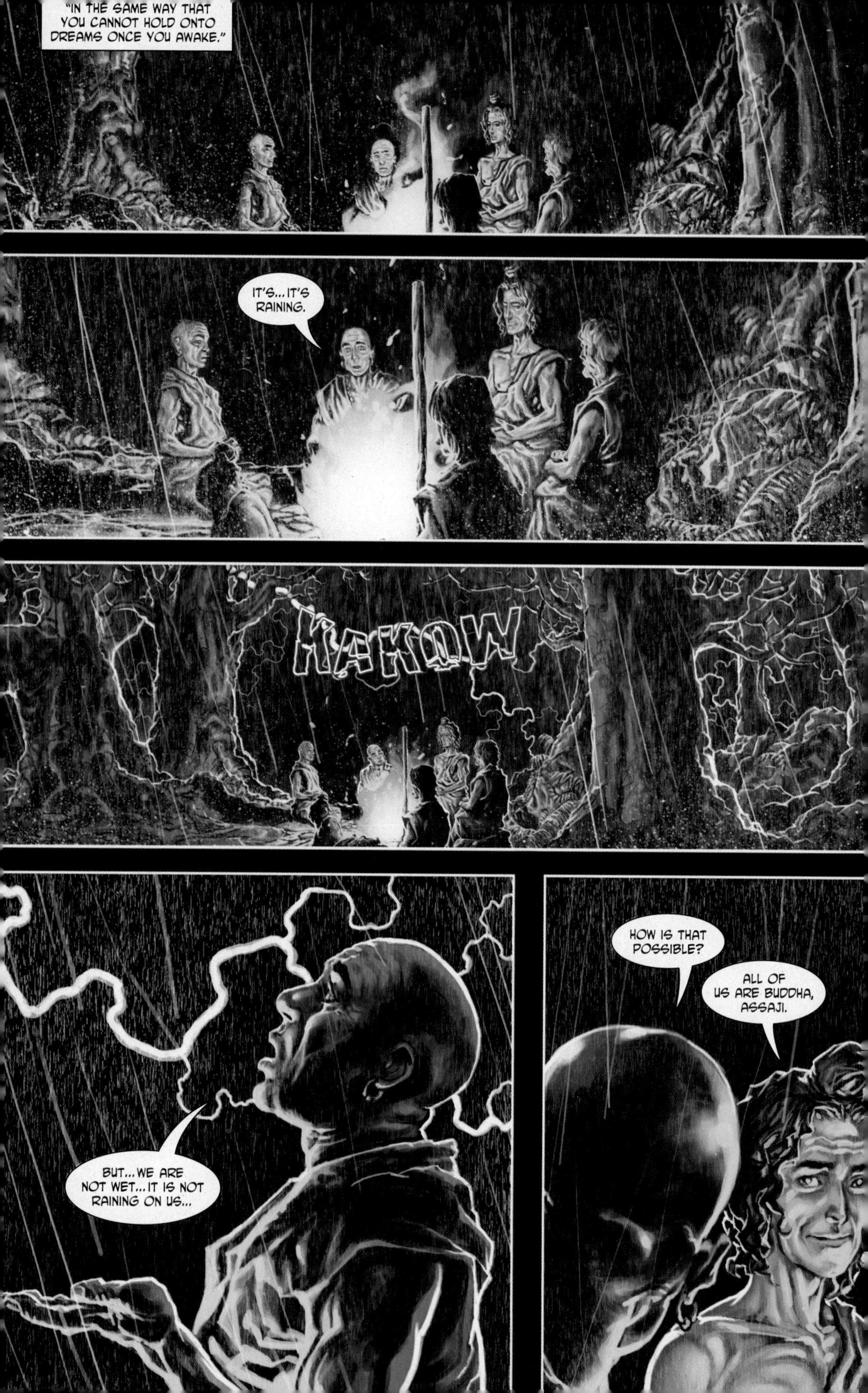
"IN THE SAME WAY THAT YOU CANNOT HOLD ONTO DREAMS ONCE YOU AWAKE."
IT'S... IT'S RAINING.
KAKOW
BUT... WE ARE NOT WET... IT IS NOT RAINING ON US...
HOW IS THAT POSSIBLE?
ALL OF US ARE BUDDHA, ASSAJI.

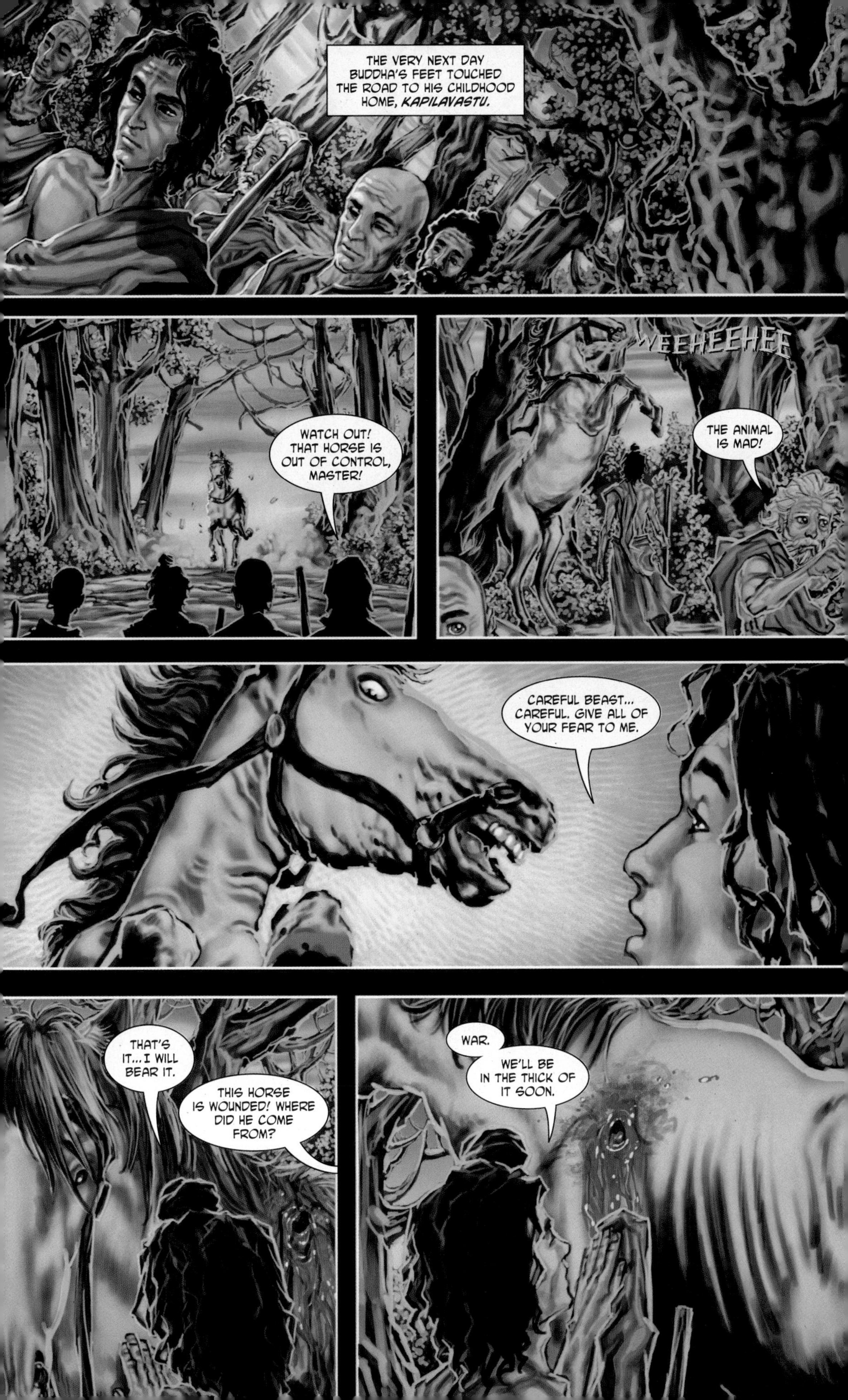
THE VERY NEXT DAY BUDDHA'S FEET TOUCHED THE ROAD TO HIS CHILDHOOD HOME, *KAPILAVASTU.*
WATCH OUT! THAT HORSE IS OUT OF CONTROL, MASTER!
WEEHEEHEE
THE ANIMAL IS MAD!
CAREFUL BEAST... CAREFUL. GIVE ALL OF YOUR FEAR TO ME.
THAT'S IT... I WILL BEAR IT.
THIS HORSE IS WOUNDED! WHERE DID HE COME FROM?
WAR.
WE'LL BE IN THE THICK OF IT SOON.

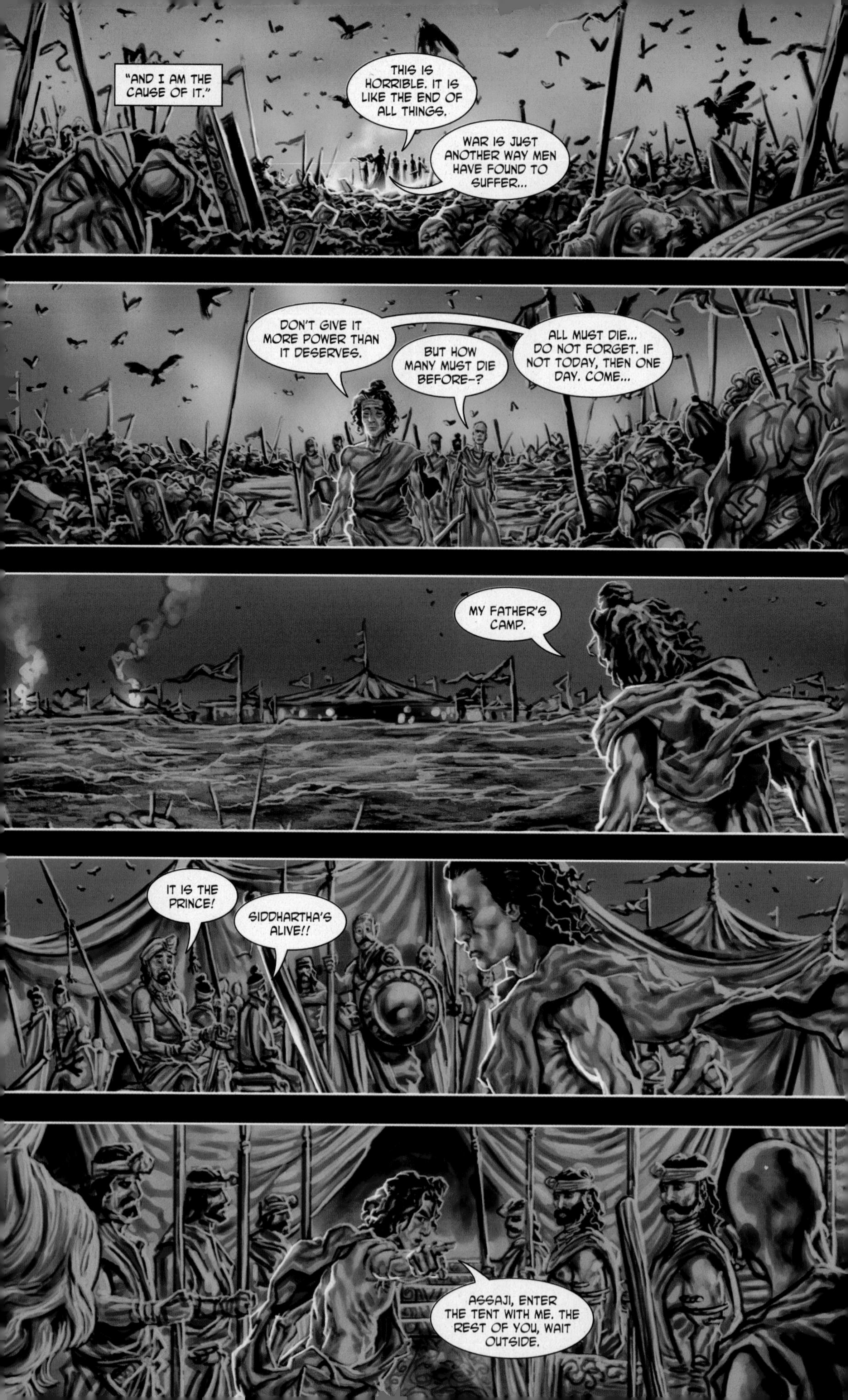
"AND I AM THE CAUSE OF IT."
THIS IS HORRIBLE. IT IS LIKE THE END OF ALL THINGS.
WAR IS JUST ANOTHER WAY MEN HAVE FOUND TO SUFFER...
DON'T GIVE IT MORE POWER THAN IT DESERVES.
BUT HOW MANY MUST DIE BEFORE–?
ALL MUST DIE... DO NOT FORGET. IF NOT TODAY, THEN ONE DAY. COME...
MY FATHER'S CAMP.
IT IS THE PRINCE!
SIDDHARTHA'S ALIVE!!
ASSAJI, ENTER THE TENT WITH ME. THE REST OF YOU, WAIT OUTSIDE.

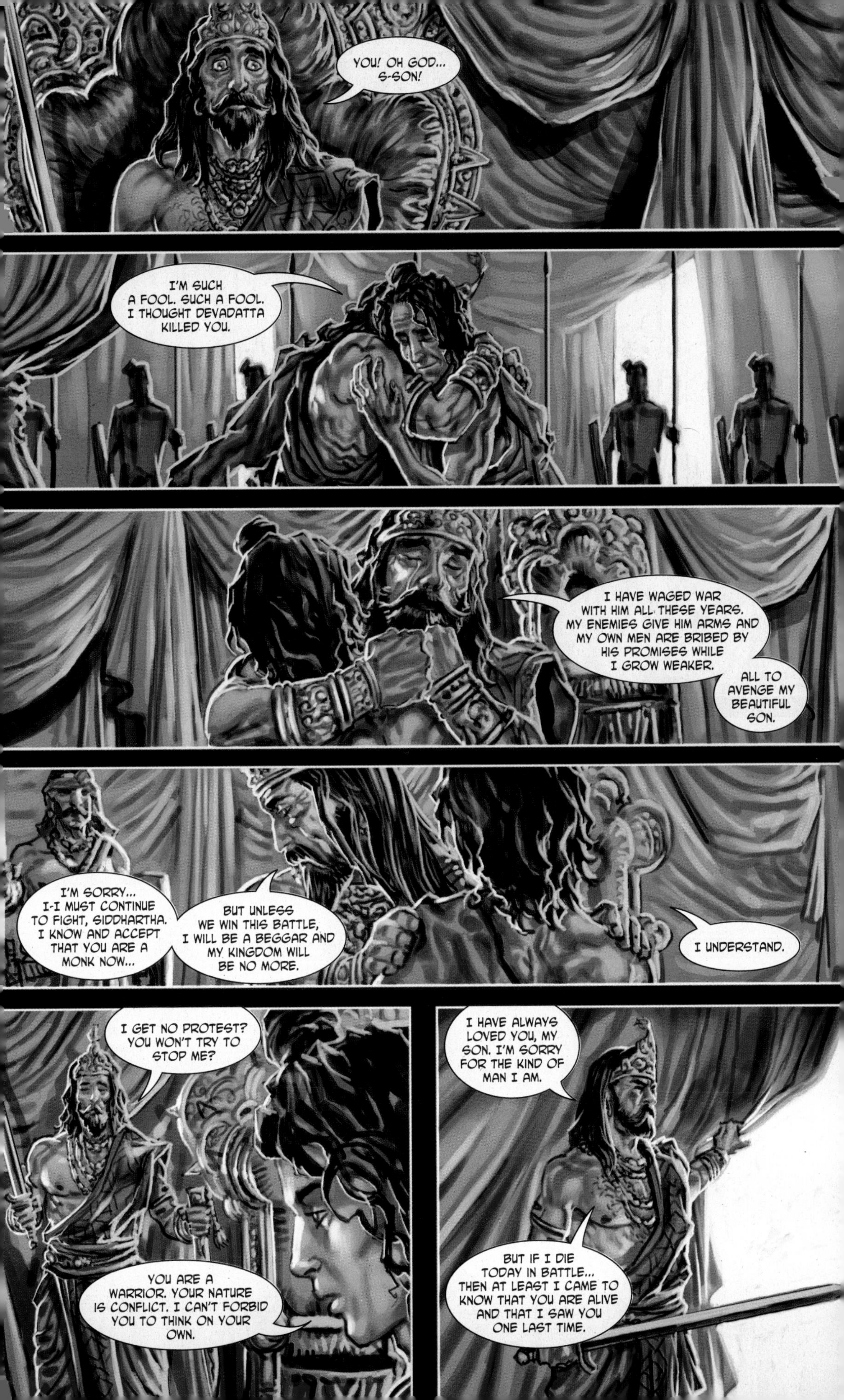
YOU! OH GOD... S-SON!
I'M SUCH A FOOL. SUCH A FOOL. I THOUGHT DEVADATTA KILLED YOU.
I HAVE WAGED WAR WITH HIM ALL THESE YEARS. MY ENEMIES GIVE HIM ARMS AND MY OWN MEN ARE BRIBED BY HIS PROMISES WHILE I GROW WEAKER.
ALL TO AVENGE MY BEAUTIFUL SON.
I'M SORRY... I-I MUST CONTINUE TO FIGHT, SIDDHARTHA. I KNOW AND ACCEPT THAT YOU ARE A MONK NOW...
BUT UNLESS WE WIN THIS BATTLE, I WILL BE A BEGGAR AND MY KINGDOM WILL BE NO MORE.
I UNDERSTAND.
I GET NO PROTEST? YOU WON'T TRY TO STOP ME?
YOU ARE A WARRIOR. YOUR NATURE IS CONFLICT. I CAN'T FORBID YOU TO THINK ON YOUR OWN.
I HAVE ALWAYS LOVED YOU, MY SON. I'M SORRY FOR THE KIND OF MAN I AM.
BUT IF I DIE TODAY IN BATTLE... THEN AT LEAST I CAME TO KNOW THAT YOU ARE ALIVE AND THAT I SAW YOU ONE LAST TIME.

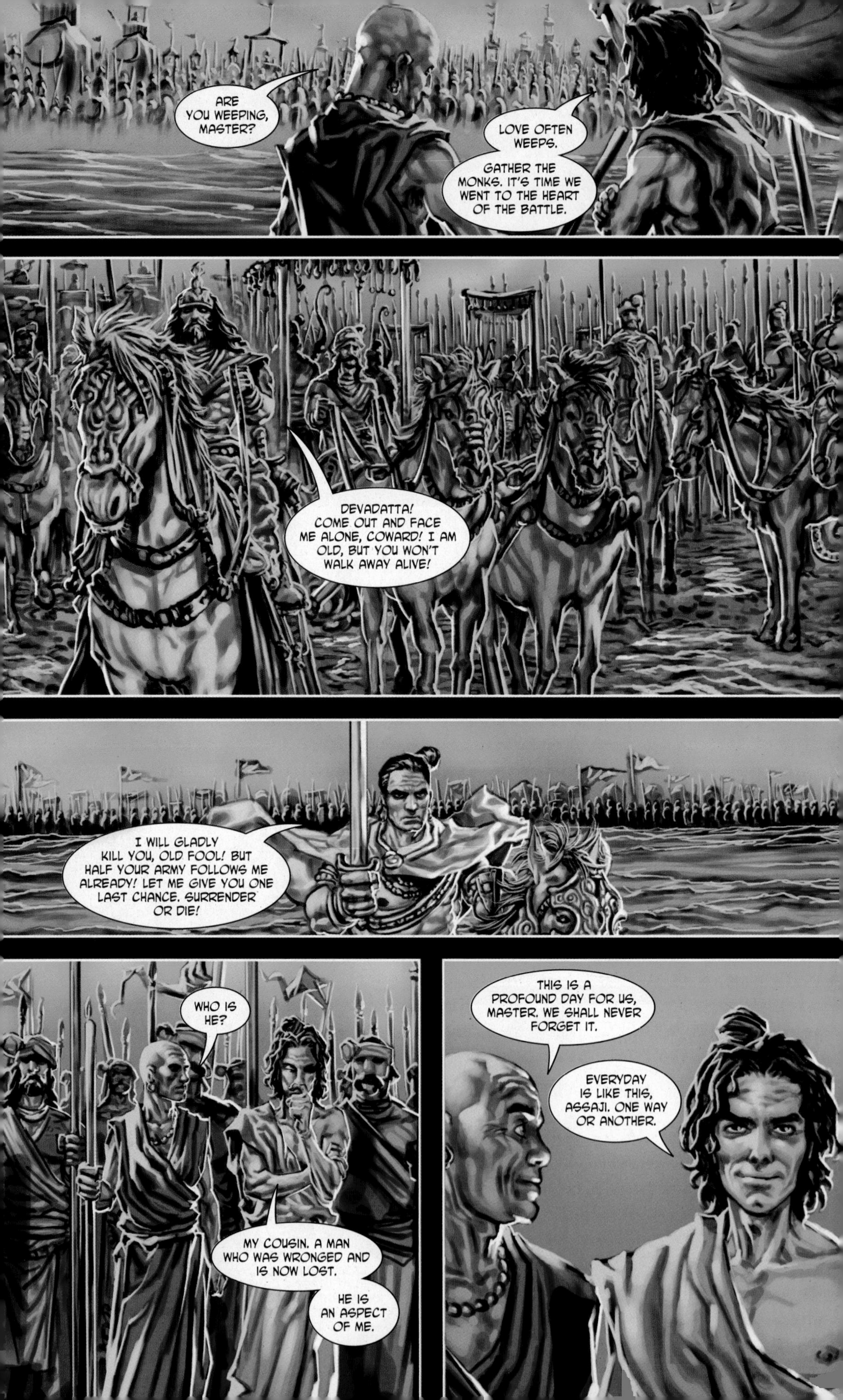

ARE YOU WEEPING, MASTER?
LOVE OFTEN WEEPS.
GATHER THE MONKS. IT'S TIME WE WENT TO THE HEART OF THE BATTLE.
DEVADATTA! COME OUT AND FACE ME ALONE, COWARD! I AM OLD, BUT YOU WON'T WALK AWAY ALIVE!
I WILL GLADLY KILL YOU, OLD FOOL! BUT HALF YOUR ARMY FOLLOWS ME ALREADY! LET ME GIVE YOU ONE LAST CHANCE. SURRENDER OR DIE!
WHO IS HE?
MY COUSIN. A MAN WHO WAS WRONGED AND IS NOW LOST.
HE IS AN ASPECT OF ME.
THIS IS A PROFOUND DAY FOR US, MASTER. WE SHALL NEVER FORGET IT.
EVERYDAY IS LIKE THIS, ASSAJI. ONE WAY OR ANOTHER.

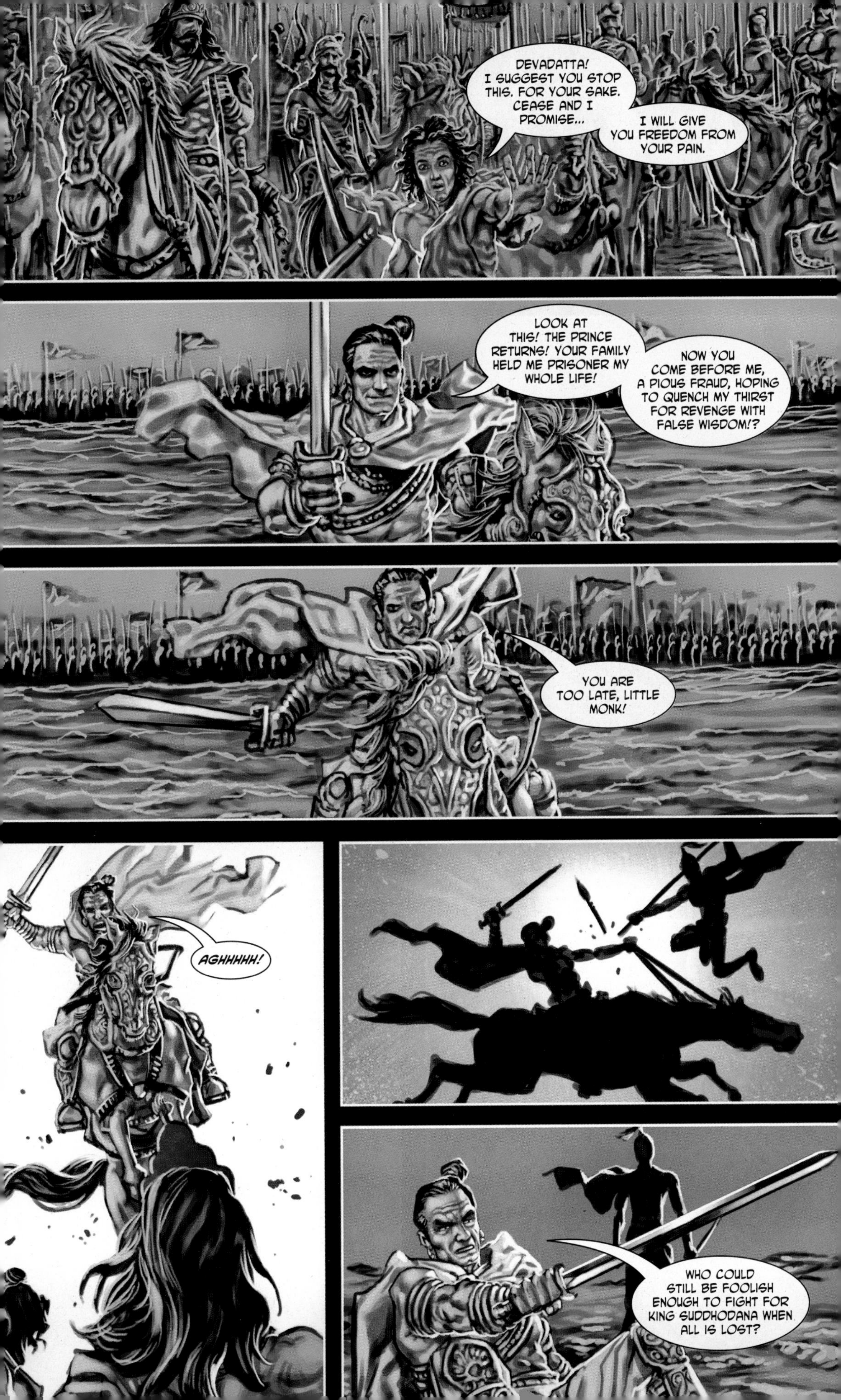
DEVADATTA! I SUGGEST YOU STOP THIS. FOR YOUR SAKE. CEASE AND I PROMISE...
I WILL GIVE YOU FREEDOM FROM YOUR PAIN.
LOOK AT THIS! THE PRINCE RETURNS! YOUR FAMILY HELD ME PRISONER MY WHOLE LIFE!
NOW YOU COME BEFORE ME, A PIOUS FRAUD, HOPING TO QUENCH MY THIRST FOR REVENGE WITH FALSE WISDOM!?
YOU ARE TOO LATE, LITTLE MONK!
AGHHHHH!
WHO COULD STILL BE FOOLISH ENOUGH TO FIGHT FOR KING SUDDHODANA WHEN ALL IS LOST?

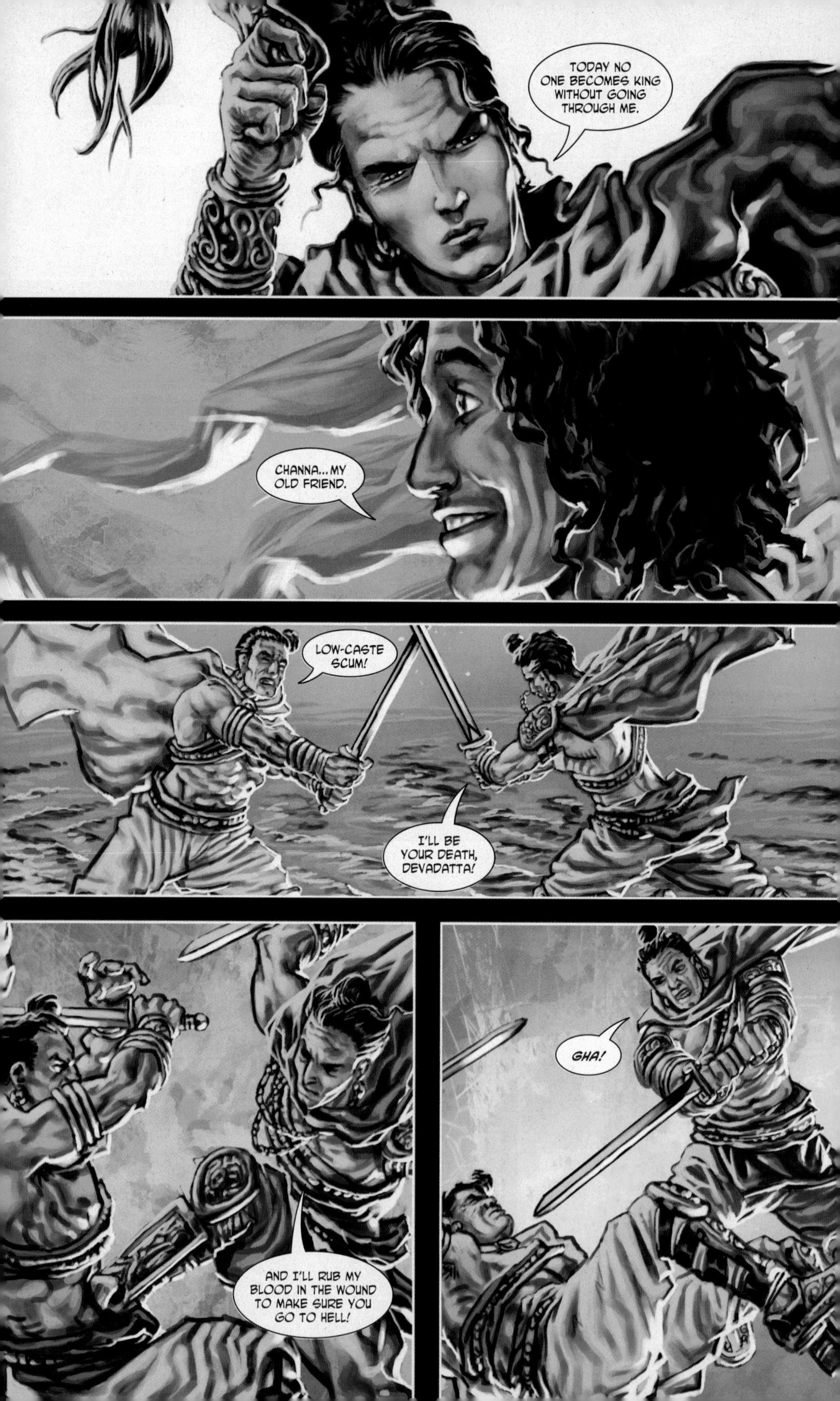
TODAY NO ONE BECOMES KING WITHOUT GOING THROUGH ME.
CHANNA... MY OLD FRIEND.
LOW-CASTE SCUM!
I'LL BE YOUR DEATH, DEVADATTA!
AND I'LL RUB MY BLOOD IN THE WOUND TO MAKE SURE YOU GO TO HELL!
GHA!

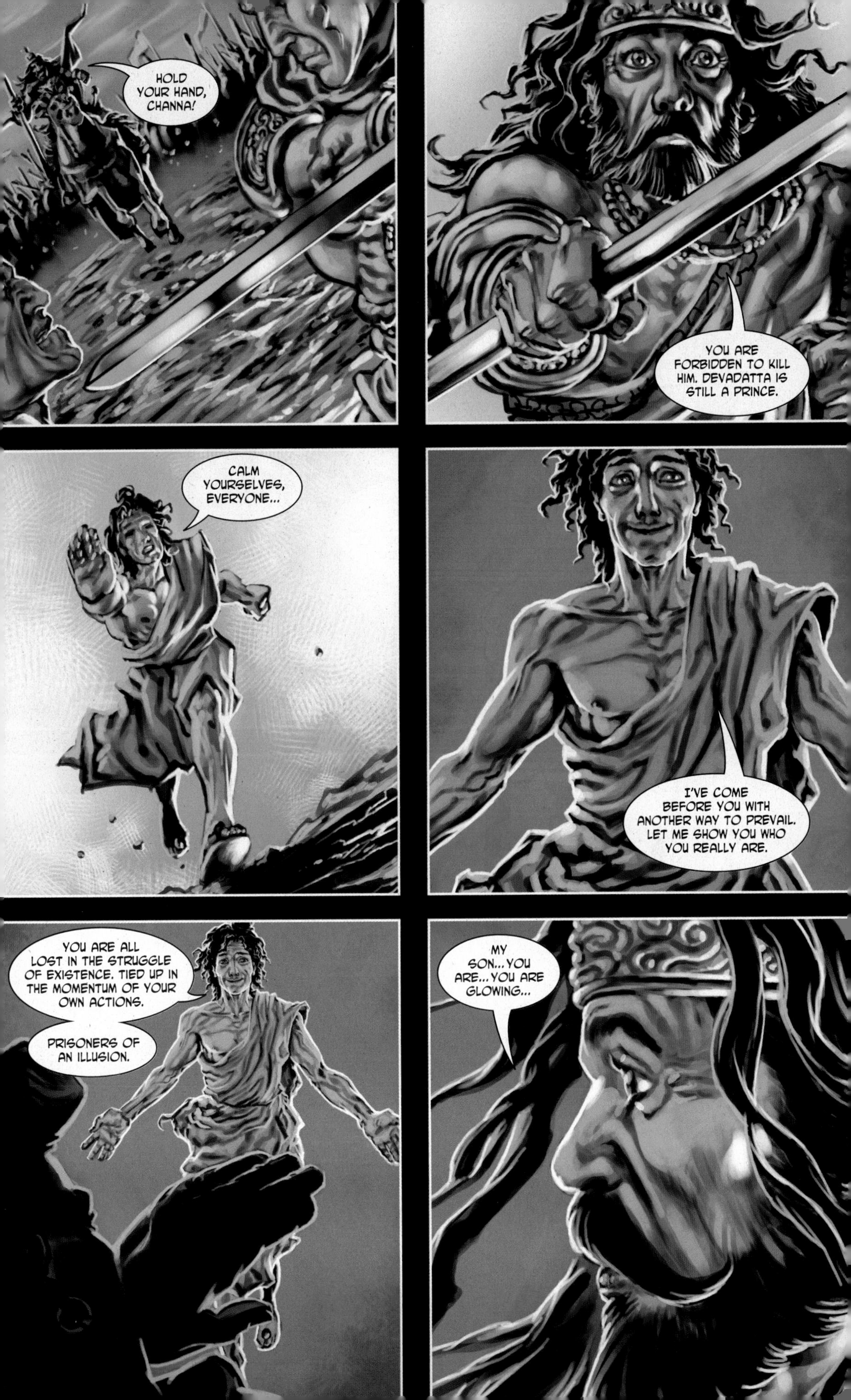
HOLD YOUR HAND, CHANNA!
YOU ARE FORBIDDEN TO KILL HIM. DEVADATTA IS STILL A PRINCE.
CALM YOURSELVES, EVERYONE...
I'VE COME BEFORE YOU WITH ANOTHER WAY TO PREVAIL. LET ME SHOW YOU WHO YOU REALLY ARE.
YOU ARE ALL LOST IN THE STRUGGLE OF EXISTENCE. TIED UP IN THE MOMENTUM OF YOUR OWN ACTIONS.
PRISONERS OF AN ILLUSION.
MY SON... YOU ARE... YOU ARE GLOWING...

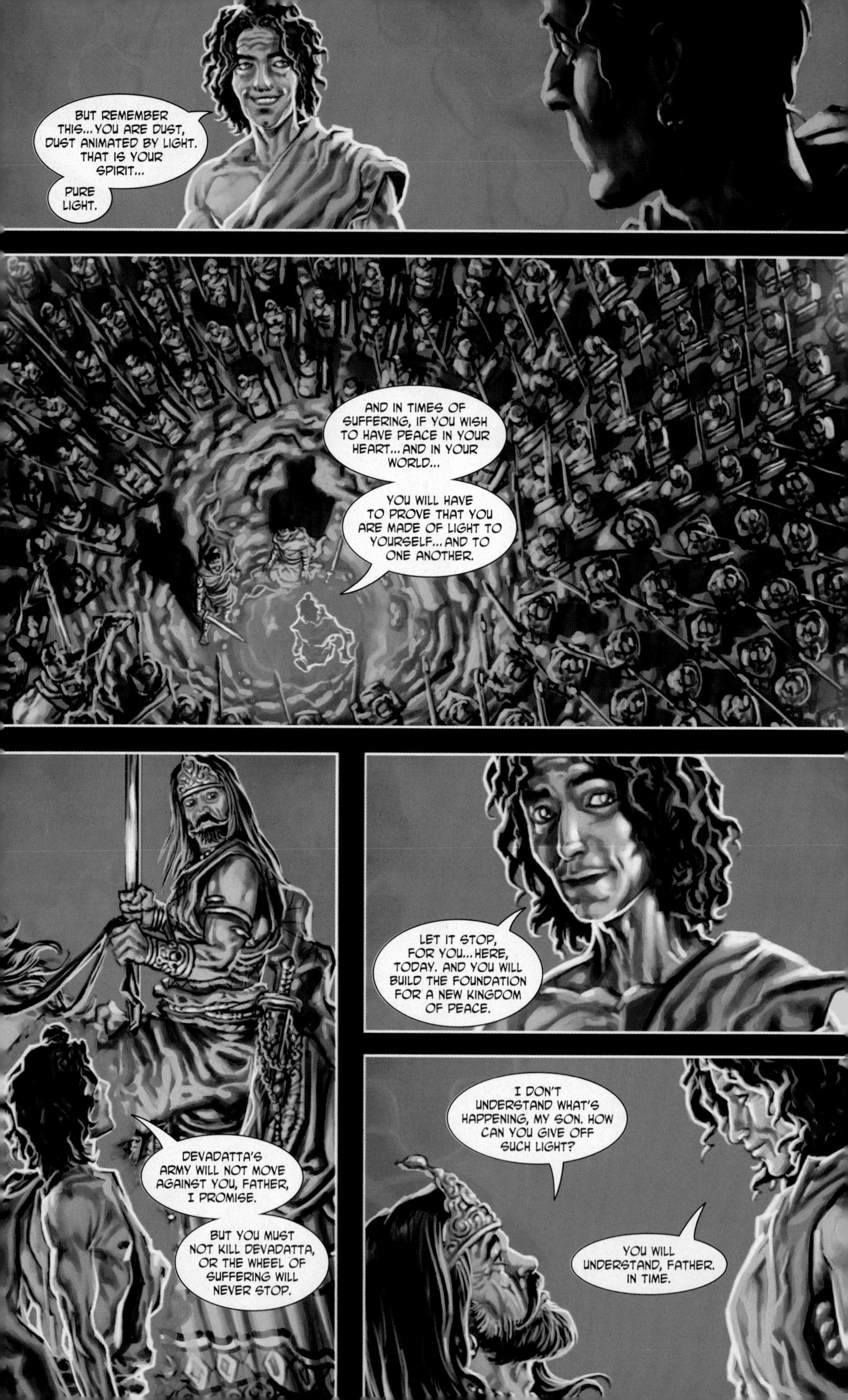
BUT REMEMBER THIS... YOU ARE DUST, DUST ANIMATED BY LIGHT. THAT IS YOUR SPIRIT...
PURE LIGHT.
AND IN TIMES OF SUFFERING, IF YOU WISH TO HAVE PEACE IN YOUR HEART... AND IN YOUR WORLD...
YOU WILL HAVE TO PROVE THAT YOU ARE MADE OF LIGHT TO YOURSELF... AND TO ONE ANOTHER.
DEVADATTA'S ARMY WILL NOT MOVE AGAINST YOU, FATHER, I PROMISE.
BUT YOU MUST NOT KILL DEVADATTA, OR THE WHEEL OF SUFFERING WILL NEVER STOP.
LET IT STOP, FOR YOU... HERE, TODAY. AND YOU WILL BUILD THE FOUNDATION FOR A NEW KINGDOM OF PEACE.
I DON'T UNDERSTAND WHAT'S HAPPENING, MY SON. HOW CAN YOU GIVE OFF SUCH LIGHT?
YOU WILL UNDERSTAND, FATHER. IN TIME.

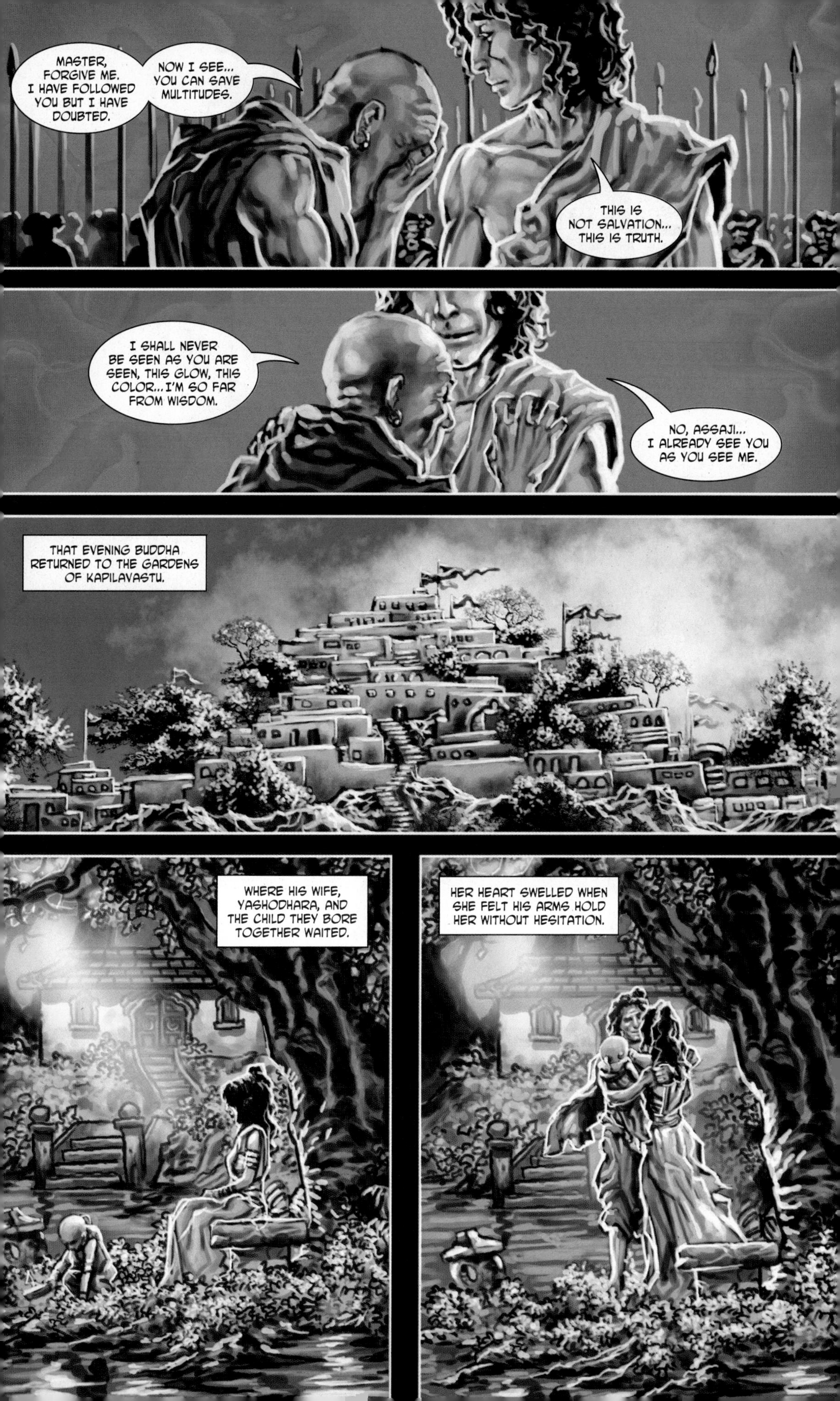

MASTER, FORGIVE ME. I HAVE FOLLOWED YOU BUT I HAVE DOUBTED.
NOW I SEE... YOU CAN SAVE MULTITUDES.
THIS IS NOT SALVATION... THIS IS TRUTH.
I SHALL NEVER BE SEEN AS YOU ARE SEEN, THIS GLOW, THIS COLOR... I'M SO FAR FROM WISDOM.
NO, ASSAJI... I ALREADY SEE YOU AS YOU SEE ME.
THAT EVENING BUDDHA RETURNED TO THE GARDENS OF KAPILAVASTU.
WHERE HIS WIFE, YASHODHARA, AND THE CHILD THEY BORE TOGETHER WAITED.
HER HEART SWELLED WHEN SHE FELT HIS ARMS HOLD HER WITHOUT HESITATION.

IN HIS PRESENCE YOSHODHARA FELT A GREAT WARMTH.

THE WORLD DISAPPEARED IN A GLOW OF WHITE LIGHT THAT HAD NO SOURCE.

IT FILLED UP HER WHOLE BEING AND SHE BEGAN TO UNDERSTAND THAT THE LIGHT CAME FROM HIM.

HE WAS NO LONGER HER HUSBAND. AND FOR THE FIRST TIME, THAT WAS OKAY.

SHE REALIZED THAT EVENTUALLY ALL OF PASSION'S FIRES BURN OUT.

AND IN THE ASHES OF PASSION ONE FINDS A GEM, ONCE OBSCURED BY THE FLAMES BUT THERE ALL ALONG.

THAT GEM HAD A NAME... SHE COULD NOW HEAR IT TUMBLING AROUND IN HER HEAD OVER AND OVER AGAIN...

A SINGLE WORD...

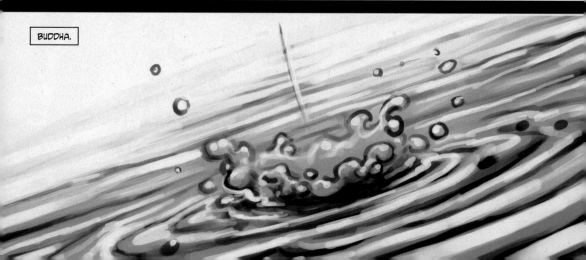

BUDDHA.

Buddha lived quietly for another
Forty-Five years, traveling throughout
northern India as a renowned teacher
before dying at the ripe old
age of eighty.

The cause of death
was eating a bad piece
of pork.